Leadership for Safe Schools

Leadership for Safe Schools is every school and district leader's guide to developing practical policies and carefully designed action plans to ensure that K–12 students are physically and psychologically safe, secure, and supported. With today's students experiencing soaring rates of depression, anxiety, trauma, loneliness, and suicidality—in addition to the effects of the COVID-19 pandemic and the normalization of school shootings—school personnel desperately need multifaceted approaches that decrease violence, facilitate social connectedness, and promote emotional well-being. This book's proactive, preventive, and responsive Three Pillar Model offers a coherent framework for creating safe and supportive schools and fostering student mental health.

Each chapter guides school leaders and administrators to implement evidence-based interventions and strategies, including:

- strategies for school safety, threat assessment, suicide prevention, and anti-violence efforts
- easy-to-apply improvements to school climate and culture
- social supports for diverse students, including the marginalized, victimized, and at-risk
- effective partnerships with families, communities, and other spheres of influence
- principles from positive psychology and social-emotional learning
- research-based strategies for trauma-informed care and crisis response

Whether you are a principal or superintendent; a school psychologist, counselor, or social worker; or a school resource officer, nurse, or proactive teacher, this book will be your all-in-one inspiration for fostering resilient learning environments and implementing multi-component prevention and intervention strategies to support students' mental health.

Philip J. Lazarus is Associate Professor and former Director of the School Psychology Program at Florida International University, USA. He is Past-President of the National Association of School Psychologists and Founder and Past-Chairperson of its National Emergency Assistance Team. He is a licensed psychologist, a NASP PREPaRE trainer, and the author or editor of several books related to mental health.

Michael L. Sulkowski is Associate Professor of School Psychology and School Psychology Program Coordinator at the University of Alabama, USA. He is a Nationally Certified School Psychologist, a NASP PREPaRE trainer, and an author of books on evidence-based interventions to facilitate student mental health.

Other Eye On Education Books Available from Routledge
(www.routledge.com/eyeoneducation)

School Psychologists as Advocates for Social Justice
Kathleen Ness

**Educators as First Responders: A Teacher's Guide to
Adolescent Development and Mental Health, Grades 6–12**
Deborah Offner

**Radical Principals: A Blueprint for Long-Term
Equity and Stability at School**
Michael S. Gaskell

**Harnessing Formative Data for K-12 Leaders:
Real-time Approaches to School Improvement**
Stepan Mekhitarian

Supporting Student Mental Health: Essentials for Teachers
Michael Hass and Amy Ardell

**Developing Your School's Student Support Teams:
A Practical Guide for K-12 Leaders, Student Services
Personnel, and Mental Health Staff**
Steve Berta, Howard Blonsky, and James Wogan

**Teaching as Protest: Emancipating Classrooms
Through Racial Consciousness**
Robert S. Harvey and Susan Gonzowitz

**Leading Schools Through Trauma: A Data-Driven
Approach to Helping Children Heal**
Michael S. Gaskell

**Abolitionist Leadership in Schools: Undoing Systemic
Injustice Through Communally Conscious Education**
Robert S. Harvey

Leadership for Safe Schools

The Three Pillar Approach to Supporting Students' Mental Health

Philip J. Lazarus and Michael L. Sulkowski

NEW YORK AND LONDON

Designed cover image: Olivia Feldman

First published 2024
by Routledge
605 Third Avenue, New York, NY 10158

and by Routledge
4 Park Square, Milton Park, Abingdon, Oxon, OX14 4RN

Routledge is an imprint of the Taylor & Francis Group, an informa business

© 2024 Philip J. Lazarus and Michael L. Sulkowski

The right of Philip J. Lazarus and Michael L. Sulkowski to be
identified as authors of this work has been asserted in accordance with
sections 77 and 78 of the Copyright, Designs and Patents Act 1988.

All rights reserved. No part of this book may be reprinted or
reproduced or utilised in any form or by any electronic, mechanical,
or other means, now known or hereafter invented, including
photocopying and recording, or in any information storage or retrieval
system, without permission in writing from the publishers.

Trademark notice: Product or corporate names may be trademarks
or registered trademarks, and are used only for identification and
explanation without intent to infringe.

ISBN: 978-0-367-20447-1 (hbk)
ISBN: 978-0-367-20448-8 (pbk)
ISBN: 978-0-429-26152-7 (ebk)

DOI: 10.4324/9780429261527

Typeset in Palatino
by Apex CoVantage, LLC

Dedications

Following the horrific bombing of the Alfred P. Murrah Building in Oklahoma City in 1995, the National Association of School Psychologists (NASP) determined that our Association needed a national crisis response team to respond to tragic events such as loss of life that impacted children and families. Consequently, the NASP National Emergency Assistance Team (NEAT) was formed in 1997. We anticipated that we would mostly respond to natural disasters. However, unexpectedly we found ourselves responding on site to multiple school shootings even before Columbine in 1999. Both individually and as a group we have responded nationally and internationally to floods, tornadoes, hurricanes, fires, environmental disasters, suicides, suicide clusters, bus accidents, 9/11, the tsunamis in Southeast Asia, and earthquakes in Turkey, as well as to dozens of school shootings including Columbine, Sandy Hook, Parkland, and Uvalde. This included providing psychological first aid, consultation to administrators, debriefings, information dissemination, school and community workshops, etc. The TEAM acronym stands for Training, Education, Advocacy and Mobile response. We provided training and education and did our best to advocate for policies, procedures, and programs to keep our youth safe and supported. I was privileged to serve as a founding member of this team. Over the years we became extremely close due to tragedies we had to confront, and the camaraderie, sense of humor, and love we shared. We consider ourselves family and all our lives have been immensely enriched. Therefore, I would like to dedicate this book to my NEAT family: Scott Poland, Ted Feinberg, Kris Sieckert, Rich Lieberman, Bill Pfohl, Frank Zenere, Shirley Pitts, Steve Brock, Cathy Paine, Cindy Dickinson, Ad Hoc member Gene Cash, and the spirit of us all, Susan Gorin.

—Philip J. Lazarus

This book is dedicated to every educator who has ever assumed a leadership position. Whether spotlighted on the national stage or working quietly backstage, your contributions are worthwhile, appreciated, and integral to the success of the millions of students who comprise our future. Thank you for being you and for all that you do!

—Michael L. Sulkowski

Contents

Acknowledgments xi

About the Front Cover Art. xiii

**1   Introduction: The Three Pillars of Safe and
Supportive Schools that Foster the Emotional
Well-Being of Students.** 1

SECTION 1
The Safe Pillar. 35

2   Physical Safety 37

3   Bullying and Violence Prevention and Intervention. . . .61

4   Suicide Prevention and Threat Assessment 91

SECTION 2
The Supportive Pillar 117

5   School Climate and Culture .119

6   Social Connectedness and Support 153

SECTION 3
The Mental Health Pillar 181

7   Promotion and Prevention. 183

8   Crisis Recovery and Advocacy 217

Index. 259

Acknowledgments

We wish to acknowledge Jane Lazarus for her thoughtful comments on the content of this text as well as her diligent and careful editing of the entire manuscript. As always she is an excellent editor and the love of my life. We thank Elisa Lage for her work on designing Figures 1.1 and 1.2. We appreciate the ongoing support and encouragement of Daniel Schwartz, our editor at Routledge. We needed to change the timetable and the focus of our book due to the impact of COVID-19 and the Black Lives Matter Movement to ensure that our content was both timely and relevant for our readers. We also acknowledge the work of the National Association of School Psychologists for their work promoting the emotional, academic, social, and behavioral needs of young people and their efforts to support diversity, equity, inclusion, and access in the delivery of school mental health services.

About the Front Cover Art

On February 14, 2018, a former student at Marjory Stoneman Douglas (MSD) High School entered the building and open fired with a semi-automatic weapon, killing 17 people, and injuring 17 others. At that time, Olivia Feldman was in the 10th grade at MSD. One year later, on the anniversary of this horrific event, students were given the option of attending school that day or commemorating the tragedy in their own way. Olivia Feldman, then an 11th-grade student and a budding artist, connected with five friends at her home. They went to the art supply store, bought paints and canvases, returned to her home, and proceeded to express their feelings through their art. On the front cover is her painting.

Olivia graduated from MSD in spring 2020. Olivia is a true leader, as she helped her friends move forward on the trajectory of healing. This is consistent with her faith and the concept of Tikkun Olam, the act of doing one's best to help repair the world. Currently, Olivia is a student at the University of South Florida where she is majoring in business. She hopes to work at Disney World in risk management one day.

May this work be a tribute to the resilience of our young people and a reminder of all the work that leaders need to do to create safe and supportive schools and foster the emotional well-being of our nation's youth. We owe this to our next generation.

1

Introduction

The Three Pillars of Safe and Supportive Schools that Foster the Emotional Well-Being of Students

On Valentine's Day in 2018, in Parkland, Florida, at 2:21 p.m., a lone gunman entered building 12 at Marjory Stoneman Douglas High School (MSD) and began shooting. The assault ended approximately six minutes later, resulting in the deaths of 14 students and three staff members. Countless others were devastated both physically and emotionally.

Responding to this calamity was daunting for the school, district, and community. This tragedy needed a multi-level, multi-district, ongoing response. The repercussions of this event will last for years, and the district's response would be a sprint, a marathon, and everything in between. Tragedies of this magnitude do not just impact the actual school itself but surrounding schools and communities as well. This assault occurred in Broward County, where the first author (PJL) lives and where a significant number of our over 400 Florida International University school psychology graduates I have trained are now employed. Following this tragedy, mental health community members throughout the state volunteered to provide crisis intervention services to the community at large. I provided crisis intervention support to students, faculty, and families at MSD, Westglades Middle, and Imagine Charter School at Broward.

In the aftermath, one young boy I spoke with at Imagine Charter School told me his plan to make schools safer. Here is what he said: "We need to have a conveyor belt to check all kids for guns, then we need to have bulletproof windows on the outside, then we need to have bulletproof closets that we can all run into in case a shooter enters the building. We need to put up a 10-foot barbed wire fence outside the playground and have more police, one at every entrance." The only thing he had yet to ask for was full body armor (Lazarus, 2023).

Though I understood the student's palpable fear, even if we could make this young boy's architectural and policing vision a reality in all schools in America, this approach would not guarantee that every child in every school would feel safe, supported, and mentally healthy. Instead, students and faculty alike would feel like prisoners in a dystopian school environment. This approach would not take into consideration all we know about how to make young people feel emotionally and physically safe in school, how to establish a school climate and culture that are conducive to learning, how to provide learning and behavioral supports to our most vulnerable youth, or how to foster coping and problem-solving skills so that all our students can grow up to be productive citizens.

The purpose of this book is not to make our schools fortresses or instruct all educators on the use of firearms. Instead, it is to provide leaders with the requisite information to create safe and supportive schools that foster students' mental health. Our intention is to provide practical strategies, policies, and procedures based on evidence-based practice informed by current science. Our approach is to lay out a broad, inclusive framework that we call the *three pillars of safe, supportive, and mentally healthy schools*. Though space limitations will not permit extensive detail on every topic described in this book, we hope that a school leader armed with the materials presented herein can gather and use

Introduction ◆ 3

information specific to their individual needs and that of their school or district.

The Purpose

The Director of the Yale Center for Emotional Intelligence, Marc Brackett, and his research team (2020) asked thousands of people across the U.S. during the COVID-19 epidemic to share things for which they were most grateful. Their number one response was good health. Dr. Antonio Guterres (2020), the United Nations Secretary General, emphasized that good health is impossible without mental health (Lazarus et al, 2021a). We wholeheartedly agree, and describing how schools can contribute to this process is one of the primary purposes of our book.

This chapter introduces the *three pillars of safe, supportive, and healthy schools*. These pillars are integral to student well-being and foundational to the approach espoused in this book. In this chapter, we discuss contemporary issues impacting students, especially those from minoritized and marginalized communities; the mental health challenges facing young people; and what schools and school leaders can do to promote safety, security, and physical and mental health. Later, in Chapters 2 through 8, we discuss fundamental knowledge, practical strategies, and interventions in each of the three pillars.

Issues Confronting Students

During children's early years, effective and loving caregivers are the primary providers who create the necessary preconditions to foster healthy development. They help engender feelings of trust (birth to 12 months), autonomy (ages 1 to 3 years), and initiative (ages 3 to 6 years). These foundational caregivers set youth on a course toward later developmental and life outcomes (Erikson, 1963). According to Maslow (1962), primary or basic needs are *physiological* (e.g., food, water, warmth, rest, shelter) and *safety*-related (e.g., security, health). When children begin attending school, the influence of immediate caregivers expands to include peers and school personnel such as educational leaders. Thus, it now takes a village to fare well; feeling safe and supported in school communities becomes fundamental to children's academic, social, and emotional growth (Sulkowski & Lazarus, 2017).

Yet, our youth are not faring well; something is amiss. From the recent increase in despair and suicide among young people; to the unbearable number of school shootings witnessed during the past three decades; to disparities that continue to afflict students, especially children of color; and to the number of students who feel disconnected from their peers, teachers, and schools; the fact that students face significant threats to their well-being is undeniable (Lazarus et al., 2021c).

As mental health scholars, trainers, and practitioners, when we have asked school psychologists to raise their hands at state conventions to indicate if they believe that we as a nation are doing a good job in fostering the emotional well-being of our youth, invariably, no one raises their hands. The people who work most closely with students are aware of the challenges they face. School psychologists in the schools every day have an accurate reading of the pulse of our nation's youth, and they recognize that our youth are struggling with mental health issues and need urgent support. They also understand that safety and support are prerequisites for good mental health.

More than 20 years ago, the U.S. Surgeon General, C. Everett Koop, told the nation that we have a mental health crisis among our nation's youth (U.S. Department of Health and Human Services, 2000). Tragically, this crisis has become even more dire since then, along with documented increases in anxiety and depression over the past two decades (Lazarus et al., 2021c). These problems have only been accelerated by the COVID-19 pandemic (Lazarus et al., 2021a).

As noted by Lazarus et al. (2021c), approximately 7.5 million children in the United States are estimated to have an unmet mental health need (Kataoka et al., 2002), and only 20% of children with severe mental disorders ever receive treatment (Merikangas et al., 2010). Further, a study by the World Health Organization indicates that mental disorders account for nearly half of all disabilities among individuals between the ages of 10 and 24 (Gore et al., 2011). The bi-annual Youth Risk Surveillance Survey has shown that three out of ten youngsters felt so sad or hopeless during the prior year that they were not able to lead fully productive lives, and one out of five students had seriously considered ending their own life (Center for Disease Control and Prevention, 2020). This amount of suffering among youth is intolerable, especially when effective treatments and practices exist. Educational leaders can embrace these practices.

National estimates on the well-being of youth are predicated on the assumption that mental health is the absence of pathology. However, the estimates are even more striking when mental health needs also include struggling children and youth, even if they do not meet the criteria for a psychiatric diagnosis. Numerous surveys indicate that excessive stress is a primary concern for high school students (Vella-Brodrick, 2016). Millions of students fail to develop essential social and emotional skills to protect their emotional well-being (Lazarus & Sulkowski, 2011; Sulkowski & Lazarus, 2017). Many of these same students are poorly bonded to supportive educational communities, and less than a third of 12th graders report that their schools provide an encouraging and supportive learning environment (Benson, 2006).

These problems are even more severe for children and youth from marginalized and minoritized communities (National Academies of Sciences, Engineering, and Medicine, 2019). Recently, since COVID-19, the storming of the U.S. Capitol, the political intransigence and unrest regarding Black Lives Matter, heightened racial trauma, our polarization as a nation related to even wearing masks and vaccinating the population, children have felt less safe, increasingly vulnerable, more disconnected, and lonelier (Murthy, 2020; National Academies of Science, Engineering and Medicine, 2021).

The COVID-19 pandemic, in particular, has caused unprecedented disruption in students' lives. These challenges include the loss of loved ones and fears about safety, school closures, social isolation, financial insecurity, food insecurity, disturbed sleep, and significant gaps in access to health care (Shah et al., 2020; Stern et al., 2020). As a result, children's learning and mental health have been negatively impacted. Currently, the breadth and depth of the impact on youth in the near term is just beginning to be understood. The effects will be much greater on marginalized youth populations because these students have less access to medical treatment, and often lack adequate supports such as health insurance (Lowenhaupt & Hopkins, 2020). Moreover, during the pandemic's early stages, these children were more fearful for their parents, who often worked in essential jobs where exposure to COVID-19 was high. In addition, these families were more likely to experience job loss and housing insecurity (Cholera et al., 2020).

Family upheaval was widespread, especially during the early stages of the pandemic. Nearly 30% of students said an adult in their home lost a job, and 24% said they went hungry for lack of food (St. George & Strauss, 2022). Most sadly of all, the pandemic left many children grieving. It has been estimated by the CDC (2022) that more than 230,000 U.S. students suffered the ultimate loss, that of a parent or caregiver during the pandemic, and that for Hispanic and Black children the loss was near twice the rate of White children.

When schools closed during the pandemic, families began to see schools' critical roles in society more clearly. Parents reported much higher levels of stress related to COVID-19 compared to non-parents. More than 70% of all parents cited online learning as a source of great stress in their children's lives (Margolius et al., 2020).

Moreover, children with disabilities had difficulty accessing online learning, and some students, especially in rural communities, did not have ready access to broadband or reliable internet. Consequently, caregivers began to appreciate, even more than before, that schools are not just for learning basic academic subjects but also for creating a web of interconnected relationships necessary for the healthy development of children. Moreover, recent reports suggest that academic skills in both reading, and math have had a precipitous decline, especially among children from minority backgrounds. According to the National Center for Education Statistics (2022), the average scores for 9-year-olds in the U.S. declined by five points in reading and seven points in math compared to 2020—the largest decline in reading since 1990, and the first ever decline in math. Moreover, struggling students, many from minority and low-income backgrounds, experienced declines in math scores by 12 points and reading scores by up to 10 points.

The Role of Schools

Schools profoundly impact children's lives, especially regarding their safety, security, mental health, and general well-being. However, schools exist within a broad ecological framework influenced by student, family, and community contexts (Nickerson et al., 2020). Thus, like people, schools are impacted by intersecting spheres of influence. Bronfenbrenner (1979) described multiple levels of influence on human development, nested within the: (a) microsystem (i.e., immediate surroundings that more directly affect the individual, such as parents, teachers, peers); (b) mesosystem (i.e., interaction among different parts of a child's microsystem, such as home, school, and neighborhood); (c) exosystem (i.e., settings in which the child does not actively participate, such as parents' workplace); (d) macrosystem (i.e., broad culture and policies); and (e) chronosystem (i.e., change over time in characteristics of the child and their environment). To these systems of influence, we would add (f) the cyber-system (i.e., the influence of the internet, social media, and social apps where children can be either supported or harmed, such as with cyberbullying). Each of these systems uniquely impacts students and interacts with each other in a dynamic multi-reciprocal manner.

It's All Interconnected

Three other points are important to make. First, youth safety, support, and mental health are all interconnected. For example, preventing school violence requires a multifaceted approach that incorporates context, addresses physical and psychological safety, and focuses not only on antiviolence policies, rules, and procedures but on developing a climate that is welcoming, and promotes order, respect, trust, and motivation to learn (Nickerson et al., 2020).

Second, if schools work in concert and are supported by multiple systems, then success is more probable and sustainable. For example, if schools (a) teach youth about cyber safety; (b) coordinate with school resource officers or local police to inform them when cyberbullying or cyberstalking occurs; (c) help parents understand how to keep their children safe from potential cyber threats; and (d) provide psychological support to victims of cyberbullying or harassment, then reducing cyber vulnerability and increasing cyber safety will have a greater impact than just incorporating one element alone.

Third, since students spend approximately 7.5 hours per day and 180 days per year in schools, it reasonably follows that most youth (60.1%) who receive entry-level mental health treatment will do so in an educational setting (Farmer et al., 2003). Moreover, many students depend on the mental health services they receive in the schools (Duong, 2020), and arguably, as one of the most trusted institutions in society, schools are optimal environments for providing mental health services (Sulkowski, 2016).

The Role of School Leaders

Following the tumultuous years after the onset of the COVID-19 pandemic, school leaders have had to play an even more prominent role in improving students' lives. By "school leaders" we mean anyone who steps up to help students feel safe and supported, and is committed to their well-being. Although this term can apply to superintendents, school board members, principals, administrators, special education directors, etc., it can also apply to school psychologists, nurses, teachers, coaches, and anyone who rises to make a difference in the life of even one student. We are not alone in this perspective. Perhaps this sentiment is best expressed by John Adams, who once noted: *"If your actions inspire others to dream more, learn more, do more, and become more, you are a leader."*

We believe all students have the right to feel safe and supported in their schools and know that all school personnel are working diligently to foster their well-being. This is especially true for those most marginalized and vulnerable—sometimes even by the institutions that purport to help them but cause harm through bad policy and practice.

We also understand that with so many competing responsibilities, what this book calls for school leaders to do is a challenge. This is especially true, as due to the pandemic, educators have been working tirelessly against immense odds, many of whom have faced daunting personal and family challenges (Diliberti et al., 2021). Moreover, since the pandemic began, educators, and especially those with children, reported an increased sense of burnout, working more hours than usual, feeling that they are almost always on the job and responding to students' and parent' concerns well after the school day is over. This has taken a toll on educators even as school has returned to more normal operations. Educators have been leaving the profession due to feeling overwhelmed, underappreciated, and underpaid. They have increasingly noted that lack of support and resources, political strife, and autonomy regarding what they can and cannot teach have made their job increasingly difficult (Edsall, 2022). Moreover, this is a societal problem, and the task is so large and multifaceted that educational leaders cannot do it alone and must unite and advocate with leaders in all segments of society to help create schools that foster the well-being of our nation's youth.

With that said, an objective of this book is to make things easier for educational leaders. Instead of recommending "more procedural things to do," it is meant to be a companion for educators who are enthusiastic about using evidence-based practices that have been shown to make a difference and transform schools. Safe, supportive, and healthy schools are the same types of schools where educators—especially educational leaders—who want to make the future brighter for the next generation, are most resilient to whatever challenges they face. As Neal Postman so eloquently said, *"Children are the living messages we send to a time we will not see."*

The Three-Pillar Model

In 2017, we co-authored the book, *Creating Safe and Supportive Schools and Fostering Students' Mental Health* with the intended audience to be school-based mental health professionals. In many ways, the current text is an outgrowth of the previous work for a broader audience. Again, anyone can be a school leader—this includes you! By picking up and reading this book, we would wager that you already are making an impact on students' lives.

As an additional extension of our work, we present a practical working model in this book that leaders can follow, which we call the *three pillars of safe, supportive, and healthy schools*. The first pillar is the Safe Pillar, the second is the Supportive Pillar, and the third is the Mental Health Pillar. One must stress that these pillars are not independent but collectively work together to uphold student well-being. If one pillar is absent or compromised, the whole structure is in jeopardy of toppling.

Introduction ◆ 11

See Figure 1.1 and Text Boxes 1.1, 1.2, and 1.3, which delineate the basic elements of the Three Pillar Model. School leaders can strive to incorporate the essential elements of the three pillars depending on the following and make it their unique approach:

- Their school's unique characteristics
- Available resources
- The school and community population
- Results of their safety audit and school climate survey
- Priorities as defined by their school board, superintendent, leadership teams, parent associations, and stakeholders.

FIGURE 1.1 The Three Pillar Model

Text Box 1.1: The Safe Pillar

- Ensuring that the school is a safe place (both physically and psychologically) for all youth
- Coordinating safety procedures and protocols with local police and hiring school resource officers (if deemed necessary)
- Establishing and training a school safety and leadership team
- Developing and training a school crisis team
- Designing schools using Crime Prevention through Universal Design
- Conducting a school safety audit
- Redesigning the school and/or policies and procedures in line with the school safety audit
- Implementing and enforcing anti-bullying policies and incorporating established bullying reducing programs, if needed
- Implementing anti-violence curricula and interventions, as necessary
- Putting systems in place that enable students to report potential threats and concerns
- Establishing threat assessment teams to investigate potential acts of violence
- Conducting active shooter drills to protect students and staff from a potentially armed intruder
- Ensuring that all staff are trained in the basics of suicide prevention and intervention
- Ensuring that all students are medically safe according to scientific guidelines, as best as possible

Text Box 1.2: The Supportive Pillar

- Improving the culture and the climate of the school to make it more responsive to student needs

Introduction ◆ 13

- Making sure that effective behavior management practices are followed in every classroom
- Fostering student connections to peers, teachers, parents, caregivers, and other adults in the community
- Establishing school-wide positive behavior supports
- Ensuring that all the requisite social supports are provided to students
- Fostering student engagement
- Establishing school-family and community partnerships
- Collaborating with colleagues across school, home, and community settings to ensure accurate assessment and service delivery
- Respecting and celebrating cultural differences among students and their families
- Providing instruction and curricula that focus on having a healthy lifestyle (e.g., developing a vigorous exercise regimen; avoiding drugs, alcohol, and tobacco; understanding nutrition and a healthy diet)
- Getting all stakeholders involved

Text Box 1.3: The Mental Health Pillar

- Ensuring the adequate provision of mental health services (i.e., following national guidelines regarding ratios of school psychologists and school counselors to students; ensuring needed support from mental health counselors and school social workers)
- Delivering social-emotional learning to all students
- Incorporating principles of positive psychology into the school curriculum.
- Providing in-service to all staff so that they have basic information about emotional and behavioral disorders
- Providing basic mental health information to all students
- Making sure that at-risk and vulnerable student populations get the additional support that they need

14 ◆ Introduction

- Identifying students who need more intensive (Tier II and Tier III) interventions.
- Providing small group interventions for at-risk students or those who have experienced a problem and need additional support (e.g., bereavement groups, anger management groups, counseling for children who have failed a grade, social skills strategies for children who have been victimized by bullies, coping skills groups for students who have attempted suicide, etc.)
- Providing school-based intensive individualized support, whenever possible, for those needing more comprehensive services
- Ensuring that effective referral sources are available for all children who require more intensive services
- Delivering crisis prevention, intervention, and postvention services

Building construction should never be rushed, and cutting corners can lead to later problems. Thus, for most schools, including everything in each pillar likely is a multi-year iterative approach. A school or a district may decide to take on one or two individual projects or priorities within a year. Essentially, leaders should strive for a balance when setting the pillars on a solid foundation. In this regard, schools should not overload one pillar while disregarding the other two; each is important and necessary.

Foundations

This text is predicated on the assumption that there are foundations or foundational principles that undergird the three pillars and the delivery of school mental health services. These are described below and listed in Text Box 1.4.

Text Box 1.4: Foundations for the Three Pillar Model

- ◆ Establish a promotion-focused multi-tiered systems of support
- ◆ Focus on the whole child
- ◆ Provide supports to all children, not just those receiving special education services
- ◆ Emphasize diversity, equity, inclusion, and access
- ◆ Use evidence-based interventions
- ◆ Focus on children's strengths and emotional well-being
- ◆ View supports through a trauma-informed lens
- ◆ Become caring communities
- ◆ Integrate the delivery of services in tandem with families and community supports

These collectively comprise the foundation that supports each pillar as well as the school mental health continuum of services. Leaders need to recognize that they should be mindful of, whenever possible, each foundational principle when developing interventions. Foundational principles function as a value, whereas under each pillar are policies, programs, and interventions. Within another context, an individual or a society can value protecting planet earth from climate change. Then they can develop policies, programs, and interventions to help make this happen. Accordingly, schools need to consider the following:

1. **Establish a promotion-focused multi-tiered system of support**

Promotion is about making good things happen. Prevention (whether primary, secondary, or tertiary) is about forestalling bad things from happening. Though both proactive and reactive

16 ◆ Introduction

approaches are necessary, it is important to consider promotion before considering prevention. For example, healthy eating is proactive and preventive whereas dieting to offset disease is reactive. Teaching emotional self-regulation strategies to young children is promotion. Providing consequences to children who display emotional or behavioral problems is reactionary. Teaching youth effective problem solving and coping skills is promotion. Teaching students how to be effective gatekeepers to inform a trusted adult when a peer is contemplating suicide is prevention. Working in leadership teams to create learning environments that create positive school climates and cultures is promotion. Dealing with discipline problems is prevention.

One of the most widely used and effective ways to change the school environment is by developing a multi-tiered system of support (MTSS; National Association of School Psychologists, 2006). However, the approach espoused in this book is the promotion-focused multi-tiered system of support (PF-MTSS) framework. See Figure 1.2. (Chapter 8 will discuss this framework in more detail.) Although promotion and prevention are closely related and often overlap, incorporating promotion as the first step in the traditional MTSS model can be transformative and reminds leaders of the value of promoting safety, security, and mental health, and establishing a climate and culture conducive to learning and well-being as well. It also reminds leaders to think proactively. Along with the traditional MTSS model, the first tier (primary prevention) represents an evidence-based curriculum or approach and incorporates intervention for all students in the school. The second tier (secondary prevention) focuses on delivering selected or targeted interventions to high-risk students which may account for about 15–20% of the student body in a typical school. The third tier (tertiary prevention) aims to deliver indicated and intensive services to those students requiring intensive support (Sulkowski & Lazarus, 2017). In a typical school, Tier III interventions may only represent 1–5% of the student population who require extensive support

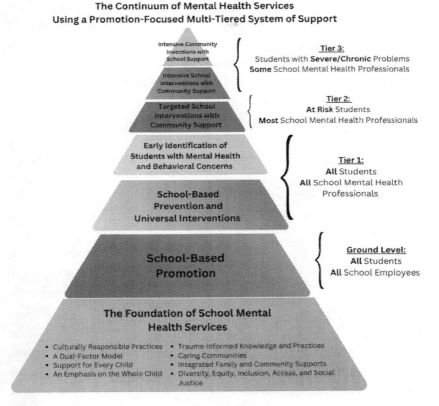

FIGURE 1.2 The Continuum of Mental Health Services

(Doll, 2019). However, as previously noted, promotion practices should be incorporated first.

For example, a school principal may be considering whether or not to include a bullying prevention program in her school. Using a *promotion*-focused approach, she and her team may decide that *all* students can be taught effective social-emotional skills and be instructed in effective problem solving and coping techniques (as discussed by Durlak et al., 2011). This would be a promotion-oriented approach and may be sufficient in eliminating any bullying problems. However, if this fails to prevent bullying and bullying continues becoming a school-wide problem, further intervention would be required. To best illustrate this

18 ◆ Introduction

MTSS model, all students could receive instruction on bullying and cyberbullying prevention and intervention at Tier I. At this level, students could also be taught how to intervene as a bystander (or "upstander") when they witness bullying. At Tier II, students who engage in chronic bullying may require an intervention to teach them how to use their power or social influence in a socially approved manner. Finally, at Tier III, a comprehensive collection of interventions (e.g., counseling, discipline of the perpetrators, family therapy, and intensive supports) would be needed for students who were chronic bullying targets and as a result often skipped school, became highly anxious, depressed, and even suicidal (See Chapter 3 for an extensive discussion on bullying).

Another example of using the PF-MTSS to ensure medical safety would entail introducing health programs that encourage students to get enough rest, eat healthy meals, and exercise to help maintain an effective immune system (Schmidt et al., 2021). This would be considered health *promotion* and the first defense against a pandemic. At the individual level amid a pandemic, *primary prevention* (Tier I) would be getting a vaccine, wearing a mask, keeping sufficient social distance, and engaging in frequent hand washing. *Secondary prevention* (Tier II) would be getting tested for possible disease if one experiences symptoms, and if positive, then going into quarantine. *Tertiary prevention* (Tier III) would be following the advice of one's physician if diagnosed with COVID-19, receiving treatment consistent with CDC guidelines, and if that is insufficient, then getting hospitalized for further treatment.

2. Focus on the whole child

One of the most comprehensive frameworks that addresses overall health in schools is the whole-child approach which focuses on the whole school, community, and child (WSCC; Jones & Miranda, 2021). This model was developed by the Centers for

Disease Control and Prevention (CDC, n.d.). It focuses on the following components: (a) physical education and physical activity, (b) nutrition environments and services, (c) health education, (d) social and emotional school climate, (e) physical environment, (f) health services, (g) counseling, psychological and social services, (h) employee wellness, (i) community involvement, and (j) family engagement.

One of the main premises of this model is that schools should shift away from traditional indicators of success such as school grades and test scores and instead focus on holistic models that also include social-emotional health and emotional well-being. A subset of the WSCC approach has been adopted by the Association for Supervision and Curriculum Development (ASCD; n.d.), and it emphasizes the core conditions necessary to support socio-emotional well-being and culturally responsive practices, as well as brings about systems-level change. Jones and Miranda (2021) state: "we often target individual problems of practice such as achievement gaps, disproportionate discipline, and fiscal disinvestment when what is required is a comprehensive approach that attacks multiple problems of practice simultaneously as *symptoms* of a systemic problem" (p. 61). The WSCC model is consistent with the Three Pillar Model undergirding this book.

3. **Provide supports to *all* children, not just those receiving special education services**

Traditionally and consistent with IDEIA, children and youth who require special education are provided with an individualized educational plan (IEP) to ensure that they receive the requisite services to learn in schools. Moreover, other students who do not require special education services can receive educational support if they qualify for 504 services. Often, the latter may require additional educational accommodations. These children may suffer from attention deficit hyperactivity disorder (ADHD) or medical or physical handicaps. The model currently used in schools is based on a disability or deficit approach. Using the Three Pillar Model, these students will continue to receive needed services.

Our model, however, recognizes that *all* children need support. It is based on a *wellness* approach. Just as all children in their early years require wellness visits to the pediatricians to get their vaccinations and check on their weight, height, overall health, etc., we emphasize not just the identification of illness, but instead the promotion of both physical and mental health. It is well recognized that students may not be physically or mentally ill, but rather may have inadequate nutrition, be food insecure, homeless, emotionally distraught, lonely, isolated, or bullied, and therefore require interventions to succeed in school and life.

4. Emphasize diversity, equity, inclusion, and access

The population of children and families served in schools has become increasingly diverse. Among the 73 million children in the United States, over 50% are members of racially and ethnically minoritized groups, more than 20% live in poverty and more than 20% do not speak English at home and are learning English as a second language (e.g., National Academies of Sciences, Engineering, and Medicine, 2019).

Unfortunately, racism and inequity pervade all aspects of public education in the United States (Lazarus et al., 2021a). White-centric norms, policies, and expectations can telegraph that minoritized students are deficient and even delinquent (Spencer et al., 2001). School practices that perpetuate inequity include the use of exclusionary discipline, zero tolerance, and school fortification with police and security technologies—all of which can criminalize Black, Indigenous, and People of Color (BIPOC) students for minor infractions (Homer & Fisher, 2020; Pearman et al., 2019). For example, exclusionary discipline practices in school have disproportionately affected the educational trajectories of Black students, along with negatively impacting their mental health. Starting early, these practices include special education placements, suspensions, alternative learning center placement, zero-tolerance discipline practices, and mandatory expulsions (Cokley et al., 2014). Compared to Asian American, Latino, and White students, Black preschoolers are three to five times more likely to be expelled. Collectively, systemic racism and structural inequity erode the well-being and mental health of students of color and other minoritized youth (Astell-Burt et al., 2012). Almost half of Black (47%) and Latino (48%) youth develop a mental health disorder before age 18 (Merikangas et al., 2010). Furthermore, the COVID-19 pandemic has exacerbated the discrepancy between White and BIPOC students in educational and mental health functioning (Grewenig et al., 2021; National Center for Education Statistics, 2022).

Accordingly, the National Association of School Psychologists (NASP, 2019) position statement on prejudice, discrimination, and racism states that "positive educational and social outcomes for all children and youth are possible only in a society—and schools within it—that guarantees equitable treatment to all people, regardless of race, class, culture, language, gender, gender identity, religion, sexual orientation, nationality, citizenship, ability, and other dimensions of difference." NASP notes that all children are entitled to an education that affirms and validates the diversity of their cultural and individual differences, facilitates well-being and positive academic and mental health outcomes, and fosters resilience.

The Three Pillar Model proposed in this book suggests that leaders should intentionally work for systems-level change that prioritizes educational equity (i.e., advocacy and activism). By doing so, leaders can help transform schools, especially those related to providing mental health services, in a way that recognizes every child's unique strengths within the context of cultural humility, respect, and agency. In other words, through culturally responsive practice, as indicated by an ever-growing body of research, disparities in providing mental health services for racially minoritized students can be reduced through school-based service delivery (Cummings et al., 2010). Therefore, in collaboration with school psychologists, school leaders can improve access to services by reducing the stigma associated with mental health problems, increasing trust in school-based mental health practitioners, and communicating and illustrating the benefit of getting help (Clauss-Ehlers et al., 2012; Harris & Plucker, 2014).

5.   Use evidence-based and research-supported interventions

A critical point: The internet is not peer reviewed. This should go without saying that much of the information on social media, in traditional media, blogs, or the internet is not backed by legitimate science. Evidence-based interventions (EBIs) have been reported in scientific journals that meet specific criteria and have been peer reviewed by a panel of experts in their respective fields before publication. Some of these criteria include a thorough understanding of the scientific literature; the quality of the research design and methodology, including the reliability, validity, and utility of the assessment tools used; the correct statistical analysis; the match between the data collected and the interpretation of the results; and a discussion of the limitations of the study. All studies have some limitations.

Both authors of this text have published dozens of articles in peer reviewed journals, serve on editorial boards devoted to the distribution of quality scientific research, and believe in science to enhance the quality of life of our nation's youth. For a manuscript to be published in a scientific peer reviewed journal, it is blindly reviewed (that is, the reviewers do not know who the researchers are) and sent to a panel of experts for their rigorous critique. Along with this process, reviewers decide to reject, suggest significant revisions, or accept a submission. In most cases, the decision is one of the first two choices. In high quality journals, only a small number of submitted manuscripts meet the scientific rigor for publication. Essentially, publishing quality research is an arduous process that is highly vetted.

One of the most respected and widely cited types of articles uses meta-analysis which refers to a research strategy where instead of conducting new research with participants, the researchers examine the results of several previous studies. This is done to gain greater confidence in the results due to the larger pool of studies and participants. For example, Durlak et al. (2011) published a study, "Impact of enhancing students' social and emotional learning: A meta-analysis of school-based universal interventions." As a result of this study, educators and social scientists understood that social-emotional learning is valuable for two reasons. First, it improved the social emotional competencies of students. Second, it also raised students' academic achievement (see Chapter 7 for further discussion of this research). Also, because the study was meta-analytic in its design, consumers can have more confidence in the results.

6. Focus on children's strengths and well-being

A dual-factor model guides the discussion of mental health in this book. This vantage point defines mental health as both the *presence* of well-being and the *absence* of pathology. Suldo and Doll (2021) noted that significant evidence exists that psychological well-being contributes to youth's school achievement and life success. The dual-factor model is predicated on assessing well-being, and it gauges the full range of emotional experiences from dissatisfied/languishing to extremely satisfied/flourishing. In other words, mental health is not a unitary concept, and the psychopathology model does not account for all the dimensions of mental health. For example, most school shooters were never classified as having an emotional behavior disorder (EBD) before the attack (Vossekuil et al., 2002). Obviously, these perpetrators did not evidence emotional well-being. They tended to be angry, frustrated, isolated, socially detached, rejected, and filled with resentment and rage, often guided by a sense of personal humiliation (Langman, 2021).

Previously, psychological models were based solely on the science of mental illness or psychopathology. They were predicated on the assumption that by decreasing youth's emotional or behavioral symptoms, the corresponding balance would ensue in well-being and quality of life. However, this point of view has been challenged within the past two decades. Research has found psychological distress or illness is negatively correlated with emotional well-being, yet still distinct. As noted by Lazarus et al. (2021a): "When considered in tandem, these two factors yield a more comprehensive understanding of human functioning" (p. 2).

It, therefore, makes sense to focus service delivery within a dual-factor model to reduce psychological distress and increase psychological well-being. The science of psychological well-being has shown how positive psychological activities can be incorporated into a school's curriculum (Masten, 2021). One of the most prominent approaches to do this, which will be discussed in Chapter 7, is social-emotional learning (SEL). This approach helps teach students skills to understand feelings, problem solve, build social relationships, and use emotional regulation (Elias et al., 2021). These skills can be taught to the entire classroom (Tier I) or in small groups (Tier II) to those needing better skills and more support.

7. View supports through a trauma-informed lens

Trauma-informed school approaches aim to establish learning environments that enable children exposed to trauma to learn to regulate their emotions, develop caring relationships with adults and peers, succeed academically, and become socially and emotionally competent (Lazarus et al., 2021b). One of the first steps to developing trauma-informed approaches is teaching educators about trauma's destructive impact on children's behavior, learning, and social-emotional development. The underlying philosophy in trauma-informed practices focuses on "what happened to the student" rather than "what is wrong with the student." This philosophy enables leaders to understand the deleterious impact that adverse experiences and trauma have on a child's life and therefore approach each child with more empathy and compassion.

As noted by Cole et al. (2005), once educators become better informed about the adverse impact of trauma on children's lives, they may be better primed to provide emotional and behavioral supports, rather than respond with punitive and disciplinary measures such as suspensions and expulsions. Instead of blaming the child, educators can take a more therapeutic approach which involves providing emotional support, teaching effective coping strategies, giving the child time to get their feelings under control, de-escalating potential power struggles, and using positive reinforcement when the child engages in prosocial behaviors. It is important to understand that a child who has experienced a great deal of trauma may react in a self-protective way and deal with any perceived threat by using anger and aggression. For example, suppose a child tends to cope with frustration with angry meltdowns. In that case, educators can teach the youngster emotional self-regulation strategies and let the child retreat to a calm corner until they control their feelings and behaviors. In addition, leaders can help foster linkages with mental health providers and advocate for specific supportive interventions and additional resources.

It is recommended that trauma-informed practices be used in all schools, especially in low-income neighborhoods where trauma in youth is more prevalent. This is in line with the National Survey of Child Health, which revealed that Black, Latino, and poorer children were more likely to experience adverse events and trauma than White and wealthier children (Slopen et al., 2016). Based on a systemic review of the extant research, it has been found that approximately two out of three youths are likely to have experienced at least one potentially traumatic event by age 17 (Perfect et al., 2016). Another national research study revealed that approximately 34 million children had experienced one potentially traumatic event during their lifetime (Bethell et al., 2017). Consequently, a trauma-informed approach has the added benefit of supporting all students, not just those receiving special education services (Chafouleas et al., 2016). As noted by Rossen and Cowan (2013), childhood trauma is one of the major causes of mental health problems in youth and will be discussed in more depth in Chapter 8.

8. Become caring and supportive communities

For schools to become caring and supportive communities, dialogues must occur among all faculty and staff and the families and communities they serve. Frequently reaching out to families and the community to provide and gather input shows that the school cares. Educational leaders can ask themselves and the families and communities they serve these questions: What are we doing as a school to become caring communities where all children belong? How do we ensure that all children and families are equally respected and supported? Are we reaching out to all children? How do we welcome new children and families into our school? Are we hiring culturally aware and sensitive professionals who are attentive to students' needs? How do we respond to our most vulnerable children? How do we establish a culture and climate that makes students eager to come to school and learn? For further discussion regarding practical ways to do this, see Chapter 5.

9. Integrate the delivery of services in tandem with families and community supports

Both families and community stakeholders are essential partners in creating safe and supportive schools and fostering students' mental health. The better partners work in tandem, the more successful schools can become. Creating school-community partnerships can be challenging but rewarding. These relationships take time to develop, with trust, mutual respect, communication, and transparency as the most essential building blocks.

We have seen the disastrous effects when agencies fail to share information, when communication is blocked, when trust has not been established, and when power struggles have occurred. This was most noteworthy during two of the major tragic events in the United States—the September 11, 2001, downing of the World Trade Center and the January 6 insurrection at the Capitol—and, more recently, during the school shooting at Robb Elementary School in Uvalde, Texas. However, often after tragedies, agencies do come together. This was seen in the aftermath of the Marjory Stoneman Douglas High School shooting. More than a dozen school districts came together to provide crisis care in the aftermath. Schools worked with a myriad of local mental health agencies; family support groups were created; religious institutions provided assistance; practitioners were taught various ways of treating PTSD in children and adolescents; the National Association of School Psychologists (NASP) shared mental health handouts with educators, parents, and students; police offered critical briefings; various local agencies provided grief counseling, art experiences, and yoga instruction; and animal support therapists were seen on campus providing care with therapy dogs, etc. Some relationships continued and were codified. Even though there were coordinated efforts to intervene, due to the severity of the tragedy, the need for more intensive services were expressed by some school members and families.

One of the most important ways schools can become caring communities is for leaders to collaborate with families and develop family-centric relationships. For further discussion regarding strategies, refer to Chapter 6.

Conclusion

In this chapter, we discussed the critical need to develop safe and supportive schools that foster the emotional well-being of our youth. We described the unique mental health challenges facing children and adolescents, the inequities in our society that make these challenges more difficult for marginalized populations, and the role of schools and school leaders to make learning environments safer and more supportive. The Three Pillar Model for safe, supportive, and mentally healthy schools was presented, the elements were listed, and the foundational principles that undergird the model were described. The next seven chapters will discuss procedures, programs, supports, and interventions. As we move forward in this book, you will learn much about what can be done to ensure safe and supportive schools that foster students' mental health. We welcome you along this journey and hope you will become an advocate for the change that promotes the emotional well-being of all our nation's youth.

References

Association of Supervision and Curriculum Development. (n.d.). The whole child approach. http://www.ascd.org/whole-child.aspx

Astell-Burt, T., Maynard, M. J., Lenguerrand, E., & Harding, S. (2012). Racism, ethnic density, and psychological well-being through adolescence: Evidence from the determinants of adolescent social well-being and health longitudinal study. *Ethnicity & Health, 17*(1–2), 71–87. https://doi.org/10.1080/13557858.2011.645153

Benson, P. L. (2006). *All kids are our kids: What communities must do to raise caring and responsible children and adolescents* (2nd ed.). Jossey-Bass.

Bethell, C. D., Davis, M. B., Gombojav, N., Stumbo, S., & Powers, K. (2017). *Issue brief: A national and across state profile on adverse childhood experiences among children and possibilities to heal and*

thrive. Johns Hopkins Bloomberg School of Public Health. http://
www.cahmi.org/wp-content/uploads/2017/10/aces_brief_final.pdf

Brackett, M. (2020, May 25). Rethinking gratitude on Memorial Day.
Blog post. https://www.marcbrackett.com/re-thinking-gratitude-
on-memorial-day/

Bronfenbrenner, U. (1979). *The ecology of human development:
Experiments by nature and design*. Harvard University Press.

Centers for Disease Control and Prevention (2018). Whole School,
Whole Community, Whole Child (WSCC) model. https://www.
cdc.gov/healthyschools/wscc/index.htm

Centers for Disease Control and Prevention (2018). *Youth risk behavior
surveillance – United States, 2017*. https://www.cdc.gov/mmwr/
volumes/67/ss/ss6708a1.htm

Chafouleas, S. M., Johnson, A. H., Overstreet, S., & Santos, N. M. (2016).
Toward a blueprint for trauma-informed service delivery in
schools. *School Mental Health, 8*, 144–162.

Cholera, R., Falusi, O. O., and Linton, J. M. (2020). Sheltering in place in
a xenophobic climate: COVID-19 and children in immigrant
families. *Pediatrics, 146*(1). https://doi.org/10.1542/peds.2020-1094.

Clauss-Ehlers, C. S., Serpell, Z. N., & Weist, M. D. (2012). *Handbook of
culturally responsive school mental health: Advancing research,
training, practice, and policy*. Springer Science & Business Media.
https://doi.org/10.1007/978-1-4614-4948-5

Cokley, K., Cody, B., Smith, L., Bealey, S., Miller, I.S.K., Hurst, A., . . ., &
Jackson, S. (2014). Bridge over troubled waters. *Phi Delta Kappan,
96*(4), 40–45.

Cole, S. F., O'Brien, J. G., Gadd, M. G., Ristuccia, J., Wallace, D. L., &
Gregory, M. (2005). *Helping traumatized children learn: Supportive
school environments for children traumatized by family violence*.
Massachusetts Advocates for Children.

Cummings, J. R., Ponce, N. A., & Mays, V. M. (2010). Comparing racial/
ethnic differences in mental health service use among high-
need subpopulations across clinical and school-based settings.
Journal of Adolescent Health, 46(6), 603–606. https://doi.org/10.
1016/j.jadohealth.2009.11.221

Diliberti, M. K., Schwartz, H. L., & Grant, D. (2021, August 29). *Stress
topped the reasons why public school teachers quit, even before*

30 ◆ Introduction

COVID-19, RAND Corporation, RR-A1121–2, 2021. https://www.rand.org/pubs/research_reports/RRA1121-2.html

Doll, B. (2019). Addressing student internalizing behavior through multi-tiered systems of support. *School Mental Health, 11,* 290–293.

Dorado, J., Martinez, S., McArthur, M., & Leibovitz, L. (2016). Healthy Environments and Response to Trauma in Schools (HEARTS): A whole-school, multi-level, prevention and intervention program for creating trauma-informed, safe and supportive schools. *School Mental Health, 8,* 163–176.

Duong, M. T., Bruns, E. J., Lee, K., Cox, S., Coifman, J., Mayworm, A., & Lyon, A. R. (2020). Rates of mental health service utilization by children and adolescents in schools and other common service settings: A systematic review and meta-analysis. *Administration and Policy in Mental Health and Mental Health Services Research.* Advance online publication. https://doi.org/10.1007/s10488-020-01080-9

Durlak, J. A., Weissberg, R. P., Dymnicki, A. B., Schellinger, K. B., & Taylor, R. D. (2011). The impact of enhancing students' social and emotional learning: A meta-analysis of school-based universal interventions. *Child Development, 82*(1), 405–432. https://doi.org/10.1111/j.1467-8624.2010.01564.x

Edsall, T. (2022, December 14). *Attacking teachers from every angle is not the way to improve schools.* New York Times. https://www.nytimes.com/2022/12/14/opinion/teacher-shortage-education.html?smid=nytcore-ios-share&referringSource=articleShare

Elias, M. J., Powlo, E. R., Lorenzo, A., & Eichert, B. (2021). Adopting a trauma informed approach to social-emotional learning. In P. J. Lazarus, S. Suldo, & B. Doll (Eds.), *Fostering the emotional well-being of our youth: A school-based approach* (pp. 96–116). Oxford University Press. doi:10.1093/med-psych/9780190918873.003.0006

Erikson, E. (1963). *Childhood and society* (2nd ed.). Norton.

Farmer, E. M. Z., Burns, B. J., Phillips, S. D., Angold, A., & Costello, E. J. (2003). Pathways into and through mental health services for children and adolescents. *Psychiatric Services, 54*(1), 60–66. https://doi.org/10.1176/appi.ps.54.1.60

Goleman, D. (2006). *Emotional intelligence: Why it can matter more than IQ.* Random House.

Gore, F., Bloem, P., Patton, G. C., Ferguson, B. J., Coffey, C., Sawyer, S. M., & Mathers, C. M. (2011). Global burden of disease in young people aged 10–24 years: A systematic analysis. *Lancet, 377*, 2093–2102. https://doi.org/10.1016/s0140-6736(11)60512-6

Grewenig, E., Lergetporer, P., Werner, K., Woessmann, L., & Zierow, L. (2021). COVID-19 and educational inequality: How school closures affect low- and high-achieving students. *European Economic Review, 140*. https://doi.org/10.1016/j.euroecorev.2021.103920

Guterres, A. (2020, May 21). We need to take action to address the mental health crisis in this pandemic. *Time*. https://time.com/5839553/un-action-mental-health-crisis/

Harris, B., & Plucker, J. (2014). Achieving equity and excellence: The role of school mental health providers in shrinking excellence gaps. *Gifted Child Today, 37*(2), 111–118. https://doi.org/10.1177/1076217514520967

Homer, E. M., & Fisher, B. W. (2020). Police in schools and student arrest rates across the United States: Examining differences by race, ethnicity, and gender. *Journal of School Violence, 19*(2), 192–204. https://doi.org/10.1080/15388220.2019.1604377

Jones, J., & Miranda, A. H. (2021). Building culturally responsive schools: A model based on the Association for Supervision and Curriculum Development's Whole Child Approach. In P. J. Lazarus, S. Suldo, & B. Doll (Eds.), *Fostering the emotional well-being of our youth: A school- based approach* (pp. 61–78). Oxford University Press. doi: 10.1093/med-psych/9780190918873.003.0004

Kataoka, S. H., Zhang, L., & Wells, K. B. (2002). Unmet need for mental health care among US children: Variation by ethnicity and insurance status. *American Journal of Psychiatry, 159*, 1548–1555. https://doi.org/10.1176/appi.ajp.159.9.1548

Langman, P. F. (2021). *Warning signs: Identifying school shooters before they strike.* Langman Psychological Associates, LLC.

Lazarus, P. J. (2023). Five years after the Parkland shooting, a school psychologist offers insights on helping students and teachers deal with grief. *The Conversation*. https://theconversation.com/five-years-after-parkland-shooting-a-school-psychologist-offers-insights-on-helping-students-and-teachers-deal-with-grief-192292.

32 ◆ Introduction

Lazarus, P. J., Doll, B., Song, S. Y., & Radliff, K. (2021a). Transforming school mental health services based on a culturally responsible dual-factor model. *School Psychology Review*. https://doi.org/10.1080/2372966X.2021.1968282

Lazarus, P. J., Overstreet, S., & Rossen, E. (2021b). Building a foundation for trauma-informed schools. In P. J. Lazarus, S. Suldo, & B. Doll (Eds.), *Fostering the emotional well-being of our youth: A school-based approach* (pp. 313–337). Oxford University Press. doi:10.1093/med-psych/9780190918873.003.0016

Lazarus, P., Suldo, S., & Doll, B. (2021c). Introduction. Are our youth all right? In P. J. Lazarus, S. Suldo, & B. Doll (Eds.), *Fostering the emotional well-being of our youth: A school- based approach* (pp. 1–19). Oxford University Press. doi:10.1093/med-psych/9780190918873.003.0001

Lazarus, P. J., & Sulkowski, M. L. (2011). The emotional well-being of our nation's youth and the promise of social-emotional learning. *Communiqué, 40*(2), 1, 16–17.

Lowenhaupt, R., & Hopkins, M. (2020). Considerations for school leaders serving US immigrant communities in the global pandemic. *Journal of Professional Capital and Community*. https://doi.org/10.1108/JPCC-05-2020-0023

Margolius, M., Doyle Lynch, A., Pufall Jones, E., & Hynes, M. (2020). *The state of young people during COVID-19: Findings from a nationally representative survey of high school youth*. Americas Promise Alliance. https://www.americaspromise.org/resource/state-young-peopleduring-

Maslow, A. (1962). *Toward a psychology of being*. Van Nostrand.

Masten, A. S., Lucke, C. M., Nelson, K. M., & Stallworthy, I. C. (2021). Resilience in development and psychopathology: Multisystem perspectives. *Annual Review of Clinical Psychology, 17*, 16.1–16.29. https://doi.org/10.1146/annurev-clinpsy-081219-120307

Merikangas, K. R., He, J., Burstein, M., Swanson, S. A., Avenevoli, S., Cui, L., . . ., & Swendsen, J. (2010). Lifetime prevalence of mental disorders in US adolescents: Results from the National Comorbidity Survey Replication–Adolescent Supplement (NCS-A). *Journal of the American Academy of Child & Adolescent Psychiatry, 49*(10), 980–989. https://doi.org/10.1016/j.jaac.2010.05.017

Murthy, V. (2020). *Together: The healing power of human connection in a sometimes lonely world.* HarperCollins.

National Academies of Sciences, Engineering, and Medicine (2019). *Fostering healthy mental, emotional, and behavioral development in children and youth: A national agenda.* The National Academies Press. https://doi.org/10.17226/25201.

National Academies of Sciences, Engineering, and Medicine (2021). *School-based strategies for addressing the mental health and well-being of youth in the wake of COVID-19.* The National Academies Press. https://doi.org/10.17226/26262.

National Association of School Psychologists (2019). NASP Policy Playbook. https://www.nasponline.org/Documents/Research and Policy/NASP Policy Playbook_FINAL 6-6-19.pdf

National Center for Education Statistics (2022). The nation's report card. NAEP long term trend assessment results: Reading and mathematics. https://www.nationsreportcard.gov/highlights/ltt/2022/

Nickerson, A. B., Randa, R., Jimerson, S., & Guerra, N. C. (2021) Safe places to learn: Advances in school safety research and practice. *School Psychology Review, 50*(2–3), 158–171. https://doi.org/10.1080/2372966X.2021.1871948

Pearman, F. A., Currashuren, F. C., Fisher, B., & Gardella, J. (2019). Are achievement gaps related to discipline gaps? Evidence from National Data. *AERA Open, 5*(4), 1–18. https://doi.org/10.1177/2332858419875440

Perfect, M. M., Turley, M. R., Carlson, J. S., Yohannan, J., & Saint Gilles. M. P. (2016). School-related outcomes of traumatic event exposure and traumatic stress symptoms in students: A systematic review of research from 1990 to 2015. *School Mental Health, 8,* 7–43.

Phifer, L. W., & Hull, R. (2016). Helping students heal: Observations of trauma- informed practices in the schools. *School Mental Health, 8*(1), 201–205. https://doi.org/10.1007/s12310-016-9183-2

Rossen, E., & Cowan, K. (2013). The role of schools in supporting traumatized students. *Principal's Research Review, 8*(6), 1–8.

Schmidt, E. M., Hamilton, T. N., & Hoffman, J. A. (2021). Promoting physical activity, nutrition and sleep. In P. J. Lazarus, S. Suldo, &

34 ◆ Introduction

B. Doll (Eds.), *Fostering the emotional well-being of our youth: A school-based approach* (pp. 243–263). Oxford University Press. doi:10.1093/med-psych/9780190918873.003.0013

Shah, K., Mann, S., Singh, R., Bangar, R., & Kulkarni, R. (2020). Impact of COVID-19 on the mental health of children and adolescents. *Cureus, 12*(8), e10051. https://doi.org/10.7759/cureus.10051

Spencer, M. B., Noll, E., Stoltzfus, J., & Harpalani, V. (2001). Identity and school adjustment: Revisiting the "acting White" assumption. *Educational Psychologist, 36*(1), 21–30. https://doi.org/10.1207/S15326985EP3601_3

Stern, M., Wagner, M.H., & Thompson, L.A. (2020). Current and COVID-19 challenges with childhood and adolescent sleep. *JAMA Pediatrics.* https://doi.org/10.1001/jamapediatrics.2020.2784.

Suldo, S. (2016*). Promoting student happiness. Positive psychology interventions in schools.* Guilford.

Suldo, S., & Doll, B. (2021). Conceptualizing youth mental health through a dual-factor model. In P. J. Lazarus, S. Suldo, & B. Doll (Eds.), *Fostering the emotional well-being of our nation's youth: A school-based approach (*pp. 20–39). Oxford University Press. doi:10.1093/med-psych/9780190918873.003.0002

Sulkowski, M. L. (2016). The student homeless crisis and the role of school psychology: Missed opportunities, room for improvement, and future directions. *Psychology in the Schools, 53*(7), 760–771. https://doi.org/10.1002/pits.21936

Sulkowski, M. L., & Lazarus, P. J. (2017). *Creating safe and supportive schools and fostering students' mental health.* Routledge.

U. S. Department of Health and Human Services. (2000). *Report of the Surgeon General's Conference on Children's Mental Health: A national action agenda.* Author.

Vella-Brodrick, D. A. (2016). Optimizing the art and science of well-being in schools. *Communiqué, 45*(1), 1, 29–31.

Vossekuil, B., Fein, R. A., Reddy, M., Borum, R., & Modzeleski, W. (2002). *The final report and findings of the Safe School Initiative: Implications for the prevention of school attacks in the United States.* Washington, DC: U.S. Secret Service and U.S. Department of Education.

Section 1
The Safe Pillar

2

Physical Safety

Environmental Design, Policies, and Approaches that Reinforce School Safety

Students are sensitive to the environment in which they learn. If the environment is favorable (e.g., is quiet, has adequate lighting, contains requisite resources and supports), the school environment can help facilitate learning. However, unfavorable school environments can make students feel uncomfortable and have a deleterious impact on learning and students' well-being. In support of this notion, one study found that seven specific environmental features accounted for up to 16% of the variance in students' academic progress over one school year, even if students were not consciously aware of these features (Barrett et al., 2015). These are light, temperature, air quality, feelings of "ownership" in the environment, flexibility in classroom design, the complexity of stimulation, and the use of color. Therefore, in addition to the interpersonal environment at school, the physical environment also is important for influencing student outcomes in subtle, yet meaningful ways. It is important to pause on this point for a second. If relatively unobvious and benign elements in the school environment can significantly impact student outcomes, what about the presence of overt and obvious elements?

This chapter discusses how elements in environmental design, organization, and functioning influence the school environment, as well as school safety and security. Most saliently, these include increasing the focus on strategic environmental design, using security technologies, employing School Resource Officers (SRO), and implementing active safety drills—all of which are now common practices in U.S. schools. However, no panacea exists for creating and maintaining physical safety in schools, and several existing practices have drawbacks and opportunity costs. Therefore, in addition to addressing the safety of the physical school environment, and consistent with research-supported practice, this chapter emphasizes developing a comprehensive and balanced safety plan to ensure the physical well-being of students and staff, as well as the steps needed to make this happen.

The Physical School Environment

Schools are increasingly faced with the dilemma of ensuring the physical safety of the school environment without turning schools into fortresses. This can be a difficult balancing act. Will students feel safer or more uncomfortable if security cameras, metal detectors, and armed guards are present on school campuses? Will they feel more ready to learn in restrictive educational settings or feel stifled and distracted by a school environment that might inadvertently broadcast that the school is unsafe and security measures are needed for protection?

The answers to these questions are varied; however, some preliminary research does speak to these questions. According to existing estimates, 57% to 68% of schools have security guards or police officers, 70% to 81% have security cameras, and 7% to 11% have metal detectors (Musu-Gillette et al., 2018;

Roberts et al., 2010). Collectively, such security strategies have been coined as "target hardening" or the purposeful strengthening of a building or setting to protect it in the event of an attack (Addington, 2009). However, constructing and running schools like correctional facilities is antithetical to the mission of schools. Instead, schools need to be open and nurturing places in which a diverse population of students feels comfortable learning and growing. Furthermore, the overuse of security technologies (e.g., metal detectors, security cameras, etc.) sends the message that schools are not safe, can make students feel anxious, and has not been found to prevent violence according to a wealth of research (Addington, 2009; Perumean-Chaney & Sutton, 2013).

Thus, balancing school security and comfort requires tact and a commitment to ensuring that all students feel welcome at school (Lamoreaux & Sulkowski, 2021). Simple strategies for achieving the former include having administrators greet students when they arrive at school and special events (e.g., ceremonies, dances), having educators present in hallways during times when a large number of students are transitioning, encouraging administrators to pop in to visit classrooms, having a clearly defined locker policy, enforcing a consistent and respectful dress code, and developing and implementing policies for parking automobiles on campus.

Other important strategies for increasing the physical safety of school campuses involve controlling campus access. In general, visitors should be required to report to a central office to check in and be provided with an identifying nametag or identification badge (Brock et al., 2001). The person checking in individuals should be familiar with the student body and be aware of school safety procedures. Additionally, all adults at school should be trained to greet and direct visitors to the main office, where they can be checked to ensure they have a legitimate reason for being at the school (Trump, 2000). Multiple entrance points in schools should be reduced by locking external doors

40 ◆ The Safe Pillar

TABLE 2.1 Strategies that Schools Can Employ to Increase Physical Safety

◆ Make school campuses safe and welcoming	◆ Display positive posters and messages
	◆ Greet all students with a smile
	◆ Have staff present in hallways during passing times
	◆ Respect diversity of all students and families
◆ Ensure that school safety is on the educational agenda	◆ Have a school safety and healthy climate segment in meetings
◆ Ensure that the school handbook includes clear language about school safety	◆ Delineate clearly defined behavioral expectations for student conduct
	◆ Reflect state, county, and local statutes and ordinances in the school handbook
◆ Have a clearly defined locker policy	◆ Inform students and families that lockers are school property
	◆ Advise students that lockers can be searched at any time
	◆ Ensure that built-in locking mechanisms for doors are used, and school staff know the combination or have access to a key
◆ Develop and enforce a school dress code	◆ Ban highly provocative and offensive clothing
	◆ Prohibit gang attire
	◆ Enforce dress code expectations
◆ Review weapons and possession policies	◆ Determine the differences and boundaries between criminal offenses and disciplinary matters
	◆ Ensure that school-related punishments fit the nature of the offense
	◆ Enforce a 12-month suspension for possession of a firearm in light of the Gun-Free School Zone Act of 1994
◆ Mandate crime reporting and tracking	◆ Report crimes immediately
	◆ Aggregate and regularly review data to identify potential trends
◆ Establish an emergency operations center	◆ Make sure that technology in the center is current
	◆ Establish a school communications network

Physical Safety ◆ 41

◆ Establish uniform visitor-screening procedures	◆ Require that name tags/badges are worn by school visitors ◆ Require picture ID cards for staff and students
◆ Back up communications sources and channels	◆ Consider using emergency emails and text messages ◆ Test Internet and phone services regularly to ensure their functioning
◆ Remove obstacles to clear observation	◆ Remove unnecessary shrubs and other objects that block clear lines of sight ◆ Remove any impediments that get in the way of navigating safely through the school ◆ Install parabolic/convex mirrors in hidden hallways/stairwells ◆ Replace double-entry doors with zig-zag designs ◆ Design or modify bathrooms to ensure better visibility by staff
◆ Have staff supervise students in high traffic areas and locker rooms	◆ Discourage students from congregating in areas where they cannot be observed by staff ◆ Rotate staff supervision responsibilities ◆ Require coaches and/or other school personnel to be in the locker rooms when students are present to ensure safety
◆ Have anonymous threat, bullying, cyberbullying, harassment, intimidation, and potential suicide reporting boxes, lines, and websites	◆ Reassure students that they will not be punished for reporting threats ◆ Tell students that all reports will be appropriately addressed ◆ Act on potential threats immediately ◆ Have a safety stop sign in the office—this sign should encourage staff to "drop everything" and immediately attend to the student who grabs the sign
◆ Quickly remove graffiti and fix broken windows/doors	◆ Ensure that the school environment is clean, functional, and orderly in order to lower rates of violence and problematic behavior

Note: With permission, this text box was adapted from Sulkowski and Lazarus (2017).

to non-staff members; pedestrian and vehicular traffic should be routed through areas that can be supervised easily; and some schools may want to consider fencing their perimeters, especially if they are located in a neighborhood with high rates of violence (Bosworth et al., 2011; Shelton et al., 2009). Table 2.1 lists additional strategies that schools can employ to increase physical safety, as well as some guidelines on how these strategies can be effectively employed.

Crime prevention through environmental design (CPTED). Crime prevention through environmental design is an architectural approach that involves building physical environments to prevent crime or delinquency. Although relatively novel, this approach is increasingly used in school design plans. For example, in 2007, Arizona's School Facilities Board officially adopted and issued a report recommending the use of CPTED as part of the state's school safety initiatives (Arizona School Facilities Board, 2007).

Regarding school design, the CPTED framework has three core components: *natural surveillance, access control,* and *territoriality/maintenance.*

Natural surveillance involves using open school layouts that maximize visibility and minimize hidden spaces in schools, where most delinquent behavior occurs. Individuals are generally less likely to engage in antisocial behavior if they think they could be observed. The CPTED concept of *access control* pertains to determining who is allowed in and out of the school building. In application, this concept generally results in limiting the number of entry points to the school, ensuring that doors are locked and secure, having visitors check in at the main office, and ensuring that unfamiliar people carry ID badges or have name tags. Lastly, the CPTED principle of *territoriality/maintenance* involves clearly demarcating spaces in the educational environment to help maintain organization and order. This principle clearly defines spaces and their use (e.g., bus circles, drop-off spots, evacuation routes, etc.). Moreover, territoriality also helps students and school staff connect to the physical school environment and develop a sense of ownership of the school (Schneider, 2010). Table 2.2 provides examples of using natural surveillance, access control, and territoriality/maintenance in school settings.

TABLE 2.2 Examples of the Use of Natural Surveillance, Access Control, and Territoriality in School Settings

- Natural surveillance
  - Increasing the number of windows to improve sight lines and natural lighting
  - Using see-through fencing around school grounds
  - Removing vegetation that can occlude natural sight lines
  - Removing unnecessary doors and clutter in shared school spaces
- Access control
  - Limiting the number of access points to a school
  - Having all visitors report to a main office
  - Keeping doors and windows locked and monitored
  - Requiring all visitors to sign in at a main office
  - Providing the main office with a way to automatically lock or open school doors electronically
  - Having emergency plans and multiple exit strategies in place
- Territoriality/Maintenance
  - Having appropriate signage in place (e.g., school rules, policies, and expectations; safety procedures)
  - Using landscaping to channel school traffic
  - Having clear access and exit points visually present
  - Maintaining school property to reduce clutter, garbage, broken furniture, and graffiti

Research on CPTED in schools. A study by Johnson et al. (2017) investigated the impact of CPTED-related factors on school violence. Key results indicated that school illumination might indirectly affect school violence because it improves natural surveillance. Further, study results suggest that changes in a school's physical environment may affect violence when those changes alter student perceptions of the environment. Similarly, consistent with the CPTED principle of territoriality/maintenance, a study by Bradshaw et al. (2014) found that physical comfort and cleanliness are important elements of school climate and propose that broken windows, trash, and graffiti are associated with a negative school climate and can increase disorder at school. Lastly, and most recently, a study by Vagi et al. (2018) found that implementing CPTED principles was associated with students feeling safer at school. In this study, students perceived that there was less violence at school, and improvements were noted in attendance because students felt that the school was more comfortable and conducive to learning.

Safety Policies and Approaches

Safe school plans and policies should be developed prospectively, continuously refined, and updated. Anticipating threats to school safety and planning how to address these in advance can mitigate many of these threats (Reeves et al., 2010). Moreover, a school can only respond effectively to chaotic and often highly distressing situations such as violent attacks with adequate forethought and planning. Safety policies and procedures are discussed next. More specifically, content is provided on forming school safety teams, conducting safety audits, developing and implementing crisis plans, collaborating with community agencies, and implementing school lockdowns and active shooter drills.

Safety teams. All schools should develop safety teams that regularly meet to discuss safety policies and procedures. These teams should generally comprise a school administrator, a school mental health professional, a school nurse, security personnel, teachers, and parents (NASP & NASRO, 2017). School safety teams aim to develop, foster, and maintain a safe and positive school climate by addressing threats of violence, emergency planning, campus security, bullying, gang violence, fighting, weapon carrying, sexual aggression, substance abuse, and vandalism. It is important for school safety teams to balance prevention, security, and crisis management practices—not just one or two of these foci. In addition, all members of school communities should know who is on the safety team, and alternate team members are needed to help manage problems that could result from a team member being absent. Many school districts are now posting contact information for school safety team members on school websites as well as resources related to ensuring student safety. Table 2.3 lists additional considerations for developing building-level school safety teams.

TABLE 2.3 Considerations in Developing Building-Level School Safety Teams

♦ Team members should include people who are familiar people in the school community (e.g., students, staff, parents/caregivers)
  ♦ Increases rapport
  ♦ Helps with identifying students who might be in crisis
  ♦ Makes it easier to make referrals and follow-up with impacted students
  ♦ Helps with identifying staff and team strengths, weaknesses, and potential needs
  ♦ Helps team members gain a greater understanding of school logistics, routines, and culture
♦ Team members must be readily available to respond to a crisis/safety concern
  ♦ Encourages immediate response
  ♦ Ensures a continuum of coverage and effective response
  ♦ Helps with communicating with outside partners and agencies
  ♦ Enables school safety team members and school-based mental health professionals to triage the needs of students who are most affected
  ♦ Provides a structure that enables teams to meet on a regular basis to be prepared as well as to review safety plans and procedures
  ♦ Ensures that evaluation and ongoing services can be coordinated and delivered more efficiently

Adapted from NASP (2009).

Safety audits. Schools are increasingly implementing audits to assess strengths and weaknesses associated with safety policies and practices. Such audits have been incorporated into state laws and typically require school districts to conduct an audit every three years. Initially, safety audits focused primarily on maintaining the school environment's physical safety, such as making sure that fire extinguishers and smoke detectors were in place and functional, that playground equipment was safe to use, and that the overall school physical environment was clean and orderly. However, safety audits have expanded to focus on the broader school climate, involve an assessment of a school's social and emotional culture, and include parent and community data sources (DeMary et al., 2000). They also increasingly involve members of school-based safety teams. This has necessitated that safety audits be conducted during school hours with students present so that they can be asked about their personal experiences in school and so that peer and staff interactions can be observed (Cornell & Gregory, 2008). Some states, such as Texas, also require an intruder assessment to be conducted during school hours, which involves having a member of the safety audit team (who is not known to the faculty) come to campus and document the accessibility of the school facilities and how sh/e is treated by school staff (e.g., Do staff stop the intruder and question them? Do they contact administration or law enforcement?).

Safety audits should include reviewing school and district data and documents related to emergency operations procedures, codes of conduct, student handbooks, and data on crime, violence, suspensions, and expulsions. Such data sources are incorporated into an audit report that is required to be submitted to the state department of education. This report typically follows a checklist format to ensure that pertinent sources of information are not overlooked. Additionally, qualitative information such as student and staff interviews and pictures of school environments may be included. Although school administrators typically lead audit teams, all members of schools can be involved, as they may have different and relevant perspectives and experiences to share about school safety. Among other ways, information can be collected from school personnel via interviews, surveys and reports of personal experiences, and critical incidents to the safety audit team. This is particularly important because schools are tasked with making safety improvements in response to data collected, analyzed, and reported as part of the audit process.

Crisis plans. Well-conceived and field-tested crisis plans can help to ensure rapid and effective responses to crises and acts of violence. Furthermore, having these plans in place and known by school community members can help individuals view crisis events as more manageable and less emotionally traumatic (Reeves et al., 2010). According to Brock et al. (2016), crisis plans should include strategies for activating response protocols; contacting law enforcement officers, emergency responders, parents, and the media; de-escalating threats; identifying all crisis response personnel; communicating with staff; and communicating with parents and other stakeholders on an ongoing basis as a crisis unfolds and is addressed. Chapter 8 goes into greater depth on the aforementioned components that a crisis plan should address.

Agency collaboration. In advance of a crisis event, schools need to establish relationships with local agencies to help ensure school safety and crisis response. If an event requires police intervention, school administrators will need to maintain regular contact with the police incident commander as well as liaison officers and public information officers to make sure that accurate and timely information is being collected and can then be disseminated to members of the school community (Reeves et al., 2010). Schools will also need to have positive and collaborative agreements set up in advance with emergency first responding agencies such as firefighters and paramedics who will need to know the layout of a school so they can nimbly navigate its infrastructure. Further, a list of community providers should be developed and regularly updated so that school members can refer students and families to competent mental health professionals, social service agencies, and shelters.

School lockdowns and active shooter drills. A lockdown is intended to secure a school to keep out a threat, whereas an active shooter (i.e., involving a firearm) or armed assailant drill (i.e., involving another type of weapon such as a knife) is designed to be practiced for when a potential assailant is approaching campus or already is on school grounds. These procedures are designed to prevent, prepare for, and respond to safety threats. According to the National Association of School Psychologists (NASP, 2018), lockdowns are considered the best practice to secure a school and ensure the safety of students and staff. The Education Department's National Center for Educational Statistics reports that nearly all public schools conduct lockdown drills—95% in 2015 and 2016 (Musu-Gillette et al., 2018). According to NASP and the National Association of School Resource Officers (2017), research is still needed regarding the effectiveness of armed assailant or active shooter drills, and the recent use of active shooter drills has garnered controversy regarding its benefits and highlighted concerns regarding potential harm.

It is most important that schools not frighten children in a place where they should feel safe. Consequently, any active shooter drill should be first preceded by extensive preparation and education. Moreover, as Erbacher and Poland (2019) noted, every student and faculty member has unique trauma history. An active shooter or armed intruder drill can trigger painful memories for some individuals. While most children will not suffer long-term meaningful consequences, a small percentage will (Cox & Rich, 2018), and with well-reasoned and extensive planning, this can and should be prevented.

If an active shooter drill is conducted, it should be coordinated by the school-based crisis team and the local police with input from mental health personnel. NASP (2018) recommends that school psychologists should always be included in the planning process of such drills because of their experience with crisis response and the mitigation of trauma. NASP also recommends that planning include considerations regarding age and developmental levels, sensory disabilities that might increase a student's distress reaction such as autism, and intellectual disabilities that might prevent the student from understanding what is happening or compromise their ability to follow instructions. One size does not fit all regarding security plans and drills. Extra care is needed to ensure the well-being of all youth—especially to minimize potential harm to at-risk or vulnerable students.

If an active shooter drill is not conducted appropriately, it can cause undue physical and psychological harm. Some schools have used real guns to shoot blanks, students pretending to be shot or dead, and simulated bullet wounds (Aronowitz, 2014; Erbacher & Poland, 2019). For example, teachers at an elementary school in Monticello, Indiana, were left bruised and bleeding after they were shot execution-style with plastic pellets during a drill. School children in Florida were left traumatized (some sobbed, fainted, or vomited and sent goodbye messages to their parents) when the school announced: "This is not a drill" when in fact it was (Erbacher & Poland, 2019). To better understand this, an analogy may help. When passengers are flying at an altitude of 30,000 feet in an airline, the pilot does not cut off the engine and allow the plane to drop 10,000 feet to teach the passengers to put on their seatbelts, nor does sh/e turn off the oxygen to force occupants to use their oxygen masks.

When considering using active shooter drills, participation should never be mandatory, deception should never be used, parental consent must be required, students or school staff should never be placed at risk of being physically or psychologically harmed, and a healthy and supportive learning environment should not be disrupted. This is especially true in elementary schools, where only 2% of school shootings occur, according to a recent study by the U.S. Secret Service's National Threat Assessment Center (2019). Children may have difficulty differentiating between a drill and reality. If a child still engages in magical thinking (e.g., believes in the tooth fairy), sh/e likely will struggle to understand the context surrounding an active shooter drill or its purpose. Furthermore, if such drills are going to be performed under any circumstances, adults must carefully monitor the well-being of students and those exhibiting signs

50 ◆ The Safe Pillar

of trauma, developmental immaturity, hypersensitivities, and reality testing deficits should not participate (NASP & NASPRO, 2017). Table 2.4 provides guidance on best practices for those schools considering lockdowns or active shooter drills.

TABLE 2.4 Recommended Practices Regarding Lockdowns and Armed Intruder Drills: Before, During, and After

◆ Provide an orientation to the drill that helps students understand what will happen.

◆ Ensure that the orientation is tailored to the age, developmental level, disability status, and second languages of the students.

◆ Always announce that this is a drill. State something like, "This is a drill. This is not a real emergency. We will now practice how to keep safe as if there were a real emergency. Please follow all directions. Remember, this is a drill. You are all safe."

◆ Make sure that all school administrators, school resource officers, and mental health personnel are present during the drill.

◆ Consider posting a message on social media and informing the newspapers that there will be a drill so that rumors do not start, or parents and the community do not panic.

◆ Work with local law enforcement to develop different types of lockdown procedures due to the specifics of an emergency. For example, if the police are chasing a robber from the local 7-Eleven a mile away, a *secured perimeter lockout* will go into effect; where all doors are locked, and no one can enter or leave the building. In contrast, when an unknown intruder enters the school building, a *full-scale lockdown* will need to go into effect. In this case, all class doors are locked, windows and blinds are closed, students sit without making a sound, and everyone follows the protocol they have been taught.

◆ During a lockdown, all staff need to model a controlled response to keep the students calm and silent. Everyone needs to silence or turn off their cellphones.

◆ Make sure all communication is clear so that everyone knows what they need to do.

◆ Staff need to reassure any panicked students using relaxation or grounding techniques. They should be taught how to do this in an in-service training.

◆ Make sure a member of the school safety team is monitoring social media and dispelling false information, if it occurs.

◆ After the drill, if some students have become overly distressed, provide mental health crisis interventions.

◆ Provide an opportunity for all students and staff members to share their reactions to the event.

◆ Evaluate the strengths and weakness of the lockdown based on feedback of all parties to improve the response.

Adapted from NASP (2018).

Most importantly, active shooter training should focus on adults. If teachers stay relatively calm, then children will reflect their emotional state, and will typically do what is being asked of them (Williamson, 2019). Scare tactics do not make students more safe, secure, prepared, or responsive—frequently, these do the opposite by ratcheting up their fears which clouds their judgment, clear thinking, and problem-solving abilities during a crisis.

School Safety Personnel

School resource officers. Commonly known as School Resource Officers (SROs), thousands of law enforcement officers have been deployed in schools across the U.S. since the 1960s (Finn & McDevitt, 2005). SROs are typically law enforcement officers from local or county law enforcement agencies assigned to schools in cooperative agreements with education officials. These officers are usually full-time, in-house school officers with police powers employed directly by the school district. Most SROs bring experience from other law enforcement positions, ranging from having worked basic patrol to narcotics, gangs, juvenile units, and other specialized squads. Thus, it is rare to see an officer come straight out of the police academy into an SRO position. Further, even with extensive law enforcement academy training and specialized police experience, effective SRO programs provide their officers with additional training specific to their jobs as SROs (Eklund et al., 2018). Thus, these programs must integrate training in topics not necessarily central to policing. Some of these topics may focus on student and school-specific issues such as working with special education students and at-risk student populations, non-violent crisis de-escalation, teen suicide, lesson plans and classroom instruction, bullying prevention and intervention, locker searches, psychiatric hospitalizations, and school emergencies. Even though they often perform educational or related functions in schools, it is important to note that SROs differ from school security officers, who are civilian district employees that perform security functions in schools yet are not sworn police officers.

The role of SROs is emerging and will likely expand in the foreseeable future. According to Girouard (2001), SROs perform a multifaceted role in that they can be expected to deliver specialized instruction or presentations (e.g., law-related education, gang violence prevention); respond to threats of violence; counsel students who are in a state of crisis; enforce school rules and codes of conduct; collaborate with school administrators to ensure school safety; and serve as a liaison between law enforcement, schools, families, and the community. Thus, in addition to balancing security concerns and enforcing the law, SROs also must be able to function effectively in school environments, understand child development, and be familiar with education laws, policies, and practices.

School resource officers have been central to federal plans for improving school safety since the Sandy Hook Elementary School massacre. Ultimately, this involved hiring thousands of SROs across the U.S. and employing them in all K–12 school settings. However, even though SROs are encouraged to receive training in school and education-focused practices and policies such as crisis management and child development, no universal training requirements have been implemented to date, and considerable variability exists in the practices of SROs across schools, districts, and states (Theriot & Orme, 2016). Additionally, research on their impact on school systems is mixed. Some studies have found SROs to improve school safety. Yet, others suggest that SROs have a negative impact on school climate and that their involvement with schools leads to increased crime and the criminalization of minor disciplinary infractions, especially for minority youth (Devlin & Gottfredson, 2018; Homer & Fisher, 2019). Therefore, SROs need to work collaboratively with school mental health professionals (e.g., school psychologists, counselors, social workers), administrators, educators, and others to ensure that appropriate disciplinary and supportive practices are in place and being followed.

Teachers as weapon-carrying personnel. Most recently, elected officials in the U.S. have been discussing the possibility of providing teachers with (or allowing them to possess) firearms to mitigate school violence and dissuade individuals from perpetrating violent attacks at school (Sulkowski & Lazarus, 2017). Although such a measure might have political appeal and potentially provide psychological comfort to some individuals who are worried about school safety, such an approach is not backed by data and is problematic for the following reasons: 1) most multiple victim violent attacks at school are over in a matter of seconds or minutes, which effectively limits the possibility of an effective immediate response (Borum et al., 2010); 2), these incidents are highly chaotic and incredibly stressful, which causes most people to flee or freeze, even if they are trained first-responders (Sulkowski & Lazarus, 2011); 3), the presence of firearms at school produces additional safety risks that would require storage practices that would render such weapons likely ineffectual when needed; 4), it is highly unlikely that teachers would be able to counterattack individuals that they might know (or be a part of their school community) during a moment of crisis as only a small minority of teachers (7%) even think they should teach about gun safety (Obeng, 2010) and even trained personnel often struggle to respond during chaotic attacks (Nieuwenhuys & Oudejans, 2010); and 5), case study research compiled across a 22-year timespan indicates that almost a third (32%) of U.S. teachers who have irresponsibly discharged a firearm did so on school grounds (Buck et al., 2013). Moreover, results from the same study found that 63% of these incidents resulted in suicide, and 70% of teachers also shot at least one other victim, which was never a student but often was a significant other (31%), administrator (20%), or another teacher (17%). Therefore, although more research is needed on the impact of school security measures, there does not appear to be an empirical or well-reasoned conceptual justification for arming educators to improve school safety or security.

Frank DeAngelis, former principal of Columbine High School, in an interview cited in Sulkowski and Lazarus (2017, p. 364), eloquently makes the case against arming educators. He states:

> I don't know if I could have pulled the trigger if I was one of the staff members to be armed. The gunmen were students of mine. Law enforcement officers who are trained to do this go through extensive training and it is much more than just doing target practice; it requires a whole different mental set. Also, the perpetrators are moving and there are other students around. Being able to hit someone without hitting innocent bystanders is extremely difficult. I can't imagine how devastating it would have been for me if I was armed and shot an innocent student accidently. Just think of the potential dangers and accompanied lawsuits of injuring or killing an innocent student in friendly fire. I am not sure how many educators would sign up for that.

Similar concerns also relate to other recently proposed target hardening strategies for improving school physical safety. For example, proposing using bullet-proof school supplies/spaces (e.g., backpacks, sleeping mats, classroom furniture) to reduce violent or homicidal behavior is impractical, unrealistic, and without any research support. Furthermore, this approach is naïve because of the low base rate of life-compromising school shootings. Schools generally are safe places contrary to media or public perceptions, and this is especially true when considering extreme incidents of school violence such as shootings and homicides (Cornell & Crowley, 2021).

A cottage industry has sprung up in response to worries about school shootings and safety largely driven by private industry.

Millions of dollars already have been invested in various untested and often impractical target hardening strategies such as fortified school entrances, smoke dispensers, biometric scanners, remote parental monitors, bullet-resistant glass, gunshot detectors, safety pods, and panic rooms (Cox & Rich, 2018; Tanner-Smith & Fisher, 2016). However, implementing many of these measures would be extremely costly. Doing so would overwhelm schools on already tight budgets, frighten students, create student privacy dilemmas, and generally interfere with school functioning. Simply stated, the use of effective, research-based, and cost-effective school safety practices, policies, and personnel must take precedence over fear-driven, unrealistic, costly, and potentially detrimental strategies to create and maintain safe schools.

Conclusion

This chapter provides foundational content for establishing and maintaining safety in school settings. Safety of the physical school environment was first discussed, including drawbacks associated with overly fortifying schools and the potential promise of CPTED to establish a balance between students' physical safety needs and their psychological comfort. Safety policies and procedures were then reviewed. An emphasis was placed on using safety teams, safety audits, agency collaboration, crisis plans, and lockdown and active shooter drills. Recommended practices and important caveats were included with the use of the aforementioned safety policies and approaches. The content was provided related to the increased use of school security personnel such as SROs. Lastly, serious dilemmas associated with arming non-trained security personnel as a safety strategy were discussed. Overall, this chapter aimed to provide a balanced review of contemporary practices, policies, and approaches that reinforce school safety. This review is complemented by the forthcoming two chapters, which cover the current state of school-based efforts to improve psychological safety in schools, as these approaches should be thought of as two sides of the same coin.

References

Addington, L. A. (2009). Cops and cameras: Public school security as a policy response to Columbine. *American Behavioral Scientist, 52,* 1426–1446. doi: 10.1177/0002764209332556

Arizona School Facilities Board (2007). *Building Arizona's 21st century schools: Ensuring innovative school facilities for the digital age.* Phoenix, AZ. https://sfb.az.gov/21st-century-schools

Aronowitz, N. W. (2014, February). *Fake blood and blanks: Schools stage active shooter drills.* https://www.nbcnews.com/news/us-news/fake-blood-blanks-schools-stage-active-shooter-drills-n28481

Barrett, P., Davies, F., Zhang, Y., & Barrett, L. (2015). The impact of classroom design on pupils' learning: Final results of a holistic, multi-level analysis. *Building and Environment, 89,* 118–133. doi: 10.1016/j.buildenv.2015.02.013

Borum, R., Cornell, D. G., Modzeleski, W., & Jimerson, S. R. (2010). What can be done about school shootings? A review of the evidence. *Educational Researcher, 39,* 27–37. doi: 10.3102/0013189X0935 7620

Bosworth, K., Ford, L., & Hernandaz, D. (2011). School climate factors contributing to student and faculty perceptions of safety in select Arizona schools. *Journal of School Health, 81,* 194–201. doi: 10.1111/j.1746–1561.2010.00579.x

Bradshaw, C. P., Waasdorp, T. E., Debnam, K. J., & Johnson, S. L. (2014). Measuring school climate in high schools: A focus on safety, engagement, and the environment. *Journal of School Health, 84,* 593–604. doi:10.1111/josh.12186

Brock, S. E., Nickerson, A. B., Reeves, M. A., Conolly, C. N., Jimerson, S. R., Pesce, R. C., & Lazzaro, B. R. (2016). *School crisis prevention and intervention: The PREPaRE model, second edition.* Bethesda, MD: National Association of School Psychologists.

Brock, S. E., Sandoval, J., & Lewis, S. (2001). *Preparing for crises in the schools: A manual for building school crisis response teams.* New York, NY: John Wiley & Sons Inc.

Buck, S., Yurvati, E., & Drake, D. (2013). *Teachers with guns: Firearms discharges by school teachers, 1980–2012.* Center for Homicide Research. http://homicidecenter.org/wp-content/uploads/2013/08/Teachers-with-Guns-RESEARCH-REPORT-FINAL1.pdf.

Cornell, D. G., & Crowley, B. (2021). Strategies to prevent school violence. In P. J. Lazarus, S. Suldo, & B. Doll (Eds.), *Fostering the emotional well-being of youth: A school-based approach.* Oxford and New York. Oxford University Press.

Cornell, D. G., & Gregory, A. (2008). *Virginia High School Safety Study: Descriptive report of survey results from ninth-grade students and teachers.* Charlottesville, VA: University of Virginia.

Cox, J. W., & Rich, S. (2018, March). Scarred by school shootings. *Washington Post.* https://www.washingtonpost.com/graphics/2018/local/us-school-shootings-history/

DeMary, J. L., Owens, M., & Ramnarain, A. K. V. (2000). *School safety audit protocol.* Reston, VA: Virginia State Education Department.

Devlin, D. N., & Gottfredson, D. C. (2018). The roles of police officers in schools: Effects on the recording and reporting of crime. *Youth Violence and Juvenile Justice, 16,* 208–223. doi: 10.1177/1541204016680405

Eklund, K., Meyer, L., & Bosworth, K. (2018). Examining the role of school resource officers on school safety and crisis response teams. *Journal of School Violence, 17,* 139–151. doi: 10.1080/15388220.2016.1263797

Erbacher, T. A., & Poland, S. (2019). School psychologists must be involved in planning and conducting active shooter drills. *NASP Communiqué, 48,* 10, 12–13.

Finn, P., & McDevitt, J. (2005). *National Assessment of School Resource Officer Programs. Final Project Report.* Washington, CD: National Institute of Justice.

Girouard, C. (2001). *School resource officer training program.* Washington, DC: US Department of Justice, Office of Justice Programs, Office of Juvenile Justice and Delinquency Prevention.

Homer, E. M., & Fisher, B. W. (2019). Police in schools and student arrest rates across the United States: Examining differences by race, ethnicity, and gender. *Journal of School Violence.* doi: 10.1080/15388220.2019.1604377

Johnson, S., Waasdorp, T., Cash, A., Debnam, K., Milam, A., & Bradshaw, C. (2017). Assessing the association between observed school disorganization and school violence: Implications for school climate interventions. *Psychology of Violence, 7*, 181–191. doi:10.1037/vio0000045

Lamoreaux, D., & Sulkowski, M. L. (2021). An alternative to fortified schools: Using crime prevention through environmental design (CPTED) to balance student safety and psychological wellbeing. *Psychology in the Schools 58*(3). https://doi.org/10.1002/pits.22459

Musu-Gillette, L., Zhang, A., Wang, K., Zhang, J., Kemp, J., Diliberti, M., & Oudekerk, B. A. (2018). *Indicators of school crime and safety: 2017.* (NCES 2017–064/NCJ 250650). Washington, D.C.: U.S. Department of Justice.

National Association of School Psychologists (2009). *Crisis prevention & preparedness: The comprehensive school crisis team. An evidence-based crisis prevention and intervention training curriculum developed by and for school crisis professionals.* Bethesda, MD: National Association of School Psychologists.

National Association of School Psychologists (2018). *Mitigating negative psychological effects of school lockdowns: Brief guidance for schools.* Bethesda, MD: National Association of School Psychologists.

National Association of School Psychologists (NASP) & National Association of School Resource Officers (NASRO). (2017). *Best practice considerations for schools in active shooter and other armed assailant drills [Brief].* Bethesda, MD: NASP. http://www.nasponline.org/Documents/Research%20and%20Policy /Advocacy%20Resources/BP_Armed_Assailant_Drills.pdf

National Threat Assessment Center (2019). *Protecting America's schools: A U.S. Secret Service analysis of targeted school violence.* Washington, DC: U.S. Secret Service, Department of Homeland Security. https://www.secretservice.gov/data/protection/ntac/Protecting_Americas_Schools.pdf

Nieuwenhuys, A., & Oudejans, R. R. (2010). Effects of anxiety on handgun shooting behavior of police officers: A pilot study. *Anxiety, Stress, & Coping, 23*, 225–233. doi: 10.1080/10615800902977494

Obeng, C. (2010). Should gun safety be taught in schools? Perspectives of teachers. *Journal of School Health*, *80*, 394–398. doi: 10.1111/j.1746–1561.2010.00519.x

Perumean-Chaney, S. E., & Sutton, L. M. (2013). Students and perceived school safety: The impact of school security measures. *American Journal of Criminal Justice*, *38*, 570–588. doi: 10.1007/s12103-012-9182-2

Reeves, M. A., Kanan, L. M., & Plog, A. E. (2010). *Comprehensive planning for safe learning environments: A school professional's guide to integrating physical and psychological safety, prevention through recovery.* New York: Routledge.

Roberts, S., Zhang, J., & Truman, J. (2010). Indicators of School Crime and Safety: 2010 (NCES 2011–002/NCJ 230812). National Center for Education Statistics, US Department of Education, and Bureau of Justice Statistics, Office of Justice Programs, US Department of Justice. Washington, DC.

Schneider, T. (2010). CPTED 101: Crime prevention through environmental design: The fundamentals for schools. *National Clearinghouse for Educational Facilities.* http://www.ncef.org/pubs/cpted101.pdf.

Shelton, A. J., Owens, E. W., & Song, H. (2009). An examination of public-school safety measures across geographic settings. *Journal of School Health*, *79*, 24–29. doi: 10.1111/j.1746–1561.2008.00370.x

Sulkowski, M. L., & Lazarus, P. J. (2011). Contemporary responses to violent attacks on college campuses. *Journal of School Violence, 10*, 338–354. doi: 10.1080/15388220.2011.602601

Sulkowski, M. L., & Lazarus, P. J. (2017). *Creating safe and supportive schools and fostering students' mental health.* New York, NY: Routledge.

Tanner-Smith, E. E., & Fisher, B. W. (2016). Visible school security measures and student academic performance, attendance, and postsecondary aspirations. *Journal of Youth and Adolescence, 45*, 195–210. doi: 10.1007/s10964-015-0265-5

Theriot, M. T., & Orme, J. G. (2016). School resource officers and students' feelings of safety at school. *Youth Violence and Juvenile Justice, 14*, 130–146. doi: 10.1177/1541204014564472

Trump, K. S. (2000). *Classroom killers? Hallway hostages? How schools can prevent and manage school crises*. New York, NY: Corwin Press.

Vagi, K. J., Stevens, M. R., Simon, T. R., Basile, K. C., Carter, S. P., & Carter, S. L. (2018). Crime Prevention Through Environmental Design (CPTED) characteristics associated with violence and safety in middle schools. *Journal of School Health*, *88*, 296–305. doi:10.1111/josh.12609

Williamson, E. (2019, September 4). When active shooter drills scare the children they hope to protect. *New York Times*. https://www.nytimes.com/2019/09/04/us/politics/active-shooter-drills-schools.html

3

Bullying and Violence Prevention and Intervention

Bullying and violence have always existed in schools and have been shown to have a detrimental impact on students' academic success, social and emotional functioning, and mental health. However, new research has emerged related to promising programs, policies, and interventions that make schools physically and psychologically safer for today's students. These approaches will be discussed in this chapter.

Bullying Prevention and Intervention

Bullying Definition

The term "bullying" generally is used to describe unwanted, intentional, aggressive behavior that involves a real or perceived power imbalance between the bully and the victim (Olweus, 1993). The power difference between bullies and victims can take many forms. For example, a bully may be physically stronger, display more adroit interpersonal skills, have a higher social

DOI: 10.4324/9780429261527-4

status, be more tech-savvy, have a more extensive social media network, or have other qualities that give them an edge or allow them to dominate a victim. Furthermore, bullying can be subdivided into various forms that include physical aggression (e.g., hitting, kicking, shoving), verbal aggression (e.g., name-calling, teasing, threatening), relational aggression (e.g., social exclusion, spreading rumors), sexual aggression (e.g., unwanted or inappropriate touching, sexting, exposure to/sharing pornography, making sexually aggressive statements), and cyberbullying, which is a combination of verbal, relational, and sexual bullying that occurs in cyberspace, on social media platforms, via text or digital messages (DMs), on gaming sites, or in comments sections on websites (Sulkowski & Lazarus, 2017).

Prevalence of Bullying

Research indicates that bullying is the most prevalent form of aggressive or violent behavior in schools (Ross, 2002). Even though specific prevalence estimates vary considerably across studies, large epidemiological studies generally find that 20–40% of students report being bullied by their peers, and more than that will be bullied at some point during their educational career (Nansel et al., 2001; Roberts et al., 2012). In addition, research indicates that about 10–25% of youth report being cyberbullied within the past year (Kowalski & Limber, 2013; Völlink et al., 2013). These findings, coupled with the belief that aggressive behavior is part of the human condition, have led some individuals to conclude that all schools (if not all classrooms) are affected by bullying to some degree.

The prevalence and nature of bullying and cyberbullying vary by a range of school characteristics and developmental considerations of students. Research suggests that bullying behaviors are extant even in preschoolers and that bullying gradually becomes more prevalent in middle childhood and adolescence (Ostrov et al., 2019). Moreover, bullying peaks in middle school and declines as children advance through high school (Swearer et al., 2012). As students mature into adolescence, bullying tends to become more complex and representative of the intimate relationships they are forming. In this regard, bullying may be expressed as sexual harassment, sexual violence, dating violence, and hurtful relationship manipulation (Taquette & Monteiro, 2019). Thus, because of variability in the prevalence and nature of bullying behaviors within and across school settings, school districts need to collect their data on the prevalence and nature of bullying in local school communities.

Cyberbullying

Before the COVID-19 pandemic, over 90% of youth regularly used the internet or web-based applications. Now virtually all U.S. students do (Montag & Elhai, 2020), which indicates that millions of youth are at-risk of being victimized by cyberbullying. Although cyberbullying is like bullying in physical settings, and most youth are bullied and victimized across these settings, some unique characteristics of cyberspace influence how aggression is transmitted in this realm (Dempsey et al., 2009). For example, cyberbullying victims may struggle to identify their victimizers because of the degree of anonymity that cyberspace can provide. In addition, cyberspace offers a potentially unlimited audience for bullying, especially in social networks where victims can be targeted at any time and information such as a nude or embarrassing photo can spread virally. Moreover, bullies often do not see how their behavior impacts victims firsthand, which can lead to cruel behavior that perpetrators might not carry out in person. This phenomenon has been called the "online disinhibition effect" and it has been observed empirically. For example, as early as 2006, Patchin and Hinduja found that 37% of teens surveyed reported that they had said things to another person via electronic communication that they would not say in face-to-face interaction. Undoubtedly, this problem has intensified in the contentious contemporary social and political climate. In this regard, Huang and Cornell (2019) found evidence of significantly increased teasing and bullying among students since the 2016 U.S. presidential election.

Bullying and School Leadership

However, from a leadership perspective, it is important to note that bullying is goal-directed behavior that can occur in myriad forms in any social environment or context (Malamut et al., 2020). It is a phenomenon that has been around as long as we have, even though educational leaders are now being increasingly held accountable for preventing and mitigating bullying. Consistent with pressure to foster a healthy school climate, school leaders are duly tasked with reducing bullying or aggressive behavior in school settings concomitantly. Thus, creating and maintaining safe, supportive, and healthy schools overlaps considerably with bullying prevention and intervention. In an exploratory study, Bosworth et al. (2018) investigated the role of leadership in implementing an approach to school climate change (positive behavior intervention and supports) that was intended to reduce bullying. Study results indicated that the involvement of school leaders in trying to improve school climate was a key component contributing to student-reported behavior change. Or, in other words, reductions in bullying resulted in a healthier school climate.

The last point is important because it suggests that school leaders can be primary change agents in providing safer, more supportive schools. In fact, school leaders who are committed to reducing bullying—especially as it impacts at-risk, vulnerable, and marginalized students—may be, to use a violent idiom, killing "two birds with one stone." An increasing amount of research clearly indicates that certain student groups are disproportionally victimized by bullying. These include LGBTQ, minoritized, immigrant students, and students with disabilities (Sulkowski et al., 2014). Although students with these identities have different backgrounds and lived experiences, and may assume intersecting or multiple identities (e.g., recently immigrating to the U.S. and identifying as LGBTQ), some similarities exist among these student groups.

First, they are non-normative because they are not part of the predominant group at school (i.e., cisgender, White, native-born, and non-disabled). Of course, this does not mean they are less than any other group of students in any important dimension. However, it does mean that they are in the minority, which can result in a power differential between them and other students at school who target different students and may not be able to marshal an equivalent degree of physical or social power (Nelson et al., 2019). In other words, on average, minority students are easier to victimize than students from the predominant group in numbers or the majority. Essentially, just about any characteristic perceived to separate a student from the majority group could be exploited. Thus, bias-based bullying against students perceived to be different or less powerful is a serious problem that victims cannot be expected to manage independently (Gönültaş & Mulvey, 2021). This is precisely where school leaders must step in. With this in mind, bullying prevention and intervention approaches are discussed under the following domains: Legal considerations and student rights, bullying prevention programs, and specific strategies school leaders can employ to combat bullying.

Bullying Prevention and Intervention

Legal considerations and student rights. As of April 2015, all U.S. states and the District of Columbia have laws that require schools to address bullying. Furthermore, results of court cases such as *Davis v. Monroe County Board of Education* (1999) suggest that schools are required to protect students from sexual harassment. Civil rights laws such as Title IV and Title VI of the Civil Rights Act of 1964, Section 504 of the Rehabilitation Act of 1973, Titles II and III of the Americans with Disabilities Act, and the Individuals with Disabilities Education Improvement Act (IDEIA), all require schools to protect youth from discrimination and harassment, especially if they are from a protected class (e.g., a class that is defined by race, disability, or religion). Although sexual orientation is not a protected class under current federal legislation, some state laws protect LGBTQ youth. Text Box 3.1 lists steps that school leaders and members of school communities should take to comply with extant laws and protect students from bullying.

Text Box 3.1: What Educational Leaders Can Do to Comply with Laws to Combat Bullying

- ◆ Investigations by schools of possible harassment must be conducted expediently, thoroughly, and consistently.
- ◆ Schools should inform students and parents of specific procedures for reporting bullying and harassment, as well as whom to contact if cases are not handled expediently.
- ◆ Schools should advise students and parents of alternative reporting mechanisms (e.g., police) in cases of violence or other criminal activity.
- ◆ Schools should assess whether bullying experiences constitute a potential civil rights violation.
- ◆ Schools should be aware that there is consistent evidence that zero-tolerance policies, originally applied to cases of school violence and weapon possession on campuses, but sometimes extended to bullying and harassment, are not effective.
- ◆ Knowledge of legal, procedural, and policy issues is central for schools in the effort to prevent bullying.
- ◆ Most legislation focuses on reporting, investigating, and intervening when bullying has occurred, but prevention efforts should be a key focus for school-based anti-bullying and harassment efforts.

Notice: These recommendations are adapted from the American Educational Research Association (2013).

Bullying prevention programs. Schools have two main options they can select to prevent and address bullying. One option involves adopting and implementing a multicomponent bullying prevention/intervention program such as the Olweus Bullying Prevention Program (Olweus & Limber, 2007), KiVA (Salmivalli et al., 2011), PeaceBuilders (Flannery et al., 2003), Steps to Respect (Brown et al., 2011), and several others. The previously mentioned programs all have empirical support. However, none are universally effective across international educational settings or in racially/ethnically diverse schools. Therefore, educational leaders need to select programs addressing bullying based on their empirical support, as well as their ability to adapt to school characteristics. Good places to start in this regard are the National Registry of Evidence-Based Programs and Practices (http://www.nrepp.samhsa.gov/), the Model Programs Guide (http://www.ojjdp.gov/mpg/), and the Blueprints for Healthy Youth Development (http://www.colorado.edu/cspvblueprints/).

Even if a school adopts a well-matched evidence-based bullying prevention/intervention program, the utility of this program and any promising results likely will be significantly compromised if it is not implemented with adequate integrity and fidelity. This means that it is unlikely that the program will be optimally effective when it is implemented if it is not delivered according to its original protocol. Even more concerning, most bullying prevention/intervention programs have little empirical support, theoretical grounding, or even practical appeal. Some even have been criticized for being insensitive, if not deleterious, to the social and educational needs of LGBTQ students and are inconsistent with research-based position papers and statements produced by organizations such as the American Psychological Association (APA) and the National Association of School Psychologists (NASP).

The second way that schools can prevent or reduce bullying involves adopting individual approaches to mitigating bullying. In this regard, research indicates that bystander interventions are the most effective (Doumas et al., 2021; Midgett et al., 2017). Most importantly, when bystanders (often called "upstanders" in the psychological literature) act as defenders of victims (or potential victims of bullying), incidents of bullying tend to reduce along with negative related effects (Polanin et al., 2012). It then behooves school leaders to encourage all members of school communities to act as active "upstanders" to defend victims from bullying.

How Educational Leaders Can Address School Bullying

Efforts of educational leaders to prevent and address school bullying ought to focus on facilitating safe and supportive learning environments for all students. Because aggressive behavior is highly prevalent and it is impossible to eradicate it from all social settings, leaders can help inoculate students and other members of school communities against the negative effects of bullying by protecting the physical safety of students, making sure that they feel socially connected to students and adults at school, championing cultural competence and social justice, and fostering a school climate that encourages pro-social behaviors (Cowie & Myers, 2017).

To protect the physical safety of students, educators should be present in loosely structured social settings or places where bullying is more likely to occur, such as in hallways, playgrounds, free periods, study halls, and the cafeteria. In addition, educational leaders should work toward increasing openness between students and adults at school so that students feel comfortable reporting incidents of bullying or problems more generally. Similarly, and consistent with an effort to improve school climate more generally, educational leaders can implement programs such as positive peer reporting in addition to having an anonymous bullying incident report box. Positive peer reporting is a research-based intervention that involves reinforcing students to engage in positive social interactions with others (e.g., helping a student pick up dropped materials, inviting other students to participate in an activity, sharing supplies with a peer, speaking up to protect a student against verbal abuse). This intervention can be implemented school-wide or classroom-wide, and it provides students an opportunity to "report" prosocial behaviors to educators who then reinforce the students who display these desirable behaviors (Collins et al., 2018).

To help establish a school climate that encourages pro-social behaviors and discourages peer aggression, educational leaders should actively communicate that bullying, teasing, and harassment will not be tolerated, and that specific consequences will occur for these behaviors. However, consequences must be consistent with extant school policies to encourage a school culture that rejects bullying. With this aim in mind, educational leaders can work with students to identify specific consequences for specific problematic behaviors to help facilitate buy-in and ownership of such policies. For example, a teacher could initiate a class activity at the beginning of the year that involves troubleshooting consequences and remediation strategies for bullying incidents involving all students' input. Text Box 3.2 lists additional strategies that educational leaders can employ to prevent

Text Box 3.2: Strategies for Bullying Prevention and Intervention

and address bullying incidents, and Text Box 3.3 debunks common myths about bullying.

- ◆ Provide workshops or materials to increase awareness and knowledge of bullying and dispel myths among all school personnel, parents, and community stakeholders.
- ◆ Provide workshops to students on safe new media use. Discuss the dangers associated with the inappropriate use of

cyberspace. Explain the concept of cyberbullying and its forms and emphasize that it is the responsibility of all students to prevent it from occurring.

♦ Survey all students using an anonymous questionnaire to determine the bullying problem in each school. Include questions related to: What types of bullying occur on campus? Where does bullying take place? How safe do students feel from bullying and harassment? How many students are involved?

♦ Develop a bullying coordinating committee consisting of a school administrator, a school psychologist or counselor, teachers, parents, and students.

♦ Develop an effective anti-bullying school policy and establish clear and enforceable rules and sanctions. In doing so, make sure that school policies are consistent with Board of Education rules and state statutes. School rules should be posted and discussed with all students so that they have a clear understanding of expectations.

♦ Consider having students sign a pledge that can include: (a) We will not bully other students; (b) We will help others who are being bullied by speaking out and by getting adult help; (c) We will use extra effort to include all students in activities at our school.

♦ Provide comprehensive training to all teachers and school staff about bullying prevention and intervention.

♦ Use survey results to make necessary changes to the school environment to create a safer and more supportive school climate. This may include extra monitoring and supervision.

♦ Develop a number of different ways that students can report bullying to adults. Investigate every report, provide follow-up, and take administrative actions as necessary.

♦ Increase adult supervision in areas found to be problematic on the survey. Bullying often occurs in school hallways, cafeteria, playground, locker rooms, and restrooms.

♦ Intervene consistently when bullying occurs—never ignore it. Empower teachers with effective strategies to confront bullying on the spot.

Bullying and Violence Prevention and Intervention ◆ 71

- Hold separate follow-up meetings with perpetrators and targets. Provide support and protection to a victimized student. Conflict resolution or peer mediation strategies are not appropriate in this process because the target is being abused by the perpetrator and there is an unequal balance of power. During this process, the teacher can help the vulnerable child learn to assert himself more effectively. Also, the educator can teach the perpetrator how to meet his or her needs in alternative ways. If possible, involve parents in the process.
- Have class meetings where students can discuss peer relations as well as any problems with bullying.
- Teach all students how to be "upstanders" and encourage them to take action to stop bullying when it occurs.
- Help foster nurturing relationships and friendship patterns within the school and classroom. This is especially important as the number and quality of friends protect children from being victimized. That is, youth who have a number of friends, especially those who are strong or popular, are less likely to become targets.
- Consider adopting a structured bully prevention program. Effective programs focus on knowledge, attitude change, and skill development taught through modeling, role play, and practice.
- Continue these efforts over time. Patience is required as it may take up to three years to change the culture of the school and make a difference.

These aforementioned strategies are based on best practices recommended by the U.S. Department of Health and Human Services through their website, Stop Bullying Now; the seminal principles of Dan Olweus (1993) and his Bullying Prevention Program; and critical components of such anti-bullying programs such as Bully Proofing Your School, Bully Busters, Steps to Respect, and PATHS (Providing Alternative THinking Strategies).

Source: Adapted from Lazarus & Pfohl (2011).

72 ◆ The Safe Pillar

Text Box 3.3

Myths about Children Who Bully

Children who bully are loners.

Children who bully have low self-esteem.

Being bullied toughens up a student and prepares him to be a man.

Most students will learn how to combat being bullied on their own.

We don't have bullying in our schools.

A student must be stronger and bigger to be a bully.

Facts about Children Who Bully

Children who bully have an easier time making friends than do victims.

Children who bully have average to high average self-esteem and feel it is their right to intimidate other students.

Being bullied creates scars. Rather than toughening up a student, it makes the victim feel more vulnerable and anxious and less able to perform academically and socially. As a result, bullied students feel less connected to the school and often less prepared for life.

Most chronic victims will need help from school staff to avoid being victimized. If handling bullying was so easy, they probably would not have been victimized in the first place.

All schools have bullying; however, for various reasons students are reluctant to report it to school staff. Also, some schools have less bullying than others.

> Rather than being bigger or stronger, a student can be more socially sophisticated, manipulative, or more technologically savvy to be a bully. In cyberspace, the disinhibition effect enables students (who may actually be weaker and smaller) to bully others who would not do so in person.

Source: Garrity et al. (2000) and Lazarus, P. J. (2011)

How Educational Leaders Can Address Cyberbullying

Because cyberbullying usually occurs outside of the watchful eyes of adults at school, educational leaders often feel powerless to address this phenomenon. However, even if educators are not part of (or even aware of) the social networks in cyberspace that allow cyberbullying to occur, they can educate students about taking precautions to help protect themselves from being bullied in cyberspace. Text Box 3.4 lists specific ways that students can make themselves less vulnerable to being a victim of cyberbullying. To help teach these strategies, educational leaders can schedule brief meetings to teach students about the perils of certain behaviors in cyberspace and help them protect themselves in this environment.

Text Box 3.4: Strategies to Prevent Being Victimized by Cyberbullying

- Never accept friend/network requests from unfamiliar people.
- Employ the "mom" principle: Do not post or share photographs or videos you would not be willing to share with your mother, father, or other important caregiver.

- Employ the "forever" principle: Assume that everything in cyberspace will be there forever.
- Employ the "no privacy" principle: Assume that everyone can get access to the information about you in cyberspace.
- Employ the "ex" principle: Would you be okay with your ex-boyfriends/girlfriends having access to content that you are planning to share?
- Block threatening or questionable people from seeing your profile and personal information.
- Do not post provocative, scandalous, or inflammatory remarks in cyberspace.
- Do not reply or retaliate to incidents of cyberbullying.
- Regularly change passwords to sites/applications and immediately delete profiles that have been hacked.
- Avoid sites, networks, and applications that have poor security, readily provide access to personal information, or encourage interactions among strangers.
- Ensure that you can approve information before it is posted or shared socially.
- Limit involvement in social networking to a few familiar sites.
- Avoid joining sites that do not have adequate privacy settings.
- Never, never, never engage in sexting!

Source: Sulkowski and Lazarus (2017).

Students regularly sign up for and quit social media platforms as they wax and wane in popularity. As parents and educational leaders often start paying attention to these platforms, students migrate to newer ones. In 2015, Facebook was the leading social media platform among teens (ages 13–17), with a 71% engagement rate. However, as the average age of Facebook users increased over the next few years, users among youth dropped to 51% in 2018, with 72% and 69% of youth reporting using Instagram and Snapchat (Seth, 2019).

School Violence Prevention and Intervention

Conceptualizing School Violence

Among students, school violence has been defined as "engagement as a perpetrator or victim in an aggressive act among peers in or related to school" (Polanin et al., 2021, p. 115). Thus, it is a broad umbrella term to describe a multifaceted problem that impacts virtually all school communities. Incidents of school violence can range in severity and intentionality from micro aggression to targeted assaults. Thus, school violence takes on a lengthy list of individual, school, and community characteristics that intersect across these levels (Thomas et al., 2018). School violence also includes bullying and peer victimization—but also other forms of aggressive behavior that do not typically get classified with bullying, such as physical or sexual assault, gang-related activity, targeted attacks, and intimate partner relations (e.g., dating violence, intimate partner violence).

Because of its range in scope, it is hard to conceptualize school violence comprehensively; however, a recent meta-analysis of 761 studies by Turanovic et al. (2022) does shed some light on its main correlates. Topping the list for violent perpetration is having a history of antisocial behavior (e.g., physical aggression, delinquency), being personally victimized, peer rejection, and having low social competence (e.g., poor social skills, negative peer relationships). Some correlates robustly linked with school violence perpetration yet weakly with victimization included having deviant peers and harboring antisocial attitudes.

School Violence Prevalence and Impact

School violence is a pervasive problem afflicting U.S. schools. National estimates indicate that over 800,000 students (aged 12–18) are afflicted by school violence each year (Wang et al., 2020), and rates of violent victimization in U.S. schools have been found to be 22% higher than in schools outside the country (Zhang et al., 2019). Moreover, loosely defined as the intent to harm another through physical force or dominance, approximately 8% of high school students reported being in a physical fight at school each year (Kann et al., 2018) and relationship/dating violence, or a pattern of coercive and abusive tactics used by one individual in a relationship to gain power or control over another has been identified as one of the most common forms of aggressive behavior affecting adolescents by the Children's Hospital of Philadelphia Center for Violence Prevention (CHOP, 2019). According to a meta-analysis by Wincentak et al. (2017), this form of violent behavior permeates school communities. Approximately, 20% of adolescents are afflicted by physical relationship violence, and 9% are afflicted by sexual relationship violence.

Although schools are almost always safer and more secure than their surrounding communities, aggressive and violent behaviors typically described as "street crime" also spill into school communities (Turanovic et al., 2022). As microcosms of their surrounding communities, schools in areas impacted by neighborhood and family violence, drug trafficking, gang activity, and gun violence are particularly at risk for school violence. Although variable across communities, gang membership among school-age populations has increased steadily since the 1990s, with prevalence rates ranging from 2% to 37% across communities (Lenzi et al., 2019). In contrast, students' reports of carrying weapons have generally declined from about 12% in 1993 to 5% in 2013 (Mayer & Jimerson, 2019). Yet, their reports of having been threatened by a weapon have remained relatively constant at about 6% during the same timeframe and until recently (Couture et al., 2022).

A full review of the deleterious effects of school violence is beyond the scope of this chapter. However, results from the most extensive investigation of school violence involvement and various student outcomes are illustrative. Overall, in a sample of 114 studies, Polanin et al. (2021) found that being a perpetrator or victim of school violence was associated with negative mental health outcomes, lower school performance, and increased risk for engaging in future criminal and delinquent acts. Regarding mental health outcomes, school violence involvement was associated with depression and reduced empathy, but perpetration was not related to low self-esteem, anxiety, or suicidal ideation. Similarly, being victimized by school violence was related to negative mental health outcomes. Specifically, students were at an elevated risk for experiencing depression and other internalizing symptoms. Still, findings connecting victimization to school performance and risk for engaging in future criminal and delinquent acts were mixed across studies. The authors conclude that being targeted by school violence exerts a clear pattern of harm on victims, negatively impacting their mental health.

School Violence and Leadership

Schools are institutions that can foster healthy interpersonal relationships and provide emotional and behavioral skill-building opportunities to protect students from engaging in school violence. School leaders are at the forefront of initiatives to reduce school violence while promoting healthy student growth and development. In collaboration with colleagues from allied disciplines and consistent with a transdisciplinary approach to addressing school violence, school leaders can collaborate to bridge research, policy, and practice (Mayer, 2012).

Because of the heterogeneity of types of school violence and its contributing factors, a transdisciplinary approach is needed to address the broad societal, political, community, and proximal drivers of school violence. Consistent with this approach, Mayer and Jimerson (2019) recommend that educational leaders (a) employ a research-to-practice focus; (b) frame key issues and challenges that are relevant across key stakeholder groups (e.g., administrators, school-based mental health professionals, school safety personnel, families, community partners); (c) stress collaborative health promotion and prevention and intervention approaches; (d) strategically target issues that are most pertinent to the local school community; (e) ground prevention and interventions in data-based decision making; and (f), navigate tensions and trade-offs associated with school violence prevention/intervention while addressing structural and systematic barriers to service delivery.

School Violence Prevention and Intervention

Most of the content covered in the current text has been shown to prevent or reduce aspects of school violence, and additional practical applications are provided in Text Box 3.5. This is because school violence is multifaceted, and there are myriad pathways to its development as well as amelioration. A healthy school climate can turn the temperature down and prevent violent escalation among students, being socially connected and supported can reduce retaliatory violence, threat assessment can increase school safety, and school-wide prevention programs (e.g., bullying prevention programs, social-emotional learning) can teach students skills they need to manage conflict effectively. However, some other emerging approaches that educational leaders can embrace to reduce school violence warrant inclusion. Additionally, some of these approaches enfranchise school community members, who might not initially see themselves as school leaders, who can be stakeholders in efforts to mitigate school violence. A salient example in this regard is restorative justice.

Text Box 3.5: Actions Leaders Can Take to Address Potentially Violent Students

- Notify guardians.
- Notify law enforcement.
- Notify appropriate school staff.

- ◆ Notify potential victims.
- ◆ Conduct a threat assessment.
- ◆ Conduct a comprehensive psychological evaluation.
- ◆ Refer to a mental health facility.
- ◆ Recommend an involuntary treatment order.
- ◆ Conduct a functional behavioral assessment (FBA).
- ◆ Implement a behavior intervention plan (BIP).
- ◆ Develop a "No Harm Contract."
- ◆ Recommend counseling or therapy.
- ◆ Teach social skills.
- ◆ Implement check-in/check-out.
- ◆ Modify schedule.
- ◆ Search students' locker and possessions.
- ◆ Recommend drug screening.
- ◆ Explore alternative educational placements.
- ◆ If suspended or hospitalized, develop a plan for school re-entry.

Restorative justice. Restorative justice addresses crime, violence, or aggressive behavior through an organized meeting between a victim and an offender, sometimes with representatives of a wider group or community (Katic et al., 2020). The goal is for the victim(s) to share their experience of what happened, to discuss who was harmed and how, and to create a consensus on what the offender can do to repair the harm that was done. In practice, restorative justice often includes facilitating restorative conversations, circles, conferences, and peer mediation, and these practices occur on a continuum ranging from informal to formal. Restorative conversations involve having a conversation between an educational leader and the individuals involved in the offense. These conversations should open the lines for communication and involve affective statements ("when you did X, I felt Y") that allow the individuals to understand how the offense impacted the involved parties and allow each side to see things from the perspective of the other.

Restorative circles can be used as a violence prevention strategy or as an intervention after an incident occurs. For prevention, restorative circles could be used in classrooms to build community, group solidarity, and social connectedness. As an intervention, restorative circles can provide victims with social support and affirm their belongingness and value in the group.

Toward the more formal end of the restorative justice continuum, restorative conferences involve avoiding labeling language, such as "you are an X," fostering and reinforcing a community of care, amplifying normally quiet student voices, and acknowledging a need for interpersonal healing among affected individuals. Lastly, peer mediation is the last component of the restorative justice process. Peer mediation involves having trained peer mediators mediate a conflict between two or more individuals. Guidance is provided during this process, and peer mediators utilize conflict resolution skills to mend or improve relationships and prevent violence. In contrast to adult-administered or system-imposed discipline policies, peer mediation aims to provide students with the opportunity to resolve conflicts and problems constructively and independently. Text Box 3.6 provides guidelines for implementing restorative justice at each step of the process.

Text Box 3.6: Guidelines for Implementing Restorative Justice

♦ Restorative conversations.
- ♦ Engender an environment that is safe for communication.
- ♦ Have an adult school leader present to help facilitate the conversation.
- ♦ Use affective statements and questions (e.g., "When you did X, I felt Y"; "I did X because I felt. . .")
- ♦ Ensure that all parties feel open to communicating and have opportunities to express their thoughts and feelings.

Bullying and Violence Prevention and Intervention ◆ 81

- ◆ Restorative circles.
  - ◆ Check in with circle members to assess their ability to participate in a prosocial and restorative process.
  - ◆ Model prosocial values and behaviors and encourage circle members to do the same.
  - ◆ Try to foster a shared group identity grounded in the healthy resolution of interpersonal conflict.
  - ◆ Positively reinforce prosocial communication and redirect or stop antisocial or problematic communication.
- ◆ Restorative conferences.
  - ◆ Assess members' readiness to engage in a collective and interactive restorative process.
  - ◆ Include all relevant stakeholders (e.g., the offender, victim(s), friends of involved parties, key bystanders and influencers).
  - ◆ Make sure that all members have their voices heard during the process.
  - ◆ Facilitate a problem-solving process that aims to find workable solutions to the conflict—not to assign blame.
- ◆ Peer mediation.
  - ◆ Select peer mediators who model prosocial behavior and are not overly enmeshed in the dynamic between the offender and the victim(s).
  - ◆ Ensure peer mediators are well-trained to facilitate restorative conversations.
  - ◆ Guide peer mediators to ensure they feel supported and encouraged.
  - ◆ Allow students to have adequate autonomy to independently resolve the conflict through their own constructive and creative thinking.

Restorative justice differs significantly from criminal justice practices. In fact, it was developed to reduce the negative consequences associated with using such practices with youth (von Hirsch et al., 2003). Whereas criminal justice practices are punitive and based on the behavior modification principle of punishment, restorative justice typically involves undoing undesirable behaviors and even possibly restitution. Restitution generally involves restoring something to its original state—not having an offender suffer a consequence beyond the infraction. One of the problems with using punishment, such as the case with criminal justice is that it does not directly help victims, and it is unclear whether perpetrators learn from their offenses (Roach, 2000). Moreover, harshly punishing offenders may cause them to feel victimized and then justified in their initial infractions or even to seek revenge for what they perceive to be undue punishment. Thus, strictly from a behavioral perspective, restorative justice has the potential to heal, whereas criminal justice practices may harm an offender while not benefiting a victim or solving the problems that led to the initial conflict. Table 3.1 lists additional comparisons between restorative and criminal justice practices.

An ever-expanding body of research supports the potential for restorative justice to reduce school violence. A recent systematic review by Katic et al. (2020) found that most existing research on restorative justice programs in schools reported positive outcomes, such as improved social relationships among students and reduced disciplinary referrals. However, the authors note that there was considerable variability in the ways that programs were implemented. A second review on the efficacy of restorative justice in school settings by Fronius et al. (2019), which had more liberal inclusion criteria, also found positive results. Specifically, across the included studies, restorative justice improved school climate, teacher-student relationships, and students' social-emotional skills while reducing behavioral infractions and incidents of physical aggression. To date, research on restorative justice is promising and should encourage school leaders who desire to reduce school violence while not criminalizing student behavior.

However, as a caveat, restorative just should not be used when there is a chance for continued conflict or violence or if an

Bullying and Violence Prevention and Intervention ◆ 83

TABLE 3.1 Differences between Restorative and Criminal Justice

Restorative Justice	Criminal Justice
◆ Violence is bad for all members of the school community, including offenders	◆ Violence is against the law or school policies
◆ Focus on repairing the harm caused by violence	◆ Focus on determining guilt and imposing punishment
◆ The people most directly affected by violence should be involved in an effective resolution process	◆ Victims and bystanders are not involved in the justice outcome
◆ Overall goal: Restitution to undue the conflict and repair harm	◆ Overall goal: Punishing the offender or perpetrator

actual crime occurred and the police need to be contacted; for example, if a student might desire revenge or retaliate against another. Moreover, it should not be used if hostile groups have a negative history with each other (Darling-Hammond et al., 2020). Nor should it be used if a student threatens another student or educator with a weapon they brought to school. Thus, it is important to use restorative justice with students who can be immersed in healing previous slights.

Conclusion

Bullying and other forms of school violence are prevalent and exist in virtually all school communities. Involvement in aggressive or violent behavior places youth at risk for experiencing problems in their social, emotional, academic, and mental health functioning. In recent years, these risks have only increased because of the ubiquity of social media and the perils that can come from being victimized anywhere and at any time. However, school leaders have an increasing array of research-supported prevention and intervention programs that they can utilize to support students at risk of being bullied or victimized by school violence in its myriad forms. Additionally, emerging approaches to reduce and respond to violent behavior (e.g., restorative justice) do not rely on criminalizing students. Collectively, through collaborating with others or taking a transdisciplinary approach to bullying and school violence, school leaders can make impressive strides toward supporting the health of school communities and the well-being of students.

References

American Educational Research Association (2013). *Prevention of bullying in schools, colleges, and universities: Research report and recommendations.* Washington, DC: American Educational Research Association.

Bosworth, K., Garcia, R., Judkins, M., & Saliba, M. (2018). The impact of leadership involvement in enhancing high school climate and reducing bullying: An exploratory study. *Journal of School Violence, 17*(3), 354–366.

Brown, E. C., Low, S., Smith, B. H., & Haggerty, K. P. (2011). Outcomes from a school-randomized controlled trial of steps to respect: A bullying prevention program. *School Psychology Review, 40,* 423–433.

Children's Hospital of Philadelphia (CHOP) (2019). *Facts about teen dating violence and how you can help prevent it.* https://www.chop.edu/news/health-tip/facts-about-teen-dating-violence-and-how-you-can-help-prevent-it

Collins, T. A., Murphy, J. M., & Heidelburg, K. (2018). Promoting supportive peer relationships using peer reporting interventions. In R. Hawkins & L. Nabors (Eds.), *Promoting prosocial behaviors in children through games and play: Making social emotional learning fun* (pp. 63–83). Nova Science Publishers.

Couture, M. C., Kang, J. E., Hemenway, D., & Grinshteyn, E. (2022). Associations between having been threatened or injured with a weapon and substance use and mental health among high school students in the United States. *International Journal of Injury Control and Safety Promotion, 29*(1), 93–102. https://doi.org/10.1080/17457300.2021.2004608

Cowie, H., & Myers, C. A. (Eds.). (2017). *School bullying and mental health: Risks, intervention and prevention.* Routledge.

Darling-Hammond, S., Fronius, T. A., Sutherland, H., Guckenburg, S., Petrosino, A., & Hurley, N. (2020). Effectiveness of restorative justice in US K–12 schools: A review of quantitative research. *Contemporary School Psychology, 24*(3), 295–308.

Davis v. Monroe County Board of Education (1999). https://www.law.cornell.edu/supremecourt/text/97-843

Dempsey, A. G., Sulkowski, M. L., Nichols, R., & Storch, E. A. (2009). Differences between peer victimization in cyber and physical settings and associated psychosocial adjustment in early adolescence. *Psychology in the Schools, 46,* 962–972. doi: 10.1002/pits.20437

Doumas, D. M., Midgett, A., & Hausheer, R. (2021). A pilot study testing the efficacy of a brief, bystander bullying intervention: Reducing bullying victimization among high school students. *Professional School Counseling, 25*(1), 215. https://doi.org/10.1177/2156759X211018651

Flannery, D. J., Vazsonyi, A. T., Liau, A.K., Guo, S., Powell, K. E., Atha, H., . . ., & Embry, D. (2003). Initial behavior outcomes for the PeaceBuilders Universal School-Based Violence Prevention Program. *Developmental Psychology, 39,* 292–308.

Fronius, T., Darling-Hammond, S., Persson, H., Guckenburg, S., Hurley, N., & Petrosino, A. (2019). *Restorative justice in US schools: An updated research review.* WestEd.

Garrity. C., Jens, K., Porter, W., Sager, N., & Short-Camilli, C. (2000). *Bully-proofing your schools: A comprehensive approach for elementary schools* (2nd ed.). Sopris West.

Gönültaş, S., & Mulvey, K. L. (2021). The role of immigration background, intergroup processes, and social-cognitive skills in bystanders' responses to bias-based bullying toward immigrants during adolescence. *Child Development, 92*(3), e296–e316.

Huang, F. L., & Cornell, D. G. (2019). School teasing and bullying after the presidential election. *Educational Researcher, 48*(2), 69–83.

Kann, L., McManus, T., Harris, W. A., Shanklin, S. L., Flint, K. H., Queen, B., . . ., & Ethier, K. A. (2018). Youth risk behavior surveillance—United States, 2017. *MMWR. Surveillance Summaries, 67*(8), 1–114. https://doi.org/10.15585/mmwr.ss6708a1

Katic, B., Alba, L. A., & Johnson, A. H. (2020). A systematic evaluation of restorative justice practices: School violence prevention and response. *Journal of School Violence, 19*(4), 579–593. https://doi.org/10.1080/15388220.2020.1783670

Kowalski, R. M., & Limber, S. P. (2013). Psychological, physical, and academic correlates of cyberbullying and traditional bullying. *Journal of Adolescent Health, 53,* S13–S20.

Lazarus, P. J. & Pfohl, W. (2011). Bullying. In A. Canter, L. Z. Paige, & S. Shaw (Eds.), *Helping children at home and school III* (pp. S4H8–1–4). National Association of School Psychologists Press.

Lenzi, M., Sharkey, J. D., Wroblewski, A., Furlong, M. J., & Santinello, M. (2019). Protecting youth from gang membership: Individual and school-level emotional competence. *Journal of Community Psychology, 47*(3), 563–578. https://doi.org/10.1002/jcop.22138

Malamut, S. T., van den Berg, Y. H., Lansu, T. A., & Cillessen, A. H. (2020). Dyadic nominations of bullying: Comparing types of bullies and their victims. *Aggressive Behavior, 46*(3), 232–243.

Mayer, M. J. (2012). Evidence-based standards and methodological issues in school violence and related prevention research in education and the allied disciplines. In S. Jimerson, A. Nickerson, M. J. Mayer, & M. J. Furlong (Eds), *The handbook of school violence and school safety: International research and practice.* Routledge.

Mayer, M. J., & Jimerson, S. R. (Eds.). (2019). The importance of school safety and violence prevention. In M. J. Mayer & S. R. Jimerson (Eds.), *School safety and violence prevention: Science, practice, policy* (pp. 3–16). American Psychological Association. https://doi.org/10.1037/0000106-001

Midgett, A., Doumas, D. M., & Johnston, A. D. (2017). Establishing school counselors as leaders in bullying curriculum delivery: Evaluation of a brief, school-wide bystander intervention. *Professional School Counseling, 21*(1). https://doi.org/10.1177/2156759X187787

Montag, C., & Elhai, J. D. (2020). Discussing digital technology overuse in children and adolescents during the COVID-19 pandemic and beyond: On the importance of considering Affective

Neuroscience Theory. *Addictive Behaviors Reports, 12,* 100313. https://doi.org/10.1016/j.abrep.2020.100313

Nansel, T. R., Overpeck, M., Pilla, R. S., Ruan, W. J., Simons-Morton, B., & Scheidt, P. (2001). Bullying behaviors among US youth: Prevalence and association with psychosocial adjustment. *JAMA, 285,* 2094–2100. doi: 10.1001/jama.285.16.2094

Nelson, H. J., Burns, S. K., Kendall, G. E., & Schonert-Reichl, K. A. (2019). Preadolescent children's perception of power imbalance in bullying: A thematic analysis. *PLoS One, 14*(3), e0211124.

Olweus, D. (1993). *Bullying at school: What we know and what we can do.* Oxford, UK: Blackwell Publishers.

Olweus, D., & Limber, S. (2007). *Olweus Bullying Prevention Program: Teacher guide.* Hazelden.

Ostrov, J. M., Kamper-DeMarco, K. E., Blakely-McClure, S. J., Perry, K. J., & Mutignani, L. (2019). Prospective associations between aggression/bullying and adjustment in preschool: Is general aggression different from bullying behavior?. *Journal of Child and Family Studies, 28*(9), 2572–2585.

Patchin, J. W., & Hinduja, S. (2006). Bullies move beyond the schoolyard a preliminary look at cyberbullying. *Youth Violence and Juvenile Justice, 4,* 148–169.

Polanin, J. R., Espelage, D. L., Grotpeter, J. K., Ingram, K., Michaelson, L., Spinney, E., . . . & Robinson, L. (2021). A systematic review and meta-analysis of interventions to decrease cyberbullying perpetration and victimization. *Prevention Science, 23,* 439–454. https://doi.org/10.1007/s11121-021-01259-y

Polanin, J. R., Espelage, D. L., & Pigott, T. D. (2012). A meta-analysis of school-based bullying prevention programs' effects on bystander intervention behavior. *School Psychology Review, 41*(1), 47–65.

Roach, K. (2000). Changing punishment at the turn of the century: Restorative justice on the rise. *Canadian Journal of Criminology, 42*(3), 249–280.

Roberts, S., Zhang, J., Truman, J., & Snyder, T. (2012). *Indicators of school crime and safety: 2011* (NCES 2012–002/NCJ 236021). Washington, DC: National Center for Education Statistics, U.S. Department of Education, and Bureau of Justice Statistics, Office of Justice Programs, U.S. Department of Justice.

Ross, D. M. (2002). Bullying. In J. Sandoval (Ed.), *Handbook of crisis counseling, intervention, and prevention in the schools* (2nd ed., pp. 105–135). Lawrence Erlbaum.

Salmivalli, C., Kärnä, A., & Poskiparta, E. (2011). Counteracting bullying in Finland: The KiVa program and its effects on different forms of being bullied. *International Journal of Behavioral Development, 35,* 405–411.

Seth, A. (2019). A new paradigm to accommodate ethical foundations in the design and management of digital platforms. *Manuscript, IIT Delhi.*

Sulkowski, M. L., Bauman, S., Wright, S., Nixon, C., & Davis, S. (2014). Peer victimization in youth from immigrant and non-immigrant U.S. families. *School Psychology International, 35,* 649–669. doi: 10.1177/0143034314554968

Sulkowski, M. L., & Lazarus, P. J. (2017). *Creating safe and supportive schools and fostering students' mental health.* Routledge.

Swearer, S. M., Wang, C., Maag, J. W., Siebecker, A. B., & Frerichs, L. J. (2012). Understanding the bullying dynamic among students in special and general education. *Journal of School Psychology, 50,* 503–520.

Taquette, S. R., & Monteiro, D. L. M. (2019). Causes and consequences of adolescent dating violence: a systematic review. *Journal of Injury and Violence Research, 11*(2), 137–147.

Thomas, H. J., Connor, J. P., & Scott, J. G. (2018). Why do children and adolescents bully their peers? A critical review of key theoretical frameworks. *Social Psychiatry and Psychiatric Epidemiology, 53*(5), 437–51

Turanovic, J. J., Pratt, T. C., Kulig, T. C., & Cullen, F. T. (2022). *Confronting school violence: A synthesis of six decades of research.* Cambridge University Press.

Völlink, T., Bolman, C. A., Dehue, F., & Jacobs, N. C. (2013). Coping with cyberbullying: Differences between victims, bully-victims and children not involved in bullying. *Journal of Community and Applied Social Psychology, 23,* 7–24.

von Hirsch, A., Roberts, J. V., Bottoms, A. E., Roach, K., & Schiff, M. (Eds.). (2003). *Restorative justice and criminal justice: Competing or reconcilable paradigms.* Bloomsbury Publishing.

Wang, K., Chen, Y., Zhang, J., & Oudekerk, B. A. (2020). *Indicators of school crime and safety: 2019*. Washington, DC: National Center for Education Statistics, US Department of Education, and Bureau of Justice Statistics, Office of Justice Programs, US Department of Justice.

Wincentak, K., Connolly, J., & Card, N. (2017). Teen dating violence: A meta-analytic review of prevalence rates. *Psychology of Violence, 7*(2), 224–241. https://doi.org/10.1037/a0040194

Zhang, A., Wang, K., Zhang, J., & Oudekerk, B. A. (2019). *Indicators of school crime and safety: 2018* (NCES 2019–047/NCJ 252571). National Center for Education Statistic.

4

Suicide Prevention and Threat Assessment

Suicide Prevention and Intervention

Suicide is the second leading cause of death among 12–18-year-old youth (CDC, 2020). As noted by Sulkowski and Lazarus (2017), few, if any, problems confronting our nation's schools are more urgent than suicidal behavior in students. Consequently, leaders need to thoroughly understand the scope of the problem and develop ways to help despairing youth from taking their own lives.

The first section begins by describing the phenomenon of youth suicide and then discusses why schools and school leaders should engage in efforts to prevent tragic self-inflicted deaths in students. Additionally, content is provided on how schools can prevent suicide and how all educators can identify and help reduce suicide risks in students. Thus, this section covers suicide risk factors, warning signs, precipitants associated with suicide, and ways that potentially suicidal students can be supported. The second section covers the essence of threat assessment in

DOI: 10.4324/9780429261527-5

schools, the characteristics of school shooters, developing threat assessment teams, the Virginia Student Threat Assessment Guidelines used in this process, and practical considerations for leaders.

The Scope of the Problems

Suicide rates among young Americans have risen dramatically from 2007 to 2018. The rate of increase is 57% and has been particularly significant among young girls (Lindsey et al., 2019). Astoundingly, more teenagers have died by suicide than from influenza, cancer, birth defects, AIDS, pneumonia, and chronic lung disease combined (U.S. Centers for Disease Control [CDC], 2007). Further, it is a tragic phenomenon that a young person dies by suicide every five hours in the U.S. and that the number of suicides has tripled since the 1950s, while rates of unintentional injury, congenital problems, and disease have decreased (Berman et al., 2006; Wagner, 2009). Clearly, youth suicide is a pressing problem that warrants urgent action.

No communities or families are immune to suicide. This tragic occurrence transcends all boundaries related to socioeconomic status, age, gender, ethnicity, geographical region, and sexual orientation (Lieberman et al., 2008). According to the World Health Organization (WHO), suicide is a global phenomenon and is the second leading cause of death among young people ages 15–29 in the world. Moreover, suicide has increased by 60% during the past 50 years (Miller, 2021) and even more dramatically following the pandemic (American Foundation for Suicide Prevention [AFSP], 2022).

According to the 2019 Youth Risk Behavior Surveillance Survey, 18.8% of U.S. high school students reported that they have seriously considered suicide, 15.7% made a suicide plan, 8.9% reported having made a suicide attempt, and 2.5% indicated that their suicide attempt required them to receive a medical intervention (CDC, 2020). Thus, consistent with these findings, one out of every five high school students has seriously considered ending his or her life. Additionally, one out of every six has developed a suicide plan, and one out of every 11 has attempted suicide (CDC, 2020). Moreover, it is estimated that there are 100 to 200 suicide attempts for each completed case (Berman et al., 2006; Miller & Eckert, 2009). Considering the implication of these findings for school communities, within a typical high school classroom, it is likely that three students (one boy and two girls) have made some type of attempt to end their lives within the past year (American Association of Suicidology, [AAS], 2014).

Research has identified high-risk groups for youth suicide, which are Native Americans; lesbian, gay, bisexual, transgender, and questioning (LGBTQ+) students; homeless students; students living in foster care; students with mental illness; students engaging in self-injury; incarcerated youth; and those bereaved of loved ones by suicide (Poland & Ivey, 2021). Moreover, there is a higher risk when an individual has multiple risk factors. For example, there has been an uptick in suicidal behavior in Black girls ages 13 to 19, and their suicide death rates have increased by 182% from 2001 to 2017 (Alessandrini, 2021; Price & Khubchandani, 2019).

It is important to emphasize that suicidal behavior is highly problematic, even if it does not result in death. Youth who attempt suicide, but do not complete, may suffer significantly due to their attempt and because of the factors that contributed to the attempt (Sulkowski & Lazarus, 2017). This suffering may include experiencing serious bodily injuries such as broken bones, possible brain damage, or organ failure (Miller, 2021). Emotionally, youth who attempt suicide often suffer from serious mental health issues such as depression, which is inexorably linked with suicidal behavior. Research indicates that feelings of depression that include sadness, hopelessness, and helplessness are major risk factors for suicide (Brock et al., 2006). In support of this link, more than 90% of children and adolescents who completed suicide suffered from a mental disorder before their death (U.S. Department of Health and Human Services, 1999).

How School Leaders Can Prevent Student Suicide

School leaders may wonder how they can help to prevent youth suicide. In response to this question, the Substance Abuse and Mental Health Services Administration (SAMHSA, 2012) has outlined four major reasons schools should address student suicide and how they can help. These are listed in the document: *Preventing Suicide: A Toolkit for High Schools*. A summary of each reason is listed below:

1. *Maintaining a safe school environment is part of a school's overall mission.* An implicit contract exists between schools and caregivers about ensuring the safety of children at school, and suicide prevention is consistent with this contract. Activities designed to prevent violence, bullying, and substance abuse can also reduce suicide risk (Epstein & Spirito, 2009). In addition, consistent with our Three Pillar Model, programs developed to improve school climate and promote connectedness have been found to help reduce the risk of suicide, bullying, and substance abuse (Blum et al., 2002). Further, efforts to promote safe schools and foster caring relationships between educators and students can help protect young people against suicidal ideation and attempts, especially among LGBTQ youth with elevated risk for suicide (LGBTQ 40.4% versus heterosexual 14.5%: CDC, 2020). Even further, some activities designed to prevent suicide and promote student mental health reinforce student wellness programs' benefits and help ensure school safety. In support of this notion, research and findings from case studies indicate that the majority (78%) of targeted school shooters have been suicidal (Vossekuil et al., 2002). Thus, if these homicidal and suicidal youth had been identified and effectively treated, some school shootings may have been prevented.

2. *Students' mental health can affect their academic performance.* Depression and other mental health issues can interfere with students' ability to learn and be successful in school. Approximately half of the students receiving grades of mostly Ds and Fs in high school report feeling sad or hopeless, yet only one out of five students excelling in school (receiving grades of mostly As and Bs) felt the same (CDC, 2010). Furthermore, the same study found that one out of five high school students receiving grades of mostly Ds and Fs attempted suicide, while only one out of 25 students who excelled in school engaged in the same behavior.

3. *A student's suicide can significantly impact other students and the entire school community.* Knowing what to do following a suicide is critical to helping students cope with loss and prevent future tragedies such as contagion suicides. Contagion suicides are often referred to as the "copycat effect," which involves attempting suicide after the recent death of someone else. Research indicates that exposure to a completed suicide has been found to increase the risk that an individual will attempt suicide, and this risk is greatest in adolescence (Hart, 2012). Although this phenomenon is rare, the possible contagion effect associated with suicide must be taken seriously. To help mitigate this risk, the American Academy of Suicidality (AAS; 1998), Hart (2012), and SAMHSA (2012) provide guidelines for managing the suicide postvention process.

4. *Reducing legal risk can help protect schools from litigation.* Schools can be liable for failing to take the necessary steps to prevent student suicide. Suppose a school employee is informed that a student may be considering suicide, in that case, sh/e has an obligation to address the risk and involve mental health professionals and emergency first responders who can help the at-risk student. In addition, as a primary step, they must contact a legal guardian of the student. Failure to notify parents if their child appears to be suicidal, failure to get assistance for a student at risk of suicide, and failure to adequately supervise a student at risk all open up a school to litigation (Juhnke et al., 2011;

Lieberman et al., 2008). Thus, in addition to having a moral prerogative to help prevent student suicide, compelling legal reasons also influence schools to help. Even if the student has been evaluated and deemed at low risk for suicide, the school still has the legal obligation to inform the parents or guardians. The first author (PJL) served as a legal consultant in such a case, and the school was obligated by the court to pay significant financial damages to the family because the parents were not contacted after a suicide risk assessment was completed, even though the student was assessed to be at low-risk at that time.

What Leaders Can Do

Educational institutions cannot do everything to prevent youth suicide. However, they need to be part of the solution. The National Association of School Psychologists (NASP) opines that it is the school's responsibility to screen students, engage in suicide risk assessments, notify parents, recommend community and mental health services, and provide follow-up and support in school. Poland and Ivey (2021) recommend that school mental health providers take these actions, and their advice is equally applicable to all leaders. Below we have listed highlights.

1. Be the advocate for suicide prevention in your district.
2. Review model policies such as the one developed jointly by the Trevor Foundation, NASP, AFSP, and ASCA in 2019 and your district policies and procedures to determine if additional strategies or resources are needed.
3. Provide suicide prevention training annually for all school staff who with direct contact with students. All school personnel should be able to recognize warning signs and know the process for reporting their observations.
4. Review all the high-quality suicide and crisis resources from NASP as well as resources from the national Suicide Prevention Resource Center.

5. Ensure that all school psychologists and mental health professionals know how to conduct a suicide risk assessment.
6. Have a system in place to document the finding of the risk assessment and ensure that the youth's guardians have been contacted.
7. Prepare for suicide postvention by downloading the latest version of the AFSP/SPRC *After a Suicide: Toolkit for Schools.*
8. Download the *Florida School Toolkit for K–12 Educators to Prevent Suicide.* Though it is written for Florida, much of the information and the forms are applicable for all states.
9. Ensure that all school staff, families, and students know about 988—the new suicide hotline and crisis response system.

School leaders may not all be experts in suicide prevention and intervention. However, they can help ensure their staff has basic information about this topic. This is especially important as we have seen the pain and anguish of school staff following a student suicide and the concerns that if staff had been better informed, they could have taken action to prevent this tragedy from occurring.

Training all school staff should include warning signs (Table 4.1), possible precipitants (Table 4.2), risk factors (Table 4.3), and protective factors that influence suicidal behavior (Table 4.4). Though there may be little that a concerned leader can do about risk factors, there is much they can do to provide protective factors within the school. Consequently, we list important suicide intervention practices for school staff (Table 4.5). For mental health providers, we list questions to ask when it has been revealed that a student is considering suicide (Text Box 4.1). Information in the Tables and Text Boxes are based on findings of the American Foundation for Suicide Prevention (AFSP, 2022: CDC, 2007; CDC, 2014; Epstein & Spirito, 2009: Kalafat & Lazarus, 2002; Lieberman et al., 2008; 2014; Poland & Ivey 2021; SAMHSA, 2012).

98 ◆ The Safe Pillar

TABLE 4.1 Warning Signs Associated with Suicide

♦ Talking about wanting to die
♦ Looking for a way to kill oneself
♦ Talking about feeling hopeless or having no purpose
♦ Talking about feeling trapped or being in unbearable pain
♦ Talking about being a burden to others
♦ Increasing use of alcohol or drugs
♦ Acting anxious, agitated, or reckless
♦ Sleeping too much or too little
♦ Withdrawing or feeling isolated
♦ Showing rage or talking about seeking revenge
♦ Displaying extreme mood swings

TABLE 4.2 Possible Precipitants of Suicide

♦ Getting into trouble with authorities (e.g., school or community, fear of the consequences)
♦ Romantic breakup
♦ Death of a loved one or significant person
♦ Disappointment and rejection such as a dispute with boy/girlfriend, failure to get a job, or rejection from college
♦ Bullying or victimization
♦ Conflict with family or family dysfunction
♦ Disappointment with school results or school failure
♦ High demands at school during examination periods
♦ Unwanted pregnancy, abortion
♦ Infection with HIV or other sexually transmitted diseases
♦ The anniversary of a death of a friend or loved one
♦ Knowing someone who died by suicide
♦ Separation from friends, boy/girlfriends
♦ Real or perceived loss
♦ Serious physical illness
♦ Serious injury that may change the individual's life course
♦ Feeling humiliated

TABLE 4.3 Risk Factors Associated with Suicide

- Previous suicide attempt (20% of those who kill themselves made a previous attempt)
- Current ideation, intent, and plan (resolve)
- Early childhood trauma, multiple adverse childhood experiences
- A confluence of multiple stressors (discipline, rejection/humiliation, end of romantic relationship, conflict with family or peers, unmet school goals)
- Hopelessness and helplessness
- Mental disorders—particularly mood disorders such as depression and bipolar disorder
- Co-occurring mental, alcohol, or substance abuse disorders
- Personality disorders (most notably conduct and borderline)
- Easy access to lethal methods, especially guns
- Isolation, a feeling of being cut off from other people
- Ineffective coping mechanisms and inadequate problem-solving skills
- Exposure to suicide and/or family history of suicide
- Influence of significant people—family members, celebrities, peers who have died by suicide—both through direct personal contact or inappropriate media representations
- Local epidemics of suicide that have a contagious influence
- Impulsive and/or aggressive tendencies
- Barriers to accessing mental health treatment
- Gender (males are four times more likely to die by suicide than females), though females are more likely to make attempts
- LGBTQ individuals are more likely to attempt and to die by suicide, especially if there is family rejection, bullying, harassment, or lack of supportive resources
- Relational, social, work, or financial loss
- Trouble with the law
- Chronic medical illnesses (e.g., HIV, traumatic brain injury)
- PTSD
- Unwillingness to seek help because of stigma attached to mental and substance abuse disorders and/or suicidal thoughts
- Cultural and religious beliefs—for instance, the belief that suicide is a noble resolution of a personal dilemma

100 ◆ The Safe Pillar

TABLE 4.4 Protective Factors that Mitigate Suicide Risk

◆ Effective problem solving and interpersonal skills including conflict resolution and nonviolent handling of disputes
◆ Contact with a caring adult
◆ A sense of involvement/belonging to one's school, based on opportunities to participate in school activities and contribute to the functioning of the school (effective school climate)
◆ Effective and appropriate clinical care for mental, physical, and substance abuse disorders
◆ Easy access to a variety of clinical interventions and support for help seeking
◆ Restricted access to highly lethal methods of suicide
◆ Family and community support
◆ Cultural and religious beliefs that discourage suicide and support self-preservation instincts
◆ Positive self-esteem
◆ Resilience and a sense of self-efficacy
◆ A sense of purpose
◆ Strong religious or spiritual connections
◆ A strong network of caring friends
◆ A positive and nurturing school climate

TABLE 4.5 Suicide Intervention Practices for School Staff

◆ Do not agree to keep a student's suicidal intention a secret. Have the student speak to a school-based mental health professional.
◆ If a staff member believes a student may be suicidal, contact the mental health staff immediately to do a suicidal risk assessment. Do not wait until the following week when the professional arrives at the school.
◆ If the school-based mental health professional is not available, then contact the school-based or district-based crisis team. In some districts, staff may be directed to contact an outside mental health agency.
◆ If the student is suicidal, make sure the student is supervised at all times.
◆ Inform the suicidal youth that professional help has been contacted and describe what the next steps will be.
◆ Do not allow the student to leave the school.
◆ If the student has the means to carry out the threatened suicide on his or her own person, determine if he or she will voluntarily relinquish it. Do not force the student to do so. Do not place yourself in danger. Call the police if they have a weapon and will not give it up.

Suicide Prevention and Threat Assessment ◆ 101

Text Box 4.1: Questions to Ask a Student with a Suicide Plan

Sometimes when people have dealt with similar things and felt the same way, they want to die or kill themselves. Every day, many people have these kinds of thoughts, and it is not uncommon. Sometimes they even surprise friends and family members because they seem so happy and put together, yet they struggle to deal with some heavy stuff. Anyway, you're not alone at all if you feel this way. Have you been thinking like this at all? If so, how often have you had these thoughts? (every day, a few times a week, a few times a month, etc.)

If so, how would you harm yourself?
Do you have a current plan?
Do you have what you need to follow through on your plan?
When are you planning on doing this?
Have you ever attempted suicide before? If the answer is yes, then ask: Does anyone know?
When was your last attempt, and how did you go about it?
What has been keeping you alive so far?
What is your hurry? Why do it now?
What do you think the future holds in store for you?

If a student is deemed to be at risk for suicide, then there are well-respected practices that leaders need to take.

Concluding Thoughts

The school leader can do a lot to make a difference to help prevent youth suicide. Most basically, the leader can ensure that all staff have been provided with workshops or training related to suicide risk factors, warning signs, and potential precipitants. They can help ensure that effective policies, practices, and procedures are in place and work with their mental health staff to provide referrals to professionals who can help potentially suicidal students. They can ensure that suicide risk assessments are completed on students who are at risk and that professionals can communicate their findings with parents/guardians.

Nonetheless, suicide in youth is complex, youth who attempt or complete most often have multiple-determinant problems. This section due to space limitations cannot be comprehensive and only provides the basic information leaders need to have. Consequently, leaders must continually educate themselves on this topic and consult other references. The good news, as stated in the *NASP President's Call to Action to Prevent Suicide* (Lazarus et al., 2009), is that "Evidenced-based research suggests that if suicidal youth are identified by the schools and if appropriate treatment is provided, suicide can be dramatically reduced (Zenere & Lazarus, 1997, 2009). If this happens, lives will be saved" (p. 4). Identification and follow-up are key.

Threat Assessment in Schools

Mass shootings in *schools* are rare. Sadly, mass shootings in the United States are not. Gun violence in the U.S. is a very serious problem. The U.S. has endured more than 600 mass shootings in 2022 alone, and as of December 1, 2022, for the first 11 months of the year, there were more than 18,500+ gun deaths, 35,900+ gun injuries, 900+ children shot, 4,700+ teenagers shot, 1,000+ defensive use incidents, 1,400+ unintentional shootings, and 22,000+ suicides (Gun Violence Archives, 2022).

Though any life lost to gun violence is tragic, no matter the setting, FBI crime statistics indicate that schools are far less likely to experience homicides than other locations (Nekvasil et al., 2015). For example, based on data from the Centers for

Disease Control and Prevention, there are approximately 1,600 shootings in the surrounding community for every shooting in a school (Cornell, 2018). The likelihood of any school experiencing a student homicide is one in every 6,000 years (Pollack et al., 2008). However, these tragic events are horrifying and galvanize the entire nation to want to take action to prevent another atrocity from happening. This has become even more true due to the proliferation of weapons of war used by school shooting perpetrators and the increasing number of fatalities and injuries. Frequent preventive strategies suggested often center on hardening schools, which aim to make schools harder to attack through implementing security technologies (e.g., metal detectors, automatic door locks, emergency call buttons, one secure school entrance, etc.), as well as increasing the number of armed law-enforcement agents and school resource officers on site potentially to neutralize an attacker, and arming teachers or other selected school personnel.

However, despite having positive intentions, many of these strategies are unlikely to *thwart* an attack before it occurs or quickly *stop it* once it does. In support of this position, most school shootings occur rapidly and are over in minutes, making it very hard for emergency response personnel to mitigate these attacks (Greenberg, 2007; Harnisch, 2008). Moreover, attackers have recently come to school equipped with weapons of war such as an AR-15 or other types of semi-automatic rifles (e.g., Robb Elementary School in Uvalde, TX; Sandy Hook Elementary in Newtown, CT; Marjory Stoneman Douglas High School in Parkland, FL), which can overwhelm one police officer or school resource officer (SRO). In addition, because of the chaos, confusion, and incidents of miscommunication that occur during the "fog" of an attack, it is even difficult for trained emergency responders to identify an attacker, protect potential victims, and secure a school campus while an attack unfolds, as can be seen in the aforementioned schools. Therefore, instead of trying to stop an attack once it occurs, preventive strategies are needed to mitigate threats of violence to school communities (Cornell, 2018; Cornell & Crowley, 2021; Sulkowski, 2011; Sulkowski & Lazarus, 2011). Yet, there is one action that schools can take to help prevent an attack from occurring. One such approach is threat assessment. However, before discussing threat assessment, the characteristics of potentially threatening students are covered.

Characteristics of Potentially Threatening Students

Even though surface characteristics cannot be used to profile or identify potentially threatening students, research by the U.S. Secret Service and U.S. DOE found that several qualities are shared by the majority of school shooters (Vossekuil et al., 2002). Researchers in these organizations studied 37 attacks that involved 41 perpetrators that took place in the U.S. between January 1974 and May 2000. Results of this investigation found that all school attackers were male, 98% had recently experienced or perceived a major personal loss (e.g., loss of a family member, breaking up with a partner), 93% had planned the attack in advance of carrying it out, 83% had difficulty coping with a recent loss/perceived loss, 78% exhibited a history of suicidal thoughts/attempts, 73% had a grievance against at least one victim, and 71% felt persecuted, bullied, or vulnerable. In contrast, relatively few school shooters (17%) had been diagnosed with a psychiatric disorder, were motivated to attack to gain notoriety (24%), had previously received a mental health evaluation (34%), and demonstrated excessive interest in explosives (32%). Although no one of the aforementioned characteristics can be used to identify a possible school attacker with accuracy, these characteristics may best be used to identify students who display psychosocial adjustment issues and could benefit from mental health support.

What Is Threat Assessment

Threat assessment is a systematic process of evaluation and intervention for individuals who have made verbal or behavioral threats of violence against others (Meloy & Hoffman, 2013). According to Cornell and Crowley (2021, p. 149):

when a threat has been reported, a threat assessment team gathers information to assess the seriousness of the threat and, when appropriate, takes actions to protect potential victims and initiate interventions intended to reduce the risk of the threat being carried out.

A few actual examples of threats are listed below:

- Student says, "I am going to do a Columbine."
- Student draws pictures of someone shooting a gun, exploding a bomb, or hanging from a noose.
- Student writes in an assignment, "I am going to kill Mr. J." (the teacher).
- Student verbally threatens to harm another student: "I am going to beat you up after school. I am going to bring my Dad's gun to school and kill you."
- Student leaves a note in the classroom or on the cafeteria floor that sh/e is going to hurt him/herself or someone else.

Cornell, as cited in his interview with Sulkowski and Lazarus (2017), has noted that the term "threat assessment" though it may sound ominous, is a constructive, supportive, problem-solving approach to student concerns. One major purpose of threat assessment is to prevent violence by addressing student problems like bullying, peer conflicts, or suicidal intent before they escalate into more severe violence or self-harm.

Cornell notes it is difficult to predict violence, but identifying that someone needs assistance is not hard. Leaders can frequently identify students who require intervention. There is a widespread misperception that we must be able to identify violent individuals and predict when they will attack to prevent violence. Cornell opines that we know how to prevent motor vehicle accidents even though accidents happen without warning. We also know how to prevent cancer by targeting risk factors long before the disease develops. We need a similar way of thinking about violence prevention. And in the rare cases where a student is actually planning and preparing to carry out a violent attack, an active threat assessment team is the most likely method of identification and intervention.

Developing Threat Assessment Teams

All schools need school threat assessment teams which generally consist of an administrative leader such as a principal or assistant principal, a school psychologist, a school counselor, a social worker, and a law enforcement officer or SRO. The main priority is to create a multidisciplinary team from school administration, mental health, and law enforcement. Prior threat assessment training is required, and team members need to be experienced and mature problem solvers.

An administrative leader has a number of responsibilities. These include ensuring all team members are well-trained and execute their responsibilities according to district policies. According to Louvar Reeves (2021), the administrative leader (a) consults with team members to screen cases to help determine if a full threat assessment needs to be conducted, (b) assists in gathering information, (c) helps in interviewing subjects, targets, witnesses, teachers, staff, parents, and students, (d) makes sure that the threat assessment plan is followed and monitored, and (e) works with the public information officer to respond to concerns and questions voiced by the community. Following the assessment, the leader (a) ensures that supports and interventions are provided, (b) enforces disciplinary consequences, if necessary, and (c) engages in a collaborative process that facilitates and monitors interventions and supports.

Mental health professionals help the team gather information concerning a student's threatening behavior and mental and emotional state. They collect information regarding developmental context and what precipitating factors may have led to a student making a threat or engaging in concerning behavior. They understand that students often do or say things without fully understanding the consequences of their behavior and have less developed reasoning ability and impulse control. Due to their understanding of typical and atypical development, they can assess the difference between a student making a threat and posing a threat (Louvar Reeves, 2021). Moreover, they can engage in counseling and help provide other interventions for distressed students (Cornell & Crowley, 2021). The vast majority of school threat assessment cases can be resolved with mental health services and disciplinary actions that do not require arrest or school exclusion.

In addition, a law enforcement representative, such as an SRO assigned to the school, should also be a team member. Most high schools typically have an SRO, but elementary and middle schools may not. In the latter case, the school might utilize the SRO in its high school feeder pattern. It is the responsibility of the SRO or the law enforcement officer to investigate cases that might involve a potential felony. They can advise the team if the threat violates the law, and in serious cases, they can investigate. They can interview other students, provide information about potential gang activity, search the home, and invoke red flag laws that enable the removal of weapons from the home (if codified in state statutes). They may also have access to information the school is not privy to, such as arrest records, criminal activity, or gang involvement (Cornell & Crowley, 2021). They can also serve as a liaison with juvenile justice, the court system, law enforcement, probation services, etc. Moreover, if the threat is imminent, they can engage in rapid response and provide security.

The Threat Assessment Process

Though there are a few models that have been developed to evaluate safety threats, this section focuses on the Virginia Student Threat Assessment Guidelines (VSTAG) that were first developed by the Youth Violence Project in the University of Virginia's Curry School of Education (Cornell & Sheras, 2006; see also Cornell, 2018). The VSTAG model, as described by Cornell and Crowley (2021), follows a five-step process[1] for conducting threat assessments and is discussed below:

Step 1. A team member interviews the student and any relevant witnesses. The aim is to determine exactly what happened and if the threat is deemed to be *transient* or *substantive.* A *transient* threat is deemed not to be serious and can be easily resolved, whereas a *substantive* threat requires more *serious* intervention.

Step 2. If the team, after interviewing the student and other witnesses determines that the threat is transient, then at the Step 2 level, the team can help resolve the conflict through some action or by an apology by the student. Sometimes it is just a matter of letting the student know that they cannot say things they said, because their words will be taken very seriously. In some circumstances, disciplinary action or consequences may be deemed necessary. According to Cornell (2018), multiple studies have found that approximately 75% of threat assessments can be resolved in two steps as they are determined to be transient.

Step 3. The team begins the third step if it considers that the student intends to cause harm. This is then deemed a *substantive* threat. At this point, the intent is to prevent violence and protect potential victims. The team will try to help resolve any problems or conflicts that precipitated the threat. They will also increase supervision of the threatening student. Additionally, disciplinary consequences will be imposed depending on the nature of the threat and the student's behavior. If the student had threatened to hit or fight someone, then the threat will be considered a *serious substantive threat* and will be resolved in Step 3. As noted by Cornell and Crowley (2021), if the student had threatened to use a weapon to shoot, stab, or severely injure a potential victim(s), then the threat is called a *"very serious substantive threat,"* and then the team initiates Step 4.

Step 4. At this point, the team will conduct a safety evaluation. This requires actions from an SRO or law enforcement officer and school-based mental health professionals. The law enforcement investigation looks for evidence of the student's planning, preparation, criminal activity, the acquisition of firearms or the making of bombs. As a result of this investigation, the SRO will advise the team regarding any security measures or legal actions that need to be taken. As noted by Cornell (2018), law enforcement involvement does not necessarily indicate that the student will be arrested or charged with crimes. He explains that in studies involving thousands of threat assessment cases, only about 1% resulted in a subsequent arrest.

In Step 4, members of the school-based mental health team will interview the student and their parents/guardians. It is best if two team members work together when questioning the student, and it is ideal if one of the members knows or has knowledge of the student. In addition, other interviews will be undertaken by the same individual or another team member with the student's peers, teachers, healthcare providers, family members, or others who have information about the student. It is important to emphasize that the mental health professional's task is threefold: 1) to figure out the reasons for the student's threat and what the student was trying to accomplish (e.g., retaliate against a bully, obtain peer respect, get attention, look tough, be suspended from school, etc.), 2) to screen the student for critical mental health issues such as suicidality, homicidal thoughts, mania, psychosis, derealization, and decomposition in functioning (Cornell & Nekvasil, 2012), and 3) to determine the need for mental health supports. The mental health professional's job is not to "make a prediction of violence, but to identify risk factors and strategies to reduce risk, using a standard protocol of questions and topics" (Cornell & Crowley, 2021, p. 153). The result of the risk assessment should lead to a short report, as documentation is important both procedurally and legally. See Text Box 4.2 for a list of questions recommended by the U.S. Secret Service when conducting a threat assessment (Fein et al., 2002).

After the law enforcement investigation and the mental health interviews have been conducted, the team then develops a safety plan. This plan will identify mental health supports needed by the student to function effectively in school. In addition, a full-scale psychological evaluation may be conducted if deemed necessary, or if the student is already in special education then a review and modification of the student's Individualized Educational Plan will need to be done.

Text Box 4.2: 11 Key Questions Provided by the U. S. Secret Service in Conducting a Threat Assessment

1. What are the student's motives or goals?
2. Any communications of intent to attack?
3. Any inappropriate interest in other attacks, weapons, or mass violence?
4. Any attack-related behaviors? Making a plan, acquiring weapons, casing sites, etc.
5. Does the student have the capacity to attack?
6. Is there hopelessness or despair?
7. Any trusting relationship with an adult?
8. Is violence regarded as a way to solve a problem? Any peer influences?
9. Are the student's words consistent with actions?
10. Are others concerned about the student?
11. What circumstances might trigger violence?

Note that all of the Secret Service questions are oriented around determining if the student is on a behavioral pathway leading to an act of violence. There is considerable emphasis on situational and relationship factors and relatively little concern with personality factors or other individual characteristics that are often identified when profiling is used.

Step 5. At this last stage, the team implements the safety plan, monitors its success or lack of, and modifies the plan as necessary. The major purpose of the safety plan is "to prevent violence by resolving the threat, addressing any school factors (such as peer conflicts that contributed to the threat situation and returning the student to school or alternative education as deemed appropriate;" Cornell & Crowley, 2021, p. 153).

Critical Considerations for Leaders

Jane Lazarus, who conducted threat assessments at the middle school level (as interviewed by Sulkowski and Lazarus, 2017), offers these important suggestions. The violence prevention process works best when schools follow this step-by-step process, educators and staff are well-trained, all teachers are involved, and the district has developed well-articulated threat assessment policies and procedures. The school leader must always be aware of any threats and be involved in taking immediate action. This may require the leader to stay late as threats may occur at the end of the day. Teachers need to understand that they have an obligation to report any threats of violence immediately to a member of the school safety team. However, they should be reassured that they are not responsible for investigating or deciding the threat's credibility. She recommends that teachers maintain a record of exactly what they saw and heard. Teachers should also receive feedback from the administrative leader regarding how the situation was handled and what will occur the next day at school.

Jane Lazarus notes that students often tell someone—usually a peer—when a dangerous situation may occur. This is called "leakage" by the U. S. Secret Service. Moreover, to increase the chances that a student will report this concern to an adult, teachers should stand in the hall during class transitions, greet students by name, and listen. Also, all schools should have a procedure where concerned students or parents can anonymously report a potential threat to the administration (Lazarus, 2001).

They need to know that rather than get a student in trouble, by informing school personnel, they can avert a potential tragedy and prevent a student from making an irreversible decision that can have terrible life-altering consequences.

Conclusion

This chapter discussed what leaders can do to reduce the risk of suicide among students and how to conduct threat assessments of troubled youth. Both of these concerns are interconnected. Even though most suicidal individuals will never engage in an attack against their school, the majority of school shooters (78%) (Vossekuil et al., 2002) are either consciously or unconsciously suicidal. Some die by "suicide by cop," and others kill themselves during the attack. Those that survive often state that they wish to end their lives. Consequently, if a school can identify a suicidal student, not only can they get the youth the help they so desperately need, but a serendipitous result may also be that a school shooting is averted.

Notes

1 The original VSTAG model (Cornell & Sheras, 2006) used a seven-step decision tree with some redundancy. The revised model (Cornell, 2018) uses five steps to cover the same process.

References

Alessandrini, K. A. (2021). Suicide among Black girls is a mental health crisis hiding in plain sight. *Time*. https://time.com/6046773/black-teenage-girls-suicide/

American Association of Suicidology (1998) *Suicide postvention guidelines: Suggestion for dealing with the aftermath of a suicide in the schools.* Washington, DC. Author.

American Association of Suicidology (2014). *Youth suicide fact sheet.* Washington, DC: Author. http://www.suicidology.org/c/document_library/get_file?folderId=262&name=DLFE-627.pdf

American Foundation for Suicide Prevention [AFSP] (2022). *Risk factors, protective factors and warning signs.* Author. https://afsp.org/risk-factors-protective-factors-and-warning-signs

Berman, A. L., Jobes, D. A., & Silverman, M. M. (2006). *Adolescent suicide: Assessment and intervention.* American Psychological Association.

Blum, R. W., McNeely, C., & Rinehart, P. M. (2002). *Improving the odds: The untapped power of schools to improve the health of teens.* Minneapolis Center for Adolescent Health and Development, University of Minnesota. http:www.med.umn.edu/peds/ahm/prod/groups/med@pub@med/documents/asset/med_21771.pdf

Brock, S. E., Sandoval, J., & Hart, S. (2006). Suicidal ideation and behaviors. In G. G. Bear & K. M. Minke (Eds.), *Children's needs III: Development, prevention, and intervention* (pp. 225–238). National Association of School Psychologists.

Centers for Disease Control and Prevention (2007). *Suicide prevention scientific information: Consequences.* http://www.cdc.gov/ncipc/dvp/Suicide/Suicide-conque.htm

Centers for Disease Control and Prevention (2010). *Youth risk behavior surveillance –United States, 2009.*

Centers for Disease Control and Prevention (2014). *Youth risk behavior surveillance –United States, 2013.* http://www.cdc.gov/mmwr/pdf/ss/ss6304.pdf?utm_source=rss&utm_medium=rss&utm_campaign=youth-risk-behavior-surveillance-united-states-2013-pdf

Centers for Disease Control and Prevention (2020). *Youth risk behavior surveillance—United States, 2019.* https://www.cdc.gov/healthyyouth/data/yrbs/index.htm

Cornell, D. (2018). *Comprehensive school threat assessment guidelines.* Charlottesville, VA: School Threat Assessment Consultants LLC.

Cornell, D., & Crowley, B. (2021). Preventing school violence and advancing school safety. In P. J. Lazarus, S. M. Suldo, & B. Doll (Eds.). *Fostering the emotional well being of our youth: A school-based approach.* (pp. 137–162). Oxford University Press.

114 ◆ The Safe Pillar

Cornell, D., & Nekvasil, E. (2012). Violent thoughts and behaviors. In S. E. Brock & S. R. Jimerson (Eds.), *Best practices in school crisis prevention and intervention* (2nd ed.) (pp. 485–502). NASP Publications.

Cornell, D., & Sheras, P. (2006). *Guidelines for responding to student threats of violence.* Sopris West.

Epstein, J. A., & Spirito, A. (2009). Risk factors for suicidality among a nationally representative sample of high school students. *Suicide and Life Threatening Behavior, 39,* 241–251.

Fein, R., Vossekuil, B., Pollack, W., Borum, R., Modzeleski, W. & Reddy, M. (2002). *Threat assessment in schools: A guide to managing threatening situations and to creating safe school climates.* Washington, DC: U.S. Secret Service and Department of Education.

Greenberg, S. F. (2007). Active shooters on college campuses: Conflicting advice, roles of the individual and first responder, and the need to maintain perspective. *Disaster Medicine and Public Health Preparedness, 1,* 57–61.

Gun Violence Archives (2022). https://www.gunviolencearchive.org/?sid=qGlCiC

Harnisch, T. L. (2008, November). *Concealed weapons on state college campuses: In pursuit of individual liberty and collective security.* A Higher Education Policy Brief. American Association of State Colleges and Universities.

Hart, S. (2012). Student suicide: Suicide postvention. In S. E. Brock & S. R. Jimerson (Eds.). *Best practices in school crisis prevention and intervention* (2nd ed.) (pp. 527–547). National Association of School Psychologists.

Juhnke, G. A., Granello, D. H., & Granello, P. F. (2011). *Suicide, self-injury, and violence in the schools: Assessment, prevention and intervention strategies.* John Wiley & Sons.

Kalafat, J., & Lazarus, P. J. (2002). Suicide prevention in schools. In S. E. Brock, P. J. Lazarus & S. R. Jimerson, (Eds.), *Best practices in school crisis prevention and intervention* (pp. 211–223). National Association of School Psychologists.

Lazarus, P. J. (2001, May). Breaking the code of silence: What schools can do about it. *NASP Communique, 29*(7), 28–29.

Lazarus, P. J., Brock, S. E., Lieberman, R., Poland, S. Zenere, F., & Feinberg, T. (2009). *NASP President"s call to action to prevent suicide.* Available from http://www.nasponline.org/advocacy/suicidecalltoaction.aspx

Lieberman, R. A., Poland, S., & Cassel, R. (2008). Best practices in suicide intervention. In A. Thomas & J. Grimes, (Eds.). *Best practices in school psychology V* (pp. 1457–1473). National Association of School Psychologists.

Lieberman, R. A., Poland, S., & Kornfeld. C. (2014). Best practices in suicide prevention and intervention. In P. L. Harrison, & A. Thomas (Eds.). *Best practices in school psychology; System level services* (pp. 273–288). National Association of School Psychologists.

Lindsey, M. A., Sheftall, A. H., Xiao, Y., & Joe, S. (2019). Trends of suicidal behaviors among high school students in the United States: 1991–2017. *Pediatrics, 144*(5). https://doi.org/10.1542/peds.2019-1187

Louvar Reeves, M. A. (2021). *Behavioral threat assessment and management for K-12 schools.* National Center for Youth Issues.

Meloy, J. R., & Hoffmann, J. (Eds.). (2013). *International handbook of threat assessment.* Oxford University Press.

Miller, D. (2021). *Child and adolescent suicidal behavior: School-based prevention, assessment and intervention* (2nd ed.). Guilford Press.

Miller, D. N., & Eckert, T. (2009). Youth suicidal behavior: An introduction and overview. *School Psychology Review, 38,* 153–167.

Nekvasil, E., & Cornell, D. (2012). Student reports of peer threats of violence: Prevalence and outcomes. *Journal of School Violence, 11,* 357–375. doi: 10.1080/15388220.2012.706764

Nekvasil, E. K., Cornell, D. G., & Huang, F. L. (2015). Prevalence and offense characteristics of multiple casualty homicides: Are schools at higher risk than other locations? *Psychology of Violence, 5,* 236–245. doi: 10.1037/a0038967

Poland, S., & Ivey, C. (2021). *Florida school toolkit for K-12 educators to prevent suicide.* Nova Southeastern University. https://www.nova.edu/publications/florida-toolkit/2021/florida-school-toolkit-educators-to-prevent-suicide/12/

Pollack, W. S., Modzeleski, W., & Rooney, G. (2008). *Prior knowledge of potential school-based violence: Information students learn may*

116 ◆ The Safe Pillar

prevent a targeted attack. Washington, DC: U.S. Secret Service & U.S. Department of Education.

Price, J. H., & Khubchandani, J. (2019). The changing characteristics of African-American adolescent suicides, 2001–2017. *Journal of Community Health, 44*(4), 756–763. https://doi.org/10.1007/s10900-019-00678-x

Substance Abuse and Mental Health Services Administration (2012). *Preventing suicide: A toolkit for high schools.* HHS Publication No. SMA-12–4669. Rockville, MD: Center for Mental Health Services, Substance Abuse and Mental Health Services Administration.

Sulkowski, M. L. (2011). An investigation of students' willingness to report threats of violence in campus communities. *Psychology of Violence, 1,* 53–65. doi: 10.1037/a0021592

Sulkowski, M. L., & Lazarus, P. J. (2011). Contemporary responses to violent attacks on college campuses. *Journal of School Violence, 10,* 338–354. doi: 10.1080/15388220.2011.602601

Sulkowski, M. L. & Lazarus, P. J. (2017). *Creating safe and supportive schools and fostering students' mental health.* Routledge.

U. S. Department of Health & Human Services (1999). *The Surgeon General's call to action to prevent suicide.* Washington, DC: Available from http://www.surgeongeneral.gov/library/calltoaction/

Vossekuil, B., Fein, R. A., Reddy, M., Borum, R. & Modzeleski, W. (2002). *The final report and findings of the Safe School Initiative: Implications for the prevention of school attacks in the United States.* Washington, DC: U.S. Secret Service and U.S. Department of Education.

Wagner, B. M. (2009). *Suicidal behavior in children and adolescents.* Yale University Press.

Zenere, F. J., III, & Lazarus, P. J. (1997). The decline of youth suicidal behavior in an urban multicultural school system following the introduction of a suicide prevention and intervention program. *Suicide and Life-Threatening Behavior, 16,* 360–378.

Zenere, F.J. III, & Lazarus, P. J. (2009). The sustained reduction of youth suicidal behavior in an urban multicultural school district. *School Psychology Review, 38,* 189–199.

Section 2
The Supportive Pillar

5

School Climate and Culture

All schools have distinct climates and cultures. These are influenced by the communities in which they reside, as well as by educational leaders, policies, broader historical events, and other contextual factors. As a primary driver of student success, school climate encompasses everything in the school's physical, social, and emotional environment. Similarly, school culture often is described as the leadership, interpersonal factors, and policies that impact individuals within a school community. Thus, although school climate and culture overlap, they are not identical. School climate is all-encompassing, and school culture pertains to the relationships among members of the school community. School leaders are, however, accountable for influencing both school climate and culture. They set the tone for the culture and are responsible for engendering a healthy school climate.

This chapter reviews the interrelated concepts of school climate and culture pertaining to school leaders. First, the definition and nature of school climate are discussed. No universal definition of school climate exists; however, similarities exist in

DOI: 10.4324/9780429261527-7

how it has been described, measured, and understood across time. Second, information is provided on the influence of school climate, as well as how it impacts students and educational communities. Although universally accepted and clear understandings of school climate have been elusive over the past 50 years (Cornell et al., 2021), members of school communities still have a palpable sense of this phenomenon and how it impacts them.

More recently, over the past couple of decades, research on school climate has expanded exponentially, consistent with a stronger emphasis on improving school safety. Similarly, the focus on school culture has increased simultaneously, largely because of increased attention being paid to systematic problems that plague school communities, such as discipline and special education practices that disproportionately harm minority students, the growing influence of social media on school climate, and bullying and peer aggression, especially as it impacts minoritized and LGBTQ students (Harris et al., 2021). Additionally, school culture is often hierarchical with school leaders at the top, teachers and educational assistants in the middle, and students and other members of the school community undergirding the bottom (Moore et al., 2017). Therefore, whereas school climate is everywhere and involves all aspects of the school environment, school culture largely relates to educational leaders and how they foster healthy interpersonal relationships among all members of school communities.

What Is School Climate?

Defining School Climate

In a seminal article, Cohen et al. (2009) define "school climate" as "the quality and character of school life that is based on patterns of people's experiences of school life and reflects norms, goals, values, interpersonal relationships, teaching and learning practices, and organizational structures" (p. 182). Further, these authors describe a positive school climate as an environment in which people are engaged and respected. Thus, such a healthy school climate fosters student development and learning, allowing them to be productive, contribute to the well-being of others, and have a satisfying life. It is integral to fitting in and feeling like you belong in the social milieu.

A positive school climate also allows for norms, values, and expectations that support people feeling socially, emotionally, and physically safe. According to Cohen et al. (2009), in such an environment, "students, families, and educators work together to develop, live, and contribute to a shared school vision; and educators model and nurture an attitude that emphasizes the benefits of, and satisfaction from, learning" (p. 182). Thus, school climate is more than an individual experience—it is a group phenomenon that reflects the character and quality of a school, which is influenced by the character and quality of school leaders.

Other descriptions of school climate refer to the collective physical, social, and emotional environment at school. In this regard, the National School Climate Council (2007) suggests that school climate is based on patterns of people's experiences of school life while also reflecting norms, goals, values, interpersonal relationships, teacher and learning practices, and organizational structures. Going even a step further, the U.S. Department of Education (U.S. DOE; 2014) describes school climate as the extent to which a school community creates and maintains a safe school campus; provides a supportive academic, disciplinary, and physical environment; and fosters respectful, trusting, and caring relationships throughout the school community. Essentially, according to the U.S. DOE, school climate encompasses the people, places, and school operations.

Considering the former, school climate is not monolithic and should be considered a multidimensional construct. "School climate" is an umbrella term that covers many conceptually related components that characterize the broad school environment.

The National School Climate Center (Thapa et al., 2013) has embraced this perspective, and it has identified five distinct—yet interrelated—school climate components:

- *Safety* (physical safety, social–emotional safety, rules, and norms)
- *Relationships* (school connectedness and engagement, social support, leadership, respect for diversity, students' race/ethnicity, and their perceptions of school climate)
- *Teaching and Learning* (social, emotional, ethical, and civic learning; service learning; support for academic learning; support for professional relationships; teachers' and students' perceptions of school climate)
- *Institutional Environment* (physical surroundings, resources, and supplies)
- *School Improvement Process* (implementation of evidence-based programs)

More recently, the U.S. Department of Education Safe and Supportive Schools also embraced a multidimensional school climate model that is hierarchically organized (U.S. DOE, 2018). This framework includes three broad school climate components: *Safety* (physical safety, social-emotional safety, substance use), *Student Engagement* (school participation, relationships, respect for diversity), and the *School Environment* (physical environment, academic environment, disciplinary environment, wellness). Figure 5.1 presents the current U.S. DOE school climate model.

As conceptions of school climate have expanded in scope, more is being demanded of school leaders to make sure students feel safe and supported. Although "school climate" is the term adopted by fields of education and psychology, perhaps "school weather" more accurately describes the environments that members of school communities inhabit. This is because schools are complex environments that are constantly changing.

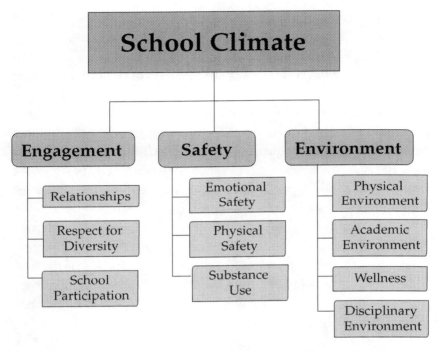

FIGURE 5.1 The U.S. Department of Education School Climate Model

Some days may be bright and sunny, and students are on task, learning, growing, and succeeding. However, other days may be dark and stormy, thus requiring school leaders to adjust quickly and batten down the hatches. Sticking with this analogy, school leaders must function like a barometer, continuously testing the pressure in the school environment, and must make decisions about what is most needed on a given day.

Types of School Climate

The pioneering work of Baumrind (1966) provides a framework to understand school climate within the context of human development. As a researcher interested in parent-child relationship dynamics, Baumrind noted that parenting styles involve prevailing patterns of discipline and affection that parents express with their children. Further, she described these practices as falling along two distinct dimensions: *control* and *responsiveness*.

Control is considered the manner and strictness by which caregivers impose limits and discipline youth. On the other hand, *responsiveness* concerns acceptance, caring, and affection. Therefore, control describes the behavioral aspects of nurturing, whereas responsiveness describes the emotional aspects of this process. Lastly, Baumrind described four parenting practices that also translate to school climate styles: uninvolved, permissive, authoritarian, and authoritative practices, each of which involves different degrees of responsiveness and control.

Using the same conceptual framework, four different types or styles of school climate can be derived from Baumrind's work. These are negligent, permissive, authoritarian, and authoritative. Out of these styles, an authoritative school climate, characterized as having appropriate warmth and disciplinary support, has been associated with the most favorable student outcomes (Cornell & Huang, 2016). Negligent school climates tend to be low in nurturing adult-student relationships and have poor structure and order, whereas permissive environments are described as having positive relationships, yet they do not have clear and consistent rules for order and safety in place. Lastly, school leaders deemphasize establishing supportive relationships in authoritarian environments and instead focus on maintaining strict order.

Thus, only an authoritative school climate has the requisite balance of warmth, support, autonomy, order, discipline, and structure. It then follows that school leaders involved with establishing an authoritative school climate have the best chance to hit the sweet spot between control and responsiveness and benefit the most students. Increasingly, to make sure schools are safe and supportive, school leaders have a responsibility to help achieve a balance between the previous qualities. Figure 5.2 lists additional characteristics associated with each style of school climate.

	Low Responsiveness	High Responsiveness
High Control	*Authoritarian* • High expectations • Clear rules • Forceful • Rigid • Low warmth • Punishment oriented • Autocratic	*Authoritative* • High expectations • Clear standards • Assertive • Flexible • Warm • Responsive • Democratic
Low Control	*Neglectful* • No expectations • Few rules • Absent • Passive • Uninterested • Competing priorities • Uninvolved	*Permissive* • Low expectations • Few rules • Indulgent • Accepting • Avoids confrontation • Warm • Lenient

FIGURE 5.2 Characteristics Associated with School Climate Styles

What Is School Culture?

Defining School Culture

As the literature describes, school culture often pertains to the underlying assumptions and beliefs within a school community that define reality and interpersonal relations within an organizational system (Roach & Kratochwill, 2004). In other words, it relates to factors that influence how people interact with each other in an environment. Early research on school culture dating back to the 1930s primarily pertained to business and industrial/organizational settings. At the time, researchers were interested in the human factors that made industry and business more efficient.

As an outgrowth of such work, school culture initially focused on making students more efficient and capable. In a seminal study, Barnard (1938) originally described organizational culture as a system's norms, sentiments, values, and emergent interactions. Thus, from this perspective, yet going a step further, Roach and Kratochwill (2004) describe school culture as "the way we do things around here" (p. 12) as "things" pertain to educational conventions. As people who influence educational practices, school leaders then have an impact on school culture. Inherently, they influence an organization's shared beliefs, rituals, ceremonies, communication patterns, practices, and policies.

However, comprehensively defining school culture has been an elusive goal. Like school climate, definitions of school culture have had to expand and become more nuanced as schools have become larger, more complex, and increasingly inclusive during the 20th century. Stemming from anthropological literature, proposed definitions of school culture vary considerably. Some scholars estimate that there are more than 100 definitions of culture (e.g., Berger, 1995); and, in an early scholarly attempt to distill various definitions of school culture, Hoy et al. (1991) describe the concept as being "a system of shared orientations (norms, core values, and tacit assumptions) held by members, which holds the unit together and gives it a distinct identity" (p. 5). But what about individuals within the organization—in the school—who do not share the same norms, core values, or tacit assumptions? What about individuals who are marginalized and excluded from the former? This is where school leaders must actively support and implement policies and practices to enfranchise traditionally disenfranchised groups of individuals.

Culturally Responsive School Culture

Some scholars argue that early definitions of school culture are incomplete and can contribute to an organizational system that is non-inclusive and discriminatory, especially for traditionally disenfranchised student populations such as students of color, Indigenous students, students who have migrated or immigrated to the United States, English language learning (ELL) students, highly mobile student populations (e.g., homeless, foster care), students with disabilities, LGBTQ students, students with non-binary gender identities, and students who claim identities that involve an intersection of these and other identities (Carrington, 1999; Franke et al., 2003; Harris et al., 2021). Thus, consistent with the U.S. DOE's definition of school climate (2014), school leaders must promote safe, supportive, and engaging schools for all students. To do so, they must flexibly adapt their efforts to be inclusive of diverse students, especially those traditionally marginalized.

Inclusive school climates and cultures. Legal imperatives exist to ensure that all students have access to healthy school climates and cultures. In general, educational laws have evolved to ensure that school cultures are non-discriminatory, more inclusive, and that all students have access to a free and appropriate education (FAPE). In support of this notion, Combes and Pazey (2020) state: "School leaders must be willing to act in concert with others to create the type of school culture that unanimously and positively responds to difference so every student can achieve full membership and feel welcomed and valued" (32).

Instead of thinking of schools as rigid brick-and-mortar structures that house organizational components and systems, schools must be considered organic institutions that socialize an increasingly diverse population of students to specific democratic values and beliefs through leadership, policies, and practices. From this perspective, school leaders have a hand in creating an environment that teaches much more than academic skills—they are teaching what it means to be a student and where he or she fits in society more generally. This is an important responsibility that must not be taken lightly.

Following a trend toward providing all students with FAPE, new definitions of school culture must be culturally responsive.

Some researchers and scholars have reframed a positive school culture to pertain to the social environment where students and educators care for one another; feel a sense of belonging, identification, inclusion, and connection; actively collaborate on shaping school activities, decisions, and discussions; have a shared sense of purpose, meaning, and common values; and provide mutual social support (e.g., Khalifa et al., 2016). Thus, a culturally responsive school culture fosters a safe, supportive, and caring learning community—a community where all students are known, respected, validated, valued, and socially connected. Such a culture also involves reinforcing an antiracist learning community, free from social identity and stereotype threats, and devoid of bigotry and discrimination, regardless of how overt or subtle it is, as is the case with microaggressions. In essence, a healthy school culture mirrors a healthy society in which democratic norms are supported, equal participation is encouraged, and individuals are unencumbered to pursue their higher ideals.

Critical race theory. Critical Race Theory (CRT) has been defined by Kimberle Crenshaw, who coined the term as "a way of looking at law's role in platforming, facilitating, producing, and even insulating racial inequality in our country" (Kendi, 2021). In the summer of 2021, CRT became highly politicized because of the highly partisan and contentious political climate in U.S. history. Many states banned the explicit teaching of CRT, even though no state department of education endorsed it as part of the curriculum. Without substantive evidence, the theory was criticized by right-leaning politicians for being polemical, accusatory, and divisive (Kendi, 2021).

Leaving politics aside, educational leaders need to know about CRT because efforts to make school climates and cultures more inclusive may be misconstrued as efforts to explicitly teach CRT. Although there is no perfect way to manage misguided accusations from parents or community members, educational leaders can prepare in advance to describe how their work is within the purview of educational law, policy, and research-based practice. Essentially, focusing on creating a healthy school climate and culture for all students involves being honest about U.S. history and contemporary society by default. Being honest in this regard is not explicitly teaching CRT—it is just accurate and inclusive instruction. In practice, a failure to reconcile history with the present during instruction is miseducation. Considering this, educational leaders do not need CRT to discuss the impact of racial injustice, they need an accurate and honest read of history.

In support of an honest discussion of history, researchers found that over 95% of Americans want high school students to learn about slavery, and 85% want them to know about racial inequality (Rogers et al., 2022). The researchers note that teaching history related to these topics is important as it helps prepare youth for growing up in a diverse and pluralistic democracy. Yet, they fear that a virulent stream of hyper-partisan political conflict has had a chilling effect on student education.

Rogers et al. (2022) recently surveyed 682 public high school principals who noted that there had been organized campaigns to intimidate public school leaders and force changes aligned with right-wing ideology. Half of the principals surveyed reported that community members or parents sought to limit or challenge teaching students about issues of race and racism, and nearly half reported challenges to school policies about practices related to LGBTQ+ rights. One-third said that challenges were made regarding school library books they deemed inappropriate. For example, one Iowa principal said that parents asked the school to remove the classic book by Harper Lee, *To Kill a Mockingbird*. Further, one Ohio principal said that parents launched an investigation into the school's curriculum using an anti-CRT playbook. When no evidence was found, the group claimed that the school was teaching "undercover CRT."

Rogers et al. (2022) stressed that this was not about parents getting involved in determining how children learn in a respectful or healthy manner, but instead, was about individuals trying to deny civil liberties, spread falsehoods, and employ intimidating action and hostile and violent rhetoric (Rubin, 2022). As a result, many educators have sought to avoid controversy by pulling back on teaching lessons about politics, civics, history, and the experiences of marginalized and minority communities. Moreover, many teachers and school leaders are considering leaving their chosen profession (Danelski, 2022), and if these threats to inclusive education continue, students will fail to acquire the skills necessary to function in a diverse society.

However, on the positive, research by Rogers et al. (2022) suggests that schools run by civilly engaged principals and where district administrators emphasized the importance of civic education, were more likely to support education for a diverse democracy. In short, effective leaders who support diversity, equity, and inclusion can make a big difference.

The Influence of School Climate and Culture

Besides having a well-established impact on improving academic outcomes for students, healthy school climates and cultures are associated with safe, supportive, caring, participatory, and effective risk-prevention and health promotion efforts (Thapa et al., 2013; Wang & Degol, 2016). Moreover, students with positive views of their school's climate tend to feel more socially bonded and less likely to experience emotional distress or attempt suicide (Benbenishty et al., 2018). This finding also has been found among sexual minority students (Hatzenbuehler et al., 2014). Having a healthy school climate and culture also mitigates problems such as aggressive behavior, misconduct, delinquency, weapons carrying, and substance use (Klein et al.,

2012). Such findings highlight how a healthy school climate can make students feel safe and supported while reducing the risk of developing mental health problems.

Although schools often are among the most trusted social institutions in their respective communities (Mitchell et al., 2018), minoritized students traditionally report having lower perceptions of school climate. In other words, they perceive the school climate as needing to be more safe and supportive because of problems with the school culture. This mirrors legitimate distrust of other social institutions (e.g., the legal system, healthcare) because of a long history of racism, other forms of bigotry, and discrimination that permeates society (Hurwitz & Peffley, 2005; Kennedy et al., 2007). However, emerging research indicates that efforts to improve school climate can benefit all students, particularly those who previously did not feel comfortable at school.

Although perceptions of school climate may differ between students of different racial or ethnic groups, a study by Konold et al. (2017) concludes that a positive school climate increases engagement and reduces victimization experiences across Black, Latino, and White groups. Similarly, a recent study by Berkowitz (2020) found that a healthy school climate exerted a strong impact on student achievement in marginalized ethnic groups of students, as well as on students from traditionally underserved backgrounds. More specifically, narrower achievement gaps were observed among students with different socioeconomic backgrounds in schools with positive climates. Moreover, a previous review of 78 studies by Berkowitz et al. (2017) found that a healthy school climate can reduce the adverse effects of poverty on student success across multiple domains. Thus, positive school climates and cultures support students who traditionally underperform because of structural or systematic social, political, and economic disadvantages.

Regarding efforts to improve school culture to transform student outcomes, a review of research by Waldron and McLeskey

(2010) concludes: "Key aspects of this reform include the development of a collaborative culture, the use of high-quality professional development to improve teacher practices, and strong leadership for school improvement activities by the principal and other school leaders" (p. 58). Thus, school leaders are at the center of efforts to improve school culture, and this is further supported by the work by MacNeil et al. (2009). In a seminal study, these researchers found that students display higher levels of achievement in schools with a healthy culture, as defined by 10 dimensions of organizational health such as cohesiveness, morale, and communication, among others. Research also suggests that school leaders who can engender a healthy school culture can benefit minoritized and disenfranchised students. As an example, Franke et al. (2003) examined the development and implementation of a program that aimed to improve school culture. This study found positive benefits for highly at-risk and vulnerable youth populations such as highly mobile or homeless students.

The Role of School Leaders

A focus on school climate and culture traditionally has taken a backseat to academic achievement. However, this began to change with research and scholarship emerging in the 1990s. One article in particular, "School Climate and Culture" by Maxwell and Thomas (1991), may exemplify a pivot toward a more holistic perspective of student success. In this article, the authors present a model that marries school climate and culture across various overlapping levels pertaining to school leadership. These include beliefs, values, norms, standards, and expected behaviors. Each level is discussed below to provide a framework for school leaders to foster a healthy culture and climate. Consistent with four different styles of school climate, Table 5.1 lists various relationships between school climate styles and aspects of school culture.

TABLE 5.1 Relationships between School Climate Styles and Aspects of School Culture

	Authoritative	Authoritarian	Permissive	Neglectful
Beliefs	• Power is balanced and distributed • Communication is balanced	• Administration dictates organizational school culture • Administration dictates communication	• Students determine school culture • Students have disproportionate control over communication	• A breakdown exists between school culture contributors • School leaders are disengaged from communicating with students
Values	• Students and staff have proportional input • Students and staff have shared responsibility	• Administration makes value-based determinations • Administration determines responsibility	• Students have strong control over values • Responsibility decisions are disproportionally influenced by students	• Values are not clearly articulated or discussed • Responsibility is not determined or discussed
Norms and Standards	• "We collaborate—but school leaders are in charge" • Students are students and leaders are leaders	• "The leaders are in charge" • Students will be students—and not challenge administrative decisions	• "What do you think—we want you to feel good about 'X'" • Students' thoughts and feelings take precedence	• "What do you want? Can't you see we're busy?" • Student needs are not addressed
Expected Behaviors	• Students and staff are responsible for behavior • There is discussion about behavioral expectations	• Students are mostly accountable to meet behavioral expectations • There is limited discussion about behavioral expectations	• Expectations are relaxed for students to meet behavioral expectations • Student input is disproportionally weighted	• Little accountability exists to meet behavioral expectations • Little discussion exists about behavioral expectations

Beliefs

The beliefs that school leaders harbor can significantly impact others in the school community. This is especially true if they are openly broadcasted and supported through policy and practice. Therefore, school leaders must carefully communicate their beliefs, whether overtly or tacitly, consciously or unconsciously.

It would be overbearing to prescribe specific beliefs for educational leaders to adopt or entertain. Therefore, instead, a general process is recommended to evaluate one's beliefs to ensure they are congruent and centered on fostering a healthy school environment. This process stems from psychological and educational leadership research involves systematically evaluating one's beliefs, which often are unknown or below the surface of consciousness, yet still profoundly influence one's behavior.

The Implicit Association Test (IAT; Greenwald et al., 1998) or the "implicit bias test" can allow a window into biases and beliefs one holds, such as unconsciously associating stereotypical Black names with words consistent with Black stereotypes that pervade American culture. The IAT can be taken online (https://implicit.harvard.edu/implicit/takeatest.html) and the test has grown since its inception to help investigate biases in racial groups, gender, sexuality, age, and religion. However, from a leadership perspective, what one does with such results is most important. If we all have biases and know what our own are, we must check in on them regularly and ensure that they are not interfering with objective leadership.

Values

Educational leaders must follow a codified set of values that should contribute to healthy school climates and cultures. Much of this comes through decades of policy work that has resulted in schools becoming increasingly more egalitarian, inclusive, and supportive of students' diverse and myriad needs. Collectively, this has resulted in FAPE being central to public education.

Therefore, it is incumbent for educational leaders to make sure that their schools are consistent with FAPE; moreover, are inclusive and supportive beyond legal guidelines. Many school cultures have been described as racist, sexist, or homophobic (Kohli et al., 2017; Moyano & del Mar Sánchez-Fuentes, 2020). Of course, this results in an unhealthy school climate that impedes the learning and well-being of students.

Simply stated, school climates that lack inclusive values that undergird contemporary public education are deleterious to society. Leaders in such environments can make a big difference to change school culture to improve the overall climate. If one is a leader in such an environment, here are some simple steps that can structure changing the environment based on the content included in this book:

1. Assess or evaluate the social environment.
2. Determine who the most influential individuals are.
3. Evaluate the values of the influential individuals and consider how they fit or do not fit with the goal of the school.
4. Work with influential individuals to help them make their behavior more consistent with school values if it is perceived to be unhealthy.
5. Re-assess the school social environment to see if progress has been made and what steps should be taken next.

Norms and Standards

Norms and standards tend to be more codified and observable than values. Norms are a social expectations for members of a group, and they serve to guide, regulate, and even control what is deemed acceptable. Standards, on the other hand, are a level of quality, achievement, attainment, or expectation. Thus, good standards should be measurable, and a specific outcome should be in mind when setting them.

A lot of recent attention has focused on state standards for measuring student, teacher, and school performance. Unfortunately, setting rigorous standards does not lead to their attainment. Furthermore, standards not anchored by meaningful criteria can do more harm than good, as they may be arbitrary, yet people and organizations will only feel like a success if they measure up to expectations.

Considering the previous, it is critically important for educational leaders to think long and hard about the standards they set and the norms they reinforce in the school environment. Setting and reinforcing standards should be a deliberate process that involves reflection, reconsideration, and challenging prevailing assumptions. Similar to reflecting on the presence and impact of implicit biases within oneself, leaders must regularly consider how norms and standards impact the climate and culture of their school. The following questions may help with this process:

- How should students and staff interact with each other in the school?
- How should students and staff interact with each other via social media?
- How should prosocial behavior be reinforced?
- What standards and thresholds should be in place for problematic behavior?
- What should be the protocol for addressing bullying incidents and peer aggression, both in physical space and online?
- What are minimal expectations for academic performance and behavior, how were these expectations determined, and how will individuals be assessed as they try to approximate them?
- What should be done about devious yet non-threatening or significantly disruptive behavior (if anything)?

- What norms are being reinforced *explicitly* and *implicitly* in the school environment?
- What desired norms are present or absent in the school climate?
- What problematic norms are present in the school climate?
- Are standards supported by research, sound or tested policy, and benefit the school climate and culture?

Expected Behaviors

School leadership is synonymous with shaping expected behaviors for school community members. The adage to lead by example holds true in this regard, but it is actually more important to foster a healthy school climate and culture to reinforce the norms, standards, values, and beliefs that contribute to a thriving school community. Pure leadership virtue and charisma are important; however, because educational environments tend to be large and complex, the impact of any particular leader might not reach certain members of the school community on a regular basis. Therefore, instead of the myth of the empowered singular leader at the top of the pyramid setting expected behaviors for a school community, a more realistic approach to accomplishing this involves a collaborative process that results in buy-in from multiple members of school communities.

As a classic example of establishing expected behaviors, consider the process of creating classroom rules or, perhaps more apt: classroom expectations. If a teacher dictates rules to the class, they will be new and possibly foreign to the students, especially for students who might have had radically different school experiences (or even no previous experiences in U.S.-styled classrooms). This then could contribute to misunderstanding, misperceptions that a student is misbehaving, and ultimately the loss of learning as time is allocated away from instruction to behavior management.

Alternatively, consistent with supportive research, a teacher could involve the class in creating, refining, and ultimately selecting classroom rules or expectations. This could be done in a way that encourages participation from all students. Ground rules could be set that none is considered as good or bad and that all will be entertained and considered—only ones that fit the class the best will be selected. The class then could go through the contributions and discuss the advantages and disadvantages of each one until a final list of a handful of expectations is adopted and agreed on.

According to research, typically, classroom rules that are devised this way end up differing little from ones that are developed by a teacher, team, or administrator (Alter & Haydon, 2017). However, buy-in from students tends to be higher because students have a hand in coming up with the expectations. When applied to other parts of the school environment or community (e.g., school-wide rules/expectations, expectations for parts of the building such as the playground), the example of collectively developing expected behaviors holds true. Collaboration and buy-in are key. From the perspective of a school leader, essential strategies for developing and establishing expected behaviors include the following:

- Make sure behaviors are clearly defined in observable terms.
- Make sure expected behaviors are clear, concise, and unambiguous.
- Make members of school communities have a shared understanding of expected behaviors.
- Make sure expected behaviors are limited to a discrete number that apply to the school setting.
- Make sure that expected behaviors are reasonable and can be performed by members of the community.
- Make sure expected behaviors enhance school climate and culture and do not detract from the former.

School Climate and Culture ◆ 139

♦ Make sure expected behaviors are unbiased, non-discriminatory, and culturally responsive.

Improving School Climate and Culture

All school climates and cultures can improve. As discussed previously, a healthy school climate and culture is associated with positive student outcomes, often over and beyond directly focusing on academics (Thapa et al., 2013; Wang & Degol, 2016). Therefore, school leaders should consider implementing strategies to improve school climate and culture as part of their general practice just like maintaining safety and an appropriate learning environment.

School Climate Data

Dating back to 1994, Gonder and Hymes published a report entitled: "Improving School Climate & Culture" on behalf of the American Association of School Administrators (AASA). In this report, the authors provide a compelling case for using shared decision-making, strategic planning, and outcomes-based education to improve school climate and culture concomitantly. They also discuss the importance of measuring school climate as a primary step to improving climate and culture.

The National Association of School Psychologists (NASP; 2019) provides guidance on measuring school climate and using the collected data to facilitate healthier school cultures. To measure school climate, in a stepwise manner, NASP recommends 1), identifying one's team; 2), identifying the intended goal of data collection; 3), selecting a valid and reliable measure of school climate (see Table 5.2 for a list of research-based school climate measures); 4), identifying how school climate data will be used among other indicators of school success; 5), involving multiple groups or parties; 6), creating a schedule for data collection; 7), creating a plan to analyze and use data; 8), and creating a plan to share data with requisite parties.

140 ◆ The Supportive Pillar

TABLE 5.2 A List of Commonly Used, Research-Based Measures of School Climate

- Authoritative School Climate Survey (Cornell, 2014): https://curry.virginia.edu/authoritative-school-climate-survey-and-school-climate-bullying-survey
- California School Climate Survey (Furlong et al., 2005): https://www.wested.org/project/california-school-climate-survey-cscs/
- Delaware School Climate Survey (Bear, Gaskins, Blank, & Chen, 2011): http://wh1.oet.udel.edu/pbs/school-climate/de-school-climate-survey/
- ED School Climate Surveys (EDSCS, 2019): https://safesupportive learning.ed.gov/edscls/administration
- Georgia School Climate Survey (Georgia Department of Education, La Salle, & Meyers, 2014): http://www.gadoe.org/Curriculum-Instruction-and-Assessment/Curriculum-and-Instruction/GSHS-II/Pages/Georgia-Student-Health-Survey-II.aspx
- Maryland Safe and Supportive Schools Climate Survey (Bradshaw et al., 2014): https://safesupportivelearning.ed.gov/survey/maryland-s3-climate-survey
- School Climate Measure (Zullig et al., 2015): https://www.ncbi.nlm.nih.gov/pubmed/25642931

Adapted from the National Association of School Psychologists (2019).

In general, selected school climate measures should be comprehensive and assess school climate across several domains consistent with prevailing models of the construct. Additionally, they should be unbiased in not discriminating based on grounds outside of their intended purpose (e.g., race/ethnicity, sex, gender, primary language), which involves assessing perceptions of the school environment. As discussed above, school climate is fluid and can change slowly or rapidly depending on significant events at a school (e.g., a crisis event). Therefore, school climate should be measured multiple times across time intervals so that school leaders have a sense of the overall "weather" of the school as it fluctuates.

More recently, in a report published by the Learning Policy Institute, an independent organization that conducts high-quality research to improve education policy and practice, Darling-Hammond and Cook-Harvey (2018) have expanded on strategies to improve school climate and culture. They specifically recommend that educational leaders embrace and implement the following four criteria to improve school climate and culture concomitantly:

1. Assessing school climate to develop positive learning environments that enable students to be well-supported in all aspects of their development.
2. Providing educative and restorative approaches to discipline that keep students in school and integrate social, emotional, and academic learning.
3. Creating multi-tiered systems of support, including health and mental health services and extended learning time focused on students' needs.
4. Strengthening educator preparation and development to enact these programs and practices grounded in the principles of learning and development.

Except for explicitly mentioning measuring school climate data to improve culture, one might notice that these strategies markedly overlap with the Three Pillars of Safe and Supportive Schools that Foster Students' Mental Health. Positive learning environments make students feel supported; restorative approaches to discipline and justice make students feel safe; and multi-tiered systems of support can be applied to school-based mental health service delivery. Essentially, schools with healthy climates and cultures are safe and supportive schools, and vice versa. These are the types of schools that this book implores school leaders to foster.

Using Data Related to Climate and Culture

The National School Climate Council (NSCC; 2007) recommends that school leaders use school climate data at various levels of student and family engagement. These include at district, school building, classroom, student, and community levels as part of a problem-solving process. This process first involves preparation followed by evaluation of data, action planning, implementation of the intervention, and re-evaluation. This process is briefly reviewed below.

1. **Preparation.** Preparation involves creating a school climate and culture team, establishing guidelines on how to move forward, gaining buy-in from important stakeholders, fostering a culture of trust, determining what resources will be needed to collect and use data, and figuring out how to procure such resources.

2. **Evaluation.** Evaluation involves using a multi-component measure of school climate to assess educational environments across multiple domains to determine strengths and weaknesses, as well as conducting a needs assessment.

3. **Action planning.** Action planning involves understanding data patterns and making decisions about school programming to improve school climate and culture. Essentially, according to NASP (2019), this step of using data involves "identifying specific ways that school climate can be maintained or enhanced for the benefit of all members of school communities" (p. 4).

4. **Implementation.** Implementation involves selecting and applying evidence-based practices to improve school climate and culture, such as those discussed in this book, consistent with the Three Pillar Model.

5. **Re-evaluation.** Re-evaluation involves revisiting and revising the assessment, preparation, evaluation, action planning, and implementing stages previously discussed. Thus, this process is iterative, and it aims to improve school climate and culture through successive approximations.

Practical Strategies

This chapter concludes with practical strategies for improving school climate and culture that educators can use at multiple student contact or engagement levels. These include the classroom- and school-level. Additionally, information is provided on tailoring these strategies (and others) to make them culturally inclusive and responsive. School leaders who desire additional information on improving school climate and culture are encouraged to visit the websites of the National School Climate Center (https://schoolclimate.org/) and the National Center for Safe Supportive Learning Environments (https://safesupportivelearning.ed.gov/).

Classroom-based Strategies

♦ Ensure that all students are socially connected and supported.
  ♦ The next chapter details the importance of ensuring that all students feel socially connected and supported at school. Along with fostering a healthy school climate and culture, these concepts constitute the Supportive Pillar of the Three Pillar Model of Safe and Supportive Schools. Therefore, this content will be covered in greater detail shortly.
♦ Provide ample opportunities to respond.
  ♦ If students have ample opportunities to respond during instruction, they remain engaged, which can indirectly impact school climate as students feel like active participants in the classroom and are less likely to display disruptive or problematic behaviors. This requires educators to pace instruction quickly and keep it interesting by making it relevant to students' lives. Similarly, school leaders must encourage

participation from all members of teams involved in efforts to improve the school climate or culture.

- Reinforce healthy values, norms, and behaviors.
  - As discussed above, healthy values and norms set the tone for the climate and culture of a school. In the classroom, strategies for modeling and reinforcing examples of behaviors consistent with healthy school norms, values, and behavioral expectations should be predetermined, and care is needed to make sure that reinforcement is being reliably implemented. Consistent reinforcement is associated with desired behaviors being adopted and maintained.
- Set clear behavioral expectations.
  - Behavioral expectations must be clearly understood by all members of the classroom. If the students do not understand the expectations, how can they possibly meet them on a consistent basis?
- Addressing bullying and victimization immediately.
  - It is critical for all incidents of bullying and overt aggressive behavior to be acknowledged and addressed, so students feel safe and supported. Of course, bullying occurs on a continuum from mild teasing to outright acts of physical violence. Thus, classroom leaders must use their judgment to determine how best to address bullying incidents and who else they might have to involve in the process to do so.

Schoolwide Strategies

- Implement schoolwide prevention programs.
  - Schoolwide prevention programs such as MTSS, Social Emotional Learning (SEL), and Positive Behavior Intervention Support (PBIS) programs have been found to support students' varied academic,

behavioral, social, and emotional needs across a spectrum. School leaders now embrace such programs to triage resources across multiple tiers of service delivery. At Tier 1 or universal service delivery, schoolwide prevention programs ensure that all students in the school community receive basic preventive services.

- Use research-based bullying prevention strategies.
  - Bullying prevention and intervention programs have proliferated over the past 30 years, largely in response to tragedies involving student loss of life (e.g., suicides, school shootings). However, not all programs have the same efficacy, especially for some populations of students like LGBTQ+ youth that traditionally have been at risk of being victimized. Therefore, school leaders need to select research-based multi-component bullying prevention/intervention programs such as the Olweus Bullying Prevention Program or KiVa, programs that were discussed along with content on the Safe Pillar of the Three Pillar Model of Safe and Supportive Schools. A benefit of such programs is that they also have been found to improve school climate in addition to reducing aggressive behavior at school. See Chapter 3 for further discussion.
- Implement restorative justice.
  - In contrast to punitive or draconian discipline practices that have been shown to push students out of school and into correctional settings such as Zero Tolerance policies, restorative justice involves addressing discipline problems through mediation, restitution, and other non-punitive practices. A major benefit of restorative justice is that it engages the school community to teach offenders how to correct or improve their behavior, thus ideally resulting in an improved school climate through improved relationships.

146 ◆ The Supportive Pillar

- ◆ Integrate trauma-informed care.
  - ◆ Trauma-informed care or trauma-focused schooling involves mitigating adverse childhood experiences (ACEs) that can have a profoundly deleterious impact on the healthy development of students. Although "trauma" is in the title, this approach aims to improve the overall functioning of all students. However, to date, several different conceptions of trauma-informed care exist, and additional research is needed to determine what components of this approach are most pertinent. (See Chapter 8 for further discussion.)

Culturally Inclusive Strategies

- ◆ Include key community stakeholders.
  - ◆ Connecting with key community stakeholders such as social workers, members of social service agencies, emergency first-responders, community activists, local politicians, clergy and religious leaders, and others can help bridge a gap between a school and a community. In turn, this can make members of school communities feel more included and give them a sense of belonging.
- ◆ Use and model respectful, inclusive, and accurate language.
  - ◆ Many students feel safer and more supported at school if they feel like their identity is respected. Therefore, consistent with school values, setting norms, and modeling behavioral expectations, school leaders should use pronouns most consistent with identities students embrace, such as gender identity, and pay attention to cultural similarities and differences.
- ◆ Modify curricula to be more diverse and inclusive.
  - ◆ Unfortunately, many schools have not embraced representative and multicultural curricula. To date, the preponderance of school curricula reflects White, heteronormative, and cisgender norms, yet many students

do not identify with these norms. Therefore, school leaders should be sensitive to this reality and actively promote curricula that may better represent the lived experiences of students who have traditionally been minoritized, marginalized, or disenfranchised.

- Evaluate expectations and codes of conduct to make sure they are culturally sensitive.
    - Consistent with restorative justice practices, school leaders should actively evaluate school policies to make sure that they are not prejudiced or biased. Further, through collecting and evaluating school climate data, school leaders can have a window into how existing policies and practices are impacting unique groups or populations in the school community and adjust accordingly.
- Encourage clubs, groups, and extra-curricular activities.
    - Extracurricular groups and activities can provide invaluable opportunities for youth to bond with others. This, in turn, can influence school climate and culture indirectly. Some students may not have many opportunities to interact with students with whom they identify during the regular school day; however, in a club, for example, they can enjoy quality time with their favorite peers.
- Provide more inclusive mental health services.
    - School leaders can help reduce the stigma of receiving mental health services. This is especially the case for students who feel most disenfranchised from school, as these youth are among those who are underrepresented when it comes to receiving care. This can produce a double-whammy effect and result in negative perceptions of school climate and culture. Yet, school leaders can intervene to ensure that such students receive the support they need, over and beyond what is typically provided in schoolwide prevention programs.

Conclusion

The importance of fostering a healthy school climate and culture was discussed in this chapter. School climate typically is described as everything that influences the physical, social, and emotional environment of the school, whereas school culture pertains to the leadership, interpersonal factors, and policies that influence the people within a school community. Thus, school climate and culture conjointly influence student success, and the influence of school leaders can impact both. The beliefs, values, norms, standards, and expected behaviors of school leaders and other members of school communities contribute to the overall school climate and culture. Therefore, care is needed to use an objective or data-based approach to assessing school climate so that leaders can ensure that schools align with practices that make all students feel safe and supported. Lastly, this chapter concluded with practical strategies to improve the school climate and culture for all students.

References

Alter, P., & Haydon, T. (2017). Characteristics of effective classroom rules: A review of the literature. *Teacher Education and Special Education, 40*(2), 114–127.

Barnard, C. (1938). *The functions of the executive.* Harvard University Press.

Baumrind, D. (1966). Effects of authoritative parental control on child behavior. *Child Development, 37*(4), 887–907.

Benbenishty, R., Astor, R. A., & Roziner, I. (2018). A school-based multilevel study of adolescent suicide ideation in California high schools. *Journal of Pediatrics, 196,* 251–257.

Berger, A. (1995). *Cultural criticism.* Routledge.

Berkowitz, R. (2020). School matters: The contribution of positive school climate to equal educational opportunities among ethnocultural minority students. *Youth & Society.* https://doi.org/10.1177/0044118X20970235

Berkowitz, R., Moore, H., Astor, R. A., & Benbenishty, R. (2017). A research synthesis of the associations between socioeconomic background, inequality, school climate, and academic achievement. *Review of Educational Research, 87*(2), 425–469.

Carrington, S. (1999). Inclusion needs a different school culture. *International Journal of Inclusive Education, 3*(3), 257–268.

Cohen, J., McCabe, L., Michelli, N. M., & Pickeral, T. (2009). School climate: Research, policy, practice, and teacher education. *Teachers College Record, 111*(1), 180–213.

Combes, B., & Pazey, B. (2020). *Principals' and school leaders' roles in inclusive education.* Oxford Research Encyclopedia of Education. https://10.1093/acrefore/9780190264093.013.1215.

Cornell, D., & Huang, F. (2016). Authoritative school climate and high school student risk behavior: A cross-sectional multi-level analysis of student self-reports. *Journal of Youth and Adolescence, 45*(11), 2246–2259.

Cornell, D. G., Mayer, M. J., & Sulkowski, M. L. (2020). History and future of school safety research. *School Psychology Review*, 50, (2–3), 143–157. https://doi.org/10.1080/2372966X.2020.1857212

Danelski, D. (2022, November 29). *Culture war battles at schools harm public education, UC report finds.* University of California at Riverside. https://news.ucr.edu/articles/2022/11/29/culture-war-battles-schools-harm-public-education-uc-report-finds

Darling-Hammond, L., & Cook-Harvey, C. M. (2018). *Educating the whole child: Improving school climate to support student success.* Learning Policy Institute.

Franke, T. M., Isken, J. A., & Parra, M. T. (2003). A pervasive school culture for the betterment of student outcomes: One school's approach to student mobility. *Journal of Negro Education, 72*(1), 150–157.

Gonder, P. O., & Hymes, D. (1994). *Improving school climate & culture.* AASA Critical Issues Report No. 27. American Association of School Administrators.

Greenwald, A. G., McGhee, D. E., & Schwartz, J. L. (1998). Measuring individual differences in implicit cognition: the implicit association test. *Journal of Personality and Social Psychology, 74*(6), 1464–1480.

Harris, R., Wilson-Daily, A. E., & Fuller, G. (2021). Exploring the secondary school experience of LGBT+ youth: An examination of school culture and school climate as understood by teachers and experienced by LGBT+ students. *Intercultural Education, 32*(4), 368–385. https://doi.org/10.1080/14675986.2021.1889987

Hatzenbuehler, M. L., Birkett, M., Van Wagenen, A., & Meyer, I. H. (2014). Protective school climates and reduced risk for suicide ideation in sexual minority youths. *American Journal of Public Health, 104*(2), 279–286.

Hoy, W. K., Tarter, C. J., & Kottkamp, R. B. (1991). *Open schools/healthy schools: Measuring organizational climate.* Sage.

Hurwitz, J., & Peffley, M. (2005). Explaining the great racial divide: Perceptions of fairness in the US criminal justice system. *The Journal of Politics, 67*(3), 762–783.

Kendi, I. X. (2021). There is no debate over critical race theory. *The Atlantic.* https://www.theatlantic.com/ideas/archive/2021/07/opponents-critical-race-theory-are-arguing-themselves/619391/

Kennedy, B. R., Mathis, C. C., & Woods, A. K. (2007). African Americans and their distrust of the health care system: healthcare for diverse populations. *Journal of Cultural Diversity, 14*(2), 56–60.

Khalifa, M. A., Gooden, M. A., & Davis, J. E. (2016). Culturally responsive school leadership: A synthesis of the literature. *Review of Educational Research, 86*(4), 1272–1311. https://doi.org/10.3102/0034654316630383

Klein, J., Cornell, D., & Konold, T. (2012). Relationships between bullying, school climate, and student risk behaviors. *School Psychology Quarterly, 27*(3), 154–169. https://doi.org/10.1037/a0029350

Kohli, R., Pizarro, M., & Nevárez, A. (2017). The "new racism" of K–12 schools: Centering critical research on racism. *Review of Research in Education, 41*(1), 182–202.

Konold, T., Cornell, D., Shukla, K., & Huang, F. (2017). Racial/ethnic differences in perceptions of school climate and its association with student engagement and peer aggression. *Journal of Youth and Adolescence, 46*(6), 1289–1303.

MacNeil, A. J., Prater, D. L., & Busch, S. (2009). The effects of school culture and climate on student achievement. *International Journal of leadership in Education, 12*(1), 73–84.

Maxwell, T. W., & Thomas, A. R. (1991). School climate and school culture. *Journal of Educational Administration, 29*(2), 72–83. https://doi.org/10.1108/09578239110003309

Mitchell, R. M., Kensler, L., & Tschannen-Moran, M. (2018). Student trust in teachers and student perceptions of safety: Positive predictors of student identification with school. *International Journal of Leadership in Education, 21*(2), 135–154.

Moore, G. F., Littlecott, H. J., Evans, R., Murphy, S., Hewitt, G., & Fletcher, A. (2017). School composition, school culture and socioeconomic inequalities in young people's health: Multi-level analysis of the Health Behaviour in School-aged Children (HBSC) survey in Wales. *British Educational Research Journal, 43*(2), 310–329.

Moyano, N., & del Mar Sánchez-Fuentes, M. (2020). Homophobic bullying at schools: A systematic review of research, prevalence, school-related predictors and consequences. *Aggression and Violent Behavior, 53.* https://doi.org/10.1016/j.avb.2020.101441

National Association of School Psychologists (2019). *Guidance for measuring and using school climate data.* Author.

National School Climate Council (2007). *The school climate challenge: Narrowing the gap between school climate research and school climate policy: Practice guidelines and teacher education policy.* https://schoolclimate.org/themes/schoolclimate/assets/pdf/policy/school-climatechallenge-web.pdf

Roach, A. T., & Kratochwill, T. R. (2004). Evaluating school climate and school culture. *Teaching Exceptional Children, 37*(1), 10–17.

Rogers, J., & Kahne, J. with Ishimoto, M., Kwako, A., Stern, S. W., Bingener, C., . . . & Conde, Y. (2022, November 29). The chilling role of political conflict in blue, purple and red communities. https://idea.gseis.ucla.edu/publications/educating-for-a-diverse-democracy/publications/files/diverse-democracy-executive-summary.

Rubin, J. (2022, November 30). Cynical MAGA censors are damaging public education. *New York Times.* https://www.washingtonpost.com/opinions/2022/11/30/maga-culture-wars-schools-education/

Thapa, A., Cohen, J., Guffey, S., & Higgins-D'Alessandro, A. (2013). A review of school climate research. *Review of Educational Research, 83,* 357–385. https://doi.org/10.3102/0034654313483907

U.S. Department of Education (2014). *Guiding Principles: A resource guide for improving school climate and discipline.* Author. https://www2.ed.gov/policy/gen/guid/school-discipline/guiding-principles.pdf

U.S. Department of Education, Office of Safe and Healthy Students to the American Institutes for Research (AIR). (2018). *School climate*. Author. https://safesupportivelearning.ed.gov/safe-and-healthy students/school-climate

Waldron, N. L., & McLeskey, J. (2010). Establishing a collaborative school culture through comprehensive school reform. *Journal of Educational and Psychological Consultation, 20*(1), 58–74.

Wang, M. T., & Degol, J. L. (2016). School climate: A review of the construct, measurement, and impact on student outcomes. *Educational Psychology Review, 28*(2), 315–352. https://doi.org/10.1007/s10648-015-9319-1

6

Social Connectedness and Support

Humans are inherently social beings. From the reflexive smiles of an infant to the complex social interactions of adults, we engage in relationships with others, which define our social and emotional lives. As humans, our most joyous and sorrowful experiences unfold and are influenced by a social context that shapes who we are, our emotional balance, and how we fit into the world. Thus, our social connections not only define us, but these connections determine how we see ourselves and our well-being across our lifespan.

This chapter discusses the importance of social relationships in students' lives. More specifically, it covers how social connectedness and social support are integral to student success in school settings and life in general. After introducing these concepts, models are provided on how social connectedness and support can be understood when working with students. Research is reviewed on associations between social relationships and key student outcomes. As part of social connection and support, information and strategies are provided regarding

DOI: 10.4324/9780429261527-8

schools' role in becoming supportive and caring communities and how school personnel can best work with families. We contend that the more support a student has from peers, teachers, school leaders, family, and the community, the better off the student will be. It is also axiomatic that struggling and vulnerable students will have a better chance to flourish if a circle of support surrounds them. The chapter also discusses how social disconnection and isolation can be addressed, especially in light of social distancing in the wake of COVID-19, and how disenfranchised students can be supported socially.

Understanding Social Connection and Support

Social connection simply is the cognitive, behavioral, and emotional experience of being attached to others. It is a basis for all interpersonal relationships and has been described as a core drive and fundamental need (Cacioppo & Patrick, 2008). However, social connection exists and is experienced in myriad ways. Some individuals maintain large social networks, whereas others stay connected to just a few close acquaintances. Some individuals branch out to have multiple layers of connections, and others maintain a small nucleus of key relationships.

Tracing back to early psychological research on personality, extroverts have been found to have larger social networks but may spread themselves out more thinly across their acquaintances, whereas introverts tend to maintain smaller yet more tightly knit networks (Flemming, 1932). In addition to temperament, countless other contextual factors influence the size of an individual's social network. These factors include age, gender, race, culture, predominant language, religion, geographic location, neighborhood, occupation, and type of school (e.g., large public, small private, charter, etc.).

Although there is not a minimal or optimal number of social connections that one can establish or maintain, there does seem to be a loose maximum threshold for most people. According to the British anthropologist Robin Dunbar, the "magic number" of meaningful social connections a person can maintain is about 150 (Dunbar, 2010). By "meaningful," Dunbar implied that such connections were strong enough for individuals to feel comfortable going out of their way to affiliate with (or make plans to spend time together with) each other in the future if they encountered each other unexpectedly. However, at this point, you might wonder: Where does the number 150 come from?

Through research involving primates, Dunbar found an association between brain size and average social group size. Then, by considering the average size of the human cerebral cortex and extrapolating from the results obtained with primates, he proposed that humans can comfortably maintain approximately 150 stable relationships. Furthermore, Dunbar postulated that most people can adequately manage five very close or loving relationships, 15 good friends, 50 friends, 150 meaningful contacts (as was previously mentioned), and 500 acquaintances, and they can recognize about 1,500 people (not including celebrities or other highly visible people in society).

Dunbar's numbers of social connections are just rough estimates and not carved into stone; other researchers and scholars have proposed different figures. However, the mere act of trying to propose a hierarchical model of social connection communicates a key message. The message is that social connectedness is important, but there are limits to how many connections we can have. Thus, perhaps the popularity of clichés and adages such as "pick and choose your friends wisely" and "you are the sum of your five closest friends" contain age-old wisdom.

It is not enough just to be connected though. In addition to social connection, or feeling socially and emotionally bonded to others, we also seek and need social support, which is defined as the overall "perception one has of being cared for, valued, and included by others within a network of caregivers, teachers, peers, and community members" (Saylor & Leach, 2009, p. 71).

156 ◆ The Supportive Pillar

Positive relationships with caregivers, peers, and others are collectively associated with mental health, physical health, and overall emotional well-being (Lee et al., 2008; Yoon et al., 2008). Furthermore, according to the belongingness hypothesis, which implies that humans have an emotional need to be an accepted member of a group, and Maslow's hierarchy of needs, the belief that basic needs must be met before individuals pursue secondary or higher-level needs, being supported by others is a fundamental human need (Baumeister & Leary, 1995; Maslow, 1943). Thus, the human desire for social connection also must be understood within the context of the support that such connections produce.

The Social Connectedness-Support Matrix

It may then be apparent that a dynamic relationship exists between social connection and support. Although these concepts can overlap (and often are for many people), they do not perfectly converge. For example, someone could have a lot of social connections but not have enough supportive people in their life. This might be especially true in contemporary times when people often have thousands of connections in social media yet still feel socially isolated. Therefore, the interplay between social connection and support must be considered to understand an individual's social adjustment and health.

Figure 6.1 presents a matrix that represents the various ways that social connectedness and support are related. Although the figure oversimplifies the relationship between these dimensions, it can help illustrate predominant tendencies in people. The top

		Social Connectedness	
		High	Low
Social Support	High	Socially attached	Loosely connected
	Low	Loosely supported	Socially detached

FIGURE 6.1 The Social Connectedness-Support Matrix

left quadrant illustrates an ideal scenario in which an individual feels like he or she has high levels of social connection and social support. Such individuals, the "socially attached" individuals, are well situated in their web of social connection and have close interpersonal connections with key people in their immediate and distal social environment. Essentially, they feel they have adequate quantity and quality in their interpersonal relationships.

In contrast, individuals in the lower right quadrant report having low levels of social connectedness and support. These individuals, "the socially detached" individuals, do not perceive that they have enough interpersonal relationships and that these relationships are not adequately nourishing. Such individuals are at risk for social disconnectedness, isolation, and loneliness—all of which are related to adverse life outcomes (Asher & Paquette, 2003; Eisenberger et al., 2010; Murthy, 2020).

The upper right matrix quadrant includes individuals who feel like they have high levels of social connection and low levels of support. As previously discussed, such individuals in the context of social media, "the loosely supported," have a lot of social connections; however, such connections may be tenuous or not highly enriching. Essentially, these individuals have many acquaintances yet not many close friends or confidants—they might feel like many of their interpersonal relationships are superficial.

Lastly, the lower left quadrant includes individuals who report having few social connections and high levels of social support. These "loosely connected" individuals probably are not social butterflies but instead have developed important supportive relations that probably involve a handful of close friends and confidants.

Conceptual Model

The following section provides a model to illustrate the concepts of social connectedness and social support within the context of schools. Although this is based on research, please remember that these models are general pedagogical tools designed to express ideas and stimulate additional thought. In other words, they are designed to be informative, thought-provoking, and not diagnostic.

Social Connectedness Web

Following a seminal study, Lee and Robbins (1995) report that social connectedness involves being "able to feel comfortable and confident within a larger social context than family or friends" (p. 232). Thus, this definition is similar to how Dunbar classifies a social contact as being "meaningful" or allowing an individual to feel like they fit into a social environment outside of one's immediate contacts such as family members. For students, this broader social context typically is school and broader school-related social contexts (e.g., extracurricular activities, sports teams, clubs, before or after school programs). At school, students may have a handful of close friends, many others in various classes, and many other meaningful contacts and acquaintances throughout the entire school. Therefore, social connectedness for students really is school connectedness or how comfortable, confident, and adjusted they feel in their social relationships in the school environment.

It can be helpful to think of social connectedness as a web of interpersonal relationships that students have at various levels, such as with immediate friends and peers, classmates, students in their grades, and more generally, in the broader school community. Strands in this web might be tightly woven around the student, including best friends, student ambassadors, a favorite teacher, a mentor on a sports team, etc. Moving out from the center of the web, the next ring might include members of a peer group or clique, students who sit at the same lunch table, friends in the same club, study buddies, trusted teachers, school staff, etc. Following this, the third ring could include classmates, peers with similar interests, friends of friends who hang out together, familiar teachers, and school staff members, etc. Lastly, the broadest ring of acquaintances could include students and other members of the school community that are familiar with but not known very well.

Some students have a few close friends at school yet feel socially disconnected because they do not have opportunities to interact with them regularly. Therefore, even though socially connected, they might score low on self-ratings of school connectedness and experience feelings of social disconnection or even isolation. It then behooves educators and other concerned adults at school to identify these students and start trying to increase their feelings of school connectedness.

Social Support Balloons

To ensure positive academic, social-emotional, and life outcomes, students must receive social support from their educators, peers, other members of the school community, and their caregivers. Research indicates that students who feel supported by their teachers and are better socially connected to the school environment, display strong academic initiative, and have higher rates of school engagement (Garcia-Reid et al., 2005; Wang & Eccles, 2012). Moreover, students who feel supported by caregivers, peers, and educators have been found to display higher school attendance rates, receive higher grades, and spend more hours studying than students who feel unsupported or socially neglected (Rosenfeld et al., 2000).

Social support also has been found to influence students' broader emotional well-being positively. Specifically, experiencing teacher, caregiver, and peer social support improves students' self-concept, self-esteem, and social competence or ability to get along with others. Yet, on the other hand, socially neglected or

Social Connectedness and Support Research

Studies suggest that students feel less socially connected and supported as they advance through their K–12 educational experience (Marks, 2000; Ryan & Patrick, 2001; Wang & Eccles, 2012). In fact, research indicates that *about half (40–60%) of students feel chronically disconnected, disengaged, and unsupported by the time they reach high school* (Furrer & Skinner, 2003). Why might this be?

One explanation relates to developmental changes that occur as students age. In early childhood, social support from primary caregivers tends to be most valued, as students in elementary school tend to select their caregivers over their friends when asked with whom they would like to spend most of their time (Nickerson & Nagle, 2005). However, students in middle school often report that they prefer to spend time with their friends over their caregivers (Malecki & Demaray, 2003; Nickerson & Nagle, 2005). Finally, many students report feeling more connected and supported by their friends than their caregivers when they transition into late adolescence (Sumter et al., 2009). Consequentially, as students advance through their K–12 education, they tend to rely more on their peers and less on their caregivers for social support.

The impact of teacher support also varies across student ages. Malecki and Demaray (2002) found that perceived teacher support decreases as students' grade level increases. Similarly, Bokhorst and colleagues (2010) found that younger students (ages 9–12) think they receive more social support from their teachers than older students (ages 13–18). These researchers also identified that older students report that their peers and caregivers were stronger sources of social support when compared to their teachers. Declines in perceived teacher support as students get older likely are associated with transitions from having a single or few teachers in elementary school to having many teachers and a rotating class schedule in secondary school. Additionally, similar to parental influences, as adolescents individualize and place a high premium on peer relationships, teacher influence, and social support also tend to diminish, even though they are still important (Wit et al., 2011).

Academic Achievement

How are social connections and supports related to student success? According to research, feeling connected and supported at school is critically important for getting good grades, staying in school, and ultimately graduating (Wang & Eccles, 2012). Additionally, the former is linked with a wide range of positive academic outcomes, such as students' academic motivation, self-esteem, self-regulation skills, attitudes toward school, academic achievement, and quality of peer relationships (Hagborg, 1994; Osterman, 2000). For facilitating student success, social relationships appear to be even more critical for at-risk students. As a prominent empirical example, a study by Niehaus and colleagues (2012) that investigated the impact of feeling connected and belonging at school found that socially connected students displayed greater resilience and had higher levels of academic achievement at the end the year. Therefore, considering existing research, the message is clear: *Social connection and support are critically important for academic success.*

Mental Health

Ensuring that students feel connected and supported at school is one of the best ways to support their mental health. A seminal study by Resnick and colleagues (1997) found that not feeling connected and supported at school was associated with emotional distress, substance use, violence, and suicidality. In another study by

Anderman (2003), feeling connected and supported at school predicted optimism and lower levels of depression and behavior problems at school. Additionally, the link between social connectedness and depression was weaker in schools with strong interpersonal connections, which suggests that these schools were also socially supportive. Thus, schools with healthy climates that foster social connection and support can improve students' mental health.

The following point is underscored by an important study. Shochet and colleagues (2006) found that students' ratings of their belongingness at school explained between 26% to 46% of the variance in their general mental health functioning and between 38% and 55% of their depression symptoms across the course of one year. This might not mean very much to the non-researcher. However, suffice it to say that feeling connected and supported at school substantially influences students' mental health. Furthermore, even after controlling for prior mental health symptoms, the previous team of researchers found that being connected and supported at school predicted fewer depression symptoms a full year later for boys and girls, fewer anxiety symptoms for girls, and overall mental health functioning for boys.

Risk and Resilience

As indicated by the Social-connectedness Support Matrix above, individuals fall into different quadrants that can either be protective or place them at risk. Essentially, having adequate social connections and supports is protective, whereas lacking the former can place a person at risk. Below, research is reviewed to flesh out what specific protections and risks have been identified related to social connection and support. Research on some general protections is first reviewed before focusing more specifically on how such protections relate to academic and mental health outcomes.

Protective factors. A considerable body of research indicates that school connectedness influences a range of other important outcomes for students, such as their engagement in risk-taking behaviors, delinquency, and violent behavior, and social relationships. A study by Catalano and colleagues (2004) found that feeling socially bonded at school was associated with lower levels of experimentation with alcohol and other drugs, as well as reduced drug abuse in later life. Further, feeling bonded at school also was related to reduced delinquency and crime, lower rates of involvement in gang activity and violence, and delayed sexual activity. Similarly, Dornbusch and colleagues (2001) found school connectedness to impact students' involvement in health-risk and deviant behavior such as the use of alcohol, marijuana, and cigarettes as well as violent behavior. The authors speculated that students who did not feel socially bonded to the school environment were likelier to associate with delinquent peers who also felt disengaged from school. Thus, school connectedness usually is described as a protective factor, and low levels of this factor can place students at risk.

Risk factors. Despite spending as much as 80% of their time around other people, such as caregivers, classmates, siblings, and friends, children may be particularly vulnerable to feeling socially disconnected and lonely (Asher & Paquette, 2003). As many as 80% of youth and 40% of adults report feeling lonely "at least some time," with levels of loneliness gradually diminishing through middle adulthood (Berguno et al., 2004). Thus, from these findings, it appears that social disconnection is more clearly related to perceptions of social isolation than objective social isolation. On the one hand, individuals can live relatively solitary lives and not feel lonely; however, others may appear to have rich social lives yet still feel lonely and socially disconnected.

In addition to social connection, at this point, you might be wondering: what about chronic loneliness, and what are its related risks? According to Hawkley and Cacioppo (2010), loneliness is defined as "a distressing feeling that accompanies the perception that one's social needs are not being met by the quantity or especially the quality of one's social relationships" (p. 218). Therefore, children without adequate peer relationships and supportive caregivers may be uniquely vulnerable to feeling socially disconnected, disengaged, and lonely.

Findings from an early study on child loneliness indicate that about 10% of elementary school-aged children report feeling lonely either "always" or "most of the time" (Asher et al., 1984). In addition to experiencing negative emotions, these students are at risk of difficulties at school as they are often rejected by their peers, perceived negatively by teachers, and generally feel misunderstood (Asher & Paquette, 2003; Woodhouse et al., 2012). Moreover, *feeling lonely or socially disconnected is associated with a range of negative outcomes such as having physical health problems* (e.g., cardiovascular disease, obesity, substance abuse, compromised immunity), *mental health problems* (e.g., anxiety, depression, heightened stress levels), *and increased risk for suicide as well as impaired cognitive performance, school dropout, and reduced executive functioning* (Hawkley & Cacioppo, 2010). Across the lifespan, chronic and intense loneliness or social disconnection has been found to be more harmful to health than being obese; loneliness has been found to reduce emotional well-being to a degree that parallels living in poverty, and social disconnection is associated with premature death (Hawkley & Cacioppo, 2010; Luo et al., 2012). Therefore, consistent with an inherent need for social connection, *a lack of social bonding and connection can literally kill.*

In further support of this notion, research has shown that the vast majority of school shooters have felt lonely, rejected, and socially disconnected from their peers and their school (Vossekuil et al., 2002). Especially when a sense of humiliation accompanied these feelings, these emotions fueled their rage and resentment, and served as a significant impetus for their attack (Langman, 2010; Langman; 2021).

The COVID-19 pandemic and social distancing. The COVID-19 pandemic has significantly altered the daily lives of students, families, the educational community, and society (Wang et al., 2020). For example, at the pandemic's beginning, many more students were learning online and families and caregivers were responsible for teaching, childcare, and supporting their children's mental health—all while managing their work, health, and well-being.

Furthermore, the pernicious effects of the COVID-19 pandemic more disproportionality harmed marginalized groups (e.g., racial/ethnic minorities, low socioeconomic status communities, undocumented Americans, people with disabilities, English language learners) that are more at-risk because of systemic inequity. Some of these inequities include structural racism, discrimination in healthcare, residential instability, harsher criminal justice and sentencing, lower quality education, and lack of access to necessities to facilitate healthy social connection and educational success (CDC COVID-19 Response Team, 2020; Ji et al., 2020; Wenham et al., 2020).

Related to the previous problem of social disconnection, sage advice to prevent the spread of COVID-19 generally involves engaging in "social distancing." This term was coined and practiced during previous outbreaks; however, it came into vogue and became widely practiced in the U.S. in the spring of 2020. Leading medical and public health experts advised individuals to avoid unnecessary social contact or proximity to help contain the spread of the dangerous virus, which has proven to be highly communicable and difficult to contain.

However, the phrase "social distancing" is a bit of a misnomer because what was really being recommended is physical distancing through physical isolation—not social isolation. As previously mentioned, social isolation is related to negative social, emotional, and mental health outcomes. Furthermore, emerging research is already illustrating increases in loneliness related to social distancing associated with COVID-19 (see Banerjee and Rai [2020]). Therefore, amid the pandemic, individuals needed to prevent the spread of the pathogen by avoiding physical contact and proximity yet maintaining social connection through whatever means are available (e.g., video-conferencing, phone calls, text and digital messages, group or family chats, social media, email, traditional letters).

Signs of Social Disconnection

Considering the negative impact of social disconnection, leaders have a unique opportunity to address this problem and ensure that all educators and staff intentionally intervene. Some common signs that might suggest that a student is socially disconnected include not participating during group activities, avoiding peer interactions (especially unstructured interactions), sitting alone or being by oneself during social times and activities (e.g., lunch, recess, physical education), not participating in extracurricular activities (even if the student is interested in the activities), being early or late to class to avoid interacting with peers, skipping class or school, refusing to participate voluntarily in class, and turning down peer support or mentoring.

Any of these signs does not mean a student may feel socially disconnected in school. Instead, one should take notice when several occur together, and it becomes clearer that the student is not engaging in regular social interactions. Many of the signs that might suggest social disconnection might also be indicative of other concerns that warrant attention, such as the presence of bullying, a mood or anxiety disorder, trauma exposure, poor self-concept, not speaking the native language, being a recent immigrant, and simply being new to the school. Thus, it is important not to pathologize, stigmatize, or do anything that could make a student feel even more socially disconnected. Instead, it is important to approach and communicate with them in a way that encourages the student to feel comfortable, open up, and feel like a valued member of the school community.

Cultural considerations. Culture influences all interpersonal relationships in important ways. Most generally, in individualistic cultures (i.e., cultures that emphasize anonymity, independence, and self-efficacy), relationships are believed to be freely chosen, and individuals often are encouraged to express their needs and concerns to individuals who may or may not be immediately close in their web of connections (Helmes, & Gallou, 2014). However, in collectivist cultures (i.e., cultures that stress interdependence and collective efficacy), relationships tend to be more group-oriented, and individuals often view their interpersonal relationships as responsibilities to individuals with whom they feel interpersonally close such as family members. Because of this, individuals in collectivist cultures can be more reluctant to seek support outside their immediate network (Tokunaga, 2009).

The former is important because feeling like one belongs is key to establishing social connections and feeling supported. White individuals often feel like they belong (or at least do not feel like they automatically do not). However, minority individuals and groups are automatically aware of their social positioning in reference to others (DiAngelo, 2018). By being in the minority, they may inherently exist as outsiders in White social groups, even if the group perceives it as welcoming and inclusive. Moreover, this dynamic is particularly daunting and pernicious for students who have traditionally been excluded, disenfranchised, marginalized, or even abused because of their race, ethnicity, skin color, religion, gender identity, sexual orientation, family income, or country of origin (DiAngelo, 2018).

In the United States, schools perpetuate White middle class norms and punish students who do not conform to such norms either through disciplinary practices or social exclusion. This then presents a major dilemma for ensuring that all students feel socially connected and supported, as racist and bigoted policies abound in public education (Anderson, 2016). For example, zero tolerance discipline policies and the disproportionate placement of minority students in special education contribute to alienating minority students and students of color (Ahram et al., 2011; American Psychological Association Zero Tolerance Task Force, 2008). Because of this, concerned adults at school must redouble their efforts to reach out to minority students and students of color to ensure that they feel welcome at school, belong, are physically and socially protected, and have a solid footing to foster social connections and receive social support (NASP, 2020).

Fostering Social Connection and Support

At the Local, State, and National Level

The science of resilience research emphasizes the "value of prevention and health promotions efforts that seek to strengthen supportive relationships across ecological contexts, including families, schools, and communities" (Yule et al., 2019, p. 423). Fortunately, countless programs provide family and student support. Through diligence and establishing a database or directory, school leaders can find and connect to resources in their local communities or at the national level. Here are just a few of these national organizations or programs that can provide assistance or information: American Academy of Pediatrics, American School Counselors Association, Autism Speaks, Big Brothers/Big Sisters, Center for Autism and Related Disorders, Children's Defense Fund, Council for Exceptional Children, Girl Scouts of the USA, GLSEN, Head Start, Kids Count Data Center, My Brother's Keeper Alliance, National Alliance on Mental Illness, National Association of Elementary School Principals, National Association of School Psychologists, National Association of Secondary School Principals, National Center for Children in Poverty, National Center for Families Learning, National Education Association, National Foster Youth Institute, National Institute on Out of School Time, National Parent Teachers Association,

Social Connectedness and Support ◆ 169

National School Social Workers Association, Prevent Child Abuse, Safe and Sound Schools, Special Olympics, YMCA of the USA, YWCA USA, and Zero to Three: National Center for Infants, Toddlers, and Families.

We will also highlight two local programs that have recently received national attention and can be adapted in schools or by connecting with outside resources. The first is Dads on Duty. This program was formed in response to fights at Southwood High School in September 2021 in Shreveport, LA, which ultimately left 23 students incarcerated. Michael LaFitte, a father, who is also the president of the Shreveport NAACP, called a meeting to address the school violence issue. The initial meeting was expected to take only 45 minutes. However, the group devised a plan four hours later (Boucher, 2021). The plan according to LaFitte was to gather a group of fathers to go to school, patrol, and walk around, and show a strong male presence. The group of 40 fathers showed up daily, according to their schedule, and took on the presence of "cool uncles." Since they began their initiative, there have been no fights. The dads talk to the kids about grooming, life skills, and self-respect. They listen to the students' concerns and provide support and connection. Mayor of Shreveport Adrian Perkins remarked, "This is the most effective mentoring programs that I have seen up close and personal" (Boucher, 2021). The Dads on Duty project has garnered national attention and was featured on CBS News (Hartman, 2021) and other news outlets.

The second program highlighted is First Star Academy at the University of California, Los Angeles, designed to work with children in foster care. In the U.S. there are approximately 400,000 children in the foster care system. Many of these students have been in numerous foster homes during their life, and after they age out, navigating life can be arduous (Strassman, 2022). According to the National Foster Youth Institute (n.d.; https://nfyi.org/mission/) only about half of all children in foster care graduate from high school, and less than 10% attend college. First Star Academy is a privately funded program that connects with foster youth when they enter high school and provides mentors who serve as positive role models throughout their four years of high school. The program also teaches youth in foster care life skills necessary for success. The result is that 97% of seniors enrolled in the First Star Academy graduate from high school, and roughly two out of three enroll in four-year colleges.

At the Individual Level

At the individual level, there is no universal way to help foster social connection and support among all students, just like there is no surefire way to engage all students academically. Nonetheless, it is exceedingly important to make an effort. Schools provide students with unparalleled opportunities to establish and maintain social connection. Schools exist in virtually all communities, typically include diverse students in terms of their backgrounds and interests, and provide rich opportunities for students to interact, both within and outside of the classroom. Moreover, they have dedicated educators and support personnel that can help forging social connections, either directly or indirectly, by including students in social activities as part of their educational experience. Even in distance education, online learning, or mixed/flexible scheduling, educators can help establish social connections among students through technology. However, creativity is needed in this regard. Educators should feel free to experiment with fostering school connectedness and aligning students with those who can provide social support.

To do this, concerned adults must consider a range of contextual factors specific to each student and make decisions to address their individual needs. To help in this regard, Table 6.1 presents a menu of options that concerned adults may utilize to promote social connectedness and support among all students and highlights approaches for those youth who are more vulnerable, at-risk, or socially detached. If these suggestions are

Social Connectedness and Support ◆ 171

implemented, the school can become a more caring community. Table 6.2 lists principles for utilizing a family-centric approach to engage family members.

TABLE 6.1 Helping to Facilitate Social Connectedness and Support at School and Fostering a Caring Community

- Learn and know all students' names—call them by their first names (we all love to hear the sound of our name)
- Find and focus on the positive. It takes three positive comments, compliments, or kind words of praise and recognition to undo one incident of criticism
- Ask students how they are feeling each day and show genuine interest in their answer
- Practice active listening so that students feel more comfortable talking to you
- Never use stigmatizing language, inappropriately label students, perpetuate stereotypes, engage in microaggressions, or judge one culture by the standards of another
- Focus on removing barriers to success in school in lieu of student problems or deficits
- Take action when bullying or peer victimization occurs. This involves addressing the perpetrator, the target, and student bystanders
- Display student work products and pictures around the classroom and school
- Have classroom pets, plants, and lounging areas accessible to students
- Have regular check-in meetings with students to understand how they are doing in and outside of school; this provides them with an opportunity to open up and it helps to solidify teacher-student relationships
- Allow students to participate in creating and buying into school and classroom rules
- Establish "new student" groups, mentoring programs/initiatives, and friendship groups
- Encourage peer mediation programs
- Give students the benefit of the doubt when they report experiencing adversity, and describe how it is negatively impacting their performance at school
- Encourage collaborative learning
- Actively invite caregivers into school and the classroom
- Invite positive community members and stakeholders to the school
- Involve all students in whole-class and collaborative instructional activities

(continued)

172 ◆ The Supportive Pillar

TABLE 6.1 Continued

♦ Provide students with healthy snacks and drinks

♦ Allow students to explore their own creative pursuits and celebrate students' creative efforts

♦ Integrate art, music, movement, and non-traditional activities into instruction and regular school practices

♦ Connect lessons and instructional activities to students' interests, hobbies, and personally meaningful topics

♦ Provide a wide range of extra-curricular learning opportunities, experiences, and opportunities for students to socialize

♦ Sponsor interest groups on a variety of topics—especially for upper-level students to enhance affiliation

♦ Consider creating roles for students who would like to contribute to the school community

♦ Have an open-door policy so students can always schedule a time to meet with you to discuss things happening in their life or at school *

♦ Become educated about the struggles of highly at-risk and vulnerable student populations, including highly mobile and economically-disadvantaged students, and actively work to make these students feel comfortable at school *

♦ Provide highly mobile students (e.g., homeless students, foster care youth) with a safe space or locker to store their personal possessions *

♦ Support and respect LGBTQ students through displaying safe-space stickers and posters that are available through the Gay, Lesbian & Straight Education Network (GLSEN) *

♦ Convey worries or concerns about at-risk students to school-based mental health professionals such as school psychologists, counselors, and social workers *

♦ Establish a process to support those students who express a desire to develop their social interactions *

♦ Establish peer buddy programs *

♦ Ensure that no student eats alone as a school policy *

♦ Create on-going lunch friendship groups for specific students where a need has been established (e.g., 6th grade girls from minority or minoritized groups, students who recently enrolled in the school) *

♦ Establish social skills group be led by a school mental health professional. These can be especially helpful for children on the Autism spectrum, lonely or shy students, and those with weak or annoying social skills *

Note: An asterisk is placed next to a strategy that may be especially important to use with more vulnerable or at-risk students, specifically those youth who appear to be socially detached. Nonetheless, most of the suggested strategies with an asterisk can be used with all students.

Adapted from Sulkowski & Lazarus (2017).

Social Connectedness and Support ◆ 173

TABLE 6.2 Principles for Utilizing a Family-centric Approach to Engage Family Member

---

◆ Establish clear, honest, and respectful communication with family members to build trust and facilitate positive partnerships

◆ Use a strength-based approach when interacting with families in which positive family factors are highlighted

◆ Use shared decision-making processes to empower caregivers to give voice to what they think will benefit their students academically, socially, and emotionally

◆ Pay attention and be sensitive to cultural and linguistic factors that influence relationships between families and schools

◆ Treat each meeting or form of communication with family members as a unique event—do not use a "cookie cutter" approach

◆ Coordinate the provision of concrete services and necessities (e.g., food, shelter, clothing) if the family lacks these resources

◆ Reach out to extended family members who may not be legal guardians yet still have a strong influence over a student

◆ Establish regular open houses and meeting times in which family members and school staff can interact, discuss ways to support students, and enrich their collaborative relationships

◆ Reinforce family members for their positive efforts to support students and acknowledge barriers that negatively impact a student's learning or problems that have a deleterious effect on the family

◆ Connect families with resources and enable the school to become a hub of support if a large-scale crisis impacts the community.

Based on Sulkowski and Lazarus (2017). Adapted with permission.

Conclusion

This chapter covered how to provide psychological support for students through fostering social connection and social support. People are inherently social beings and need adequate healthy and nourishing social relationships to thrive. This is also true for students throughout their K–12 educational experience. Without such relationships, students are more likely to experience distress, mental health problems, and academic underperformance. However, by activating resilience or building on protective factors through social connection and support, concerned adults at school can protect against risk and help ensure positive academic and life outcomes.

This chapter provides two models (i.e., the social connectedness web and the social support balloons) for help in understanding social connections and social support. It describes research that elucidates the relationship between the two and student functioning. Attention is paid to considering cultural factors that influence interpersonal relationships at school and how social disconnection stemming from the COVID-19 crisis has negatively impacted students. The chapter concludes with a listing of national resources that serve to help youth and families and numerous practical strategies for assisting a range of students who may be socially disconnected and need increased support. In addition, advice is provided to help schools become more caring communities and support families in this process.

References

Ahram, R., Fergus, E., & Noguera, P. (2011). Addressing racial/ethnic disproportionality in special education: Case studies of suburban school districts. *Teachers College Record, 113*(10), 2233–2266.

American Psychological Association Zero Tolerance Task Force (2008). Are zero tolerance policies effective in the schools? An evidentiary review and recommendations. *American Psychologist, 63*(9), 852–862. doi: 10.1037/0003-066X.63.9.852

Anderman, L. H. (2003). Academic and social perceptions as predictors of change in middle school students' sense of school belonging. *Journal of Experimental Education, 72*(1), 5–22. https://doi.org/10.1080/00220970309600877

Anderson, C. (2016). *White rage. The unspoken truth of our racial divide.* Bloomsbury Publishing.

Asher, S. R., Hymel, S., & Renshaw, P. D. (1984). Loneliness in children. *Child Development, 55*(4), 1456–1464. doi: 10.2307/1130015

Asher, S. R., & Paquette, J. A. (2003). Loneliness and peer relations in childhood. *Current Directions in Psychological Science, 12*(3), 75–78. https://doi.org/10.1111/1467-8721.01233

Banerjee, D., & Rai, M. (2020). Social isolation in Covid-19: The impact of loneliness. *International Journal of Social Psychiatry.* https://doi.org/10.1177/0020764020922269

Baumeister, R. F., & Leary, M. R. (1995). The need to belong: Desire for interpersonal attachments as a fundamental human motivation. *Psychological Bulletin, 117*(3), 497–529.

Berguno, G., Leroux, P., McAinsh, K., & Shaikh, S. (2004). Children's experience of loneliness at school and its relation to bullying and the quality of teacher interventions. *The Qualitative Report, 9*(3), 483–499.

Bokhorst, C. L., Sumter, S. R., & Westenberg, P. M. (2010). Social support from parents, friends, classmates, and teachers in children and adolescents aged 9 to 18 years: Who is perceived as most supportive? *Social Development, 19*(2), 417–426. https://doi.org/10.1111/j.1467-9507.2009.00540.x

Boucher, M. (2021, October, 31). Dads on Duty: Louisiana fathers fan out at school to prevent violence and mentor kids. USA Today. https://www.usatoday.com/story/news/education/2021/10/30/louisiana-high-school-dads-bring-calm-campus-after-fights-arrests/6197862001/

Cacioppo, J. T., & Patrick, W. (2008). *Loneliness: Human nature and the need for social connection.* New York, NY: WW Norton & Company.

Catalano, R. F., Haggerty, K. P., Oesterle, S., Fleming, C. B., & Hawkins, J. D. (2004). The importance of bonding to school for healthy development: Findings from the Social Development Research Group. *Journal of School Health, 74*(7), 252–261. doi: 10.1111/j.1746-1561.2004.tb08281.x.

CDC COVID-19 Response Team (2020). Preliminary estimates of the prevalence of selected underlying health conditions among patients with coronavirus disease 2019—United States, February 12–March 28, 2020. *Morbidity and Mortality Weekly Report, 69,* 382–386. https://stacks.cdc.gov/view/cdc/87230

DiAngelo, R. (2018). *White fragility: Why it's so hard for white people to talk about racism.* Beacon Press.

Dornbusch, S. M., Erickson, K. G., Laird, J., & Wong, C. A. (2001). The relation of family and school attachment to adolescent deviance in diverse groups and communities. *Journal of Adolescent Research, 16*(4), 396–422. https://doi.org/10.1177/0743558401164006

Dunbar, R. (2010). *How many friends does one person need? Dunbar's number and other evolutionary quirks.* Cambridge, MA: Harvard University Press.

Eisenberger, N. I., Inagaki, T. K., Mashal, N. M., & Irwin, M. R. (2010). Inflammation and social experience: an inflammatory challenge induces feelings of social disconnection in addition to depressed mood. *Brain, Behavior, and Immunity, 24*(4), 558–563. https://doi.org/10.1016/j.bbi.2009.12.009

Flemming, E. G. (1932) Testing some aspects of personality, *Journal of Social Psychology, 3*(3) 376–384. https://doi.org/10.1080/00224545.1932.9919163

Froiland, J. M., Worrell, F. C., & Oh, H. (2019). Teacher–student relationships, psychological need satisfaction, and happiness among diverse students. *Psychology in the Schools, 56*(5), 856–870. https://doi.org/10.1002/pits.22245

Furrer, C., & Skinner, E. (2003). Sense of relatedness as a factor in children's academic engagement and performance. *Journal of Educational Psychology, 95*(1), 148–162. https://doi.org/10.1037/0022-0663.95.1.148

Garcia-Reid, P., Reid, R. J., & Peterson, N. A. (2005). School engagement among Latino youth in an urban middle school context: Valuing the role of social support. *Education and Urban Society, 37*(3), 257–275. https://doi.org/10.1177/0013124505275534

Hagborg, W. J. (1994). An exploration of school membership among middle-and high-school students. *Journal of Psychoeducational Assessment, 12*(4), 312–323. https://doi.org/10.1177/073428299401200401

Hartman, S. (2021, October 22). *Dads spend time in Louisiana high school after 23 students were arrested in string of violence.* CBS News. https://www.cbsnews.com/amp/news/dads-louisiana-high-school-student-violence/

Hawkley, L. C., & Cacioppo, J. T. (2010). Loneliness matters: A theoretical and empirical review of consequences and mechanisms. *Annals of Behavioral Medicine, 40*(2), 218–227. https://doi.org/10.1007/s12160-010-9210-8

Helmes, E., & Gallou, L. (2014). Culture and attitudes toward psychological help-seeking influence clients' self-disclosure. *European Journal of Psychotherapy & Counselling, 16*(2), 163–176. https://doi.org/10.1080/13642537.2014.895771

Ji, Y., Ma, Z., Peppelenbosch, M. P., & Pan, Q. (2020). Potential association between COVID-19 mortality and health-care resource availability. *Lancet Global Health, 8,* e480. doi: 10.1016/S2214-109X(20)30068-1

Kennedy-Moore, E. (2012). Children's growing friendships: How children's understanding of friendship changes and develops with age. *Psychology Today.* https://www.psychologytoday.com/us/blog/growing-friendships/201202/childrens-growing-friendships

Langman, P. F. (2010). *Why kids kill: Inside the minds of school shooters.* St. Martins Griffin.

Langman, P. F. (2021). *Warning signs: Identifying school shooters before they strike.* Langman Psychological Associates, LLC

Lee, R. M., Dean, B. L., & Jung, K. R. (2008). Social connectedness, extraversion, and subjective well-being: Testing a mediation model. *Personality and Individual Differences, 45*(5), 414–419. https://doi.org/10.1016/j.paid.2008.05.017

Lee, R. M., & Robbins, S. B. (1995). Measuring belongingness: The social connectedness and the social assurance scales. *Journal of Counseling Psychology, 42*(2), 232–241. https://doi.org/10.1037/0022-0167.42.2.232

Luo, Y., Hawkley, L. C., Waite, L. J., & Cacioppo, J. T. (2012). Loneliness, health, and mortality in old age: A national longitudinal study. *Social Science & Medicine, 74*(6), 907–914. https://doi.org/10.1016/j.socscimed.2011.11.028

Malecki, C. K., & Demaray, M. K. (2002). Measuring perceived social support: Development of the child and adolescent social support scale (CASSS). *Psychology in the Schools, 39*(1), 1–18.

Malecki, C. K., & Demaray, M. K. (2003). What type of support do they need? Investigating student adjustment as related to emotional, informational, appraisal, and instrumental support. *School Psychology Quarterly, 18*(3), 231–252.

Marks, H. M. (2000). Student engagement in instructional activity: Patterns in the elementary, middle, and high school years.

American Educational Research Journal, 37(1), 153–184. https://doi.org/10.3102/00028312037001153

Maslow, A. H. (1943). A theory of human motivation. *Psychological Review, 50*(4), 370–96.

Murthy, V. (2020). *Together: The healing power of human connection in a sometimes lonely world.* HarperCollins.

National Association of School Psychologists (2020). *NASP calls for action to end racism and violence against people of color.* https://www.nasponline.org/about-school-psychology/media-room/press-releases/nasp-calls-for-action-to-end-racism-and-violence-against-people-of-color

Nickerson, A. B., & Nagle, R. J. (2005). Parent and peer attachment in late childhood and early adolescence. *Journal of Early Adolescence, 25*(2), 223–249. https://doi.org/10.1177/0272431604274174

Niehaus, K., Rudasill, K. M., & Rakes, C. R. (2012). A longitudinal study of school connectedness and academic outcomes across sixth grade. *Journal of School Psychology, 50*(4), 443–460. https://doi.org/10.1016/j.jsp.2012.03.002

Osterman, K. F. (2000). Students' need for belonging in the school community. *Review of Educational Research, 70*(3), 323–367. https://doi.org/10.3102/00346543070003323

Resnick, H. S., Acierno, R., & Kilpatrick, D. G. (1997). Health impact of interpersonal violence 2: Medical and mental health outcomes. *Behavioral Medicine, 23*(2), 65–78. https://doi.org/10.1080/08964289709596730

Rosenfeld, L. B., Richman, J. M., & Bowen, G. L. (2000). Social support networks and school outcomes: The centrality of the teacher. *Child and Adolescent Social Work Journal, 17*(3), 205–226. doi: 10.1023/A:1007535930286

Rueger, S., Malecki, C., & Demaray, M. (2008). Gender differences in the relationship between perceived social support and student adjustment during early adolescence. *School Psychology Quarterly, 23,* 496–514. doi: 10.1037/1045-3830.23.4.496

Ryan, A. M., & Patrick, H. (2001). The classroom social environment and changes in adolescents' motivation and engagement during middle school. *American Educational Research Journal, 38*(2), 437–460. https://doi.org/10.3102/00028312038002437

Saylor, C. F., & Leach, J. B. (2009). Perceived bullying and social support in students accessing special inclusion programming. *Journal of Developmental and Physical Disabilities, 21*(1), 69–80. doi: 10.1007/s10882-008-9126-4

Shochet, I. M., Dadds, M. R., Ham, D., & Montague, R. (2006). School connectedness is an underemphasized parameter in adolescent mental health: Results of a community prediction study. *Journal of Clinical Child & Adolescent Psychology, 35*(2), 170–179. https://doi.org/10.1207/s15374424jccp3502_1

Strassman, M. (2022, December 8). *Program helps foster kids achieve college dreams. Consistency is the key.* CBS news. https://www.cbsnews.com/news/foster-care-kids-college-first-star-academy-ucla/

Sulkowski, M. L., & Lazarus, P. J. (2017). *Creating safe and supportive schools and fostering students' mental health.* Routledge.

Sumter, S. R., Bokhorst, C. L., & Westenberg, P. M. (2009). Social fears during adolescence: Is there an increase in distress and avoidance? *Journal of Anxiety Disorders, 23*(7), 897–903. https://doi.org/10.1016/j.janxdis.2009.05.004

Tokunaga, R. S. (2009). High-speed internet access to the other: The influence of cultural orientations on self-disclosures in offline and online relationships. *Journal of Intercultural Communication Research, 38*(3), 133–147. https://doi.org/10.1080/17475759.2009.505058

Vossekuil, B., Fein, R. A., Reddy, M., Borum, R., & Modzeleski, W. (2002). *The final report and findings of the Safe School Initiative: Implications for the prevention of school attacks in the United States.* Washington, DC: U.S. Secret Service and U.S. Department of Education.

Wang, G., Zhang, Y., Zhao, J., Zhang, J., & Jiang, F. (2020). Mitigate the effects of home confinement on children during the COVID-19 outbreak. *Lancet, 395,* 945–947. doi: 10.1016/S0140-6736(20)30547-X

Wang, M. T., & Eccles, J. S. (2012). Social support matters: Longitudinal effects of social support on three dimensions of school engagement from middle to high school. *Child Development, 83*(3), 877–895. https://doi.org/10.1111/j.1467-8624.2012.01745.x

Wenham, C., Smith, J., & Morgan, R. (2020). COVID-19: The gendered impacts of the outbreak. *Lancet, 395,* 846–848. doi: 10.1016/S0140-6736(20)30526-2

Wit, D. J. D., Karioja, K., Rye, B. J., & Shain, M. (2011). Perceptions of declining classmate and teacher support following the transition to high school: Potential correlates of increasing student mental health difficulties. *Psychology in the Schools, 48*(6), 556–572. https://doi.org/10.1002/pits.20576

Woodhouse, S. S., Dykas, M. J., & Cassidy, J. (2012). Loneliness and peer relations in adolescence. *Social Development, 21*(2), 273–293. https://doi.org/10.1111/j.1467-9507.2011.00611.x

Yoon, E., Lee, R. M., & Goh, M. (2008). Acculturation, social connectedness, and subjective well-being. *Cultural Diversity and Ethnic Minority Psychology, 14*(3), 246–255.

Yule, K., Houston, J., & Grych, J. (2019). Resilience in children exposed to violence: A meta-analysis of protective factors across ecological contexts. *Clinical Child and Family Psychology Review, 22,* 406–431. https://doi.org/10.1007/s10567-019-00293-1

Zaff, J. F., Ginsberg, K. K., Boyd, M. J., & Kakli, Z. (2014). Reconnecting disconnected youth: Examining the development of productive engagement. *Journal of Research on Adolescence, 24*(3), 526–540. https://doi.org/10.1111/jora.12109

Section 3
The Mental Health Pillar

7

Promotion and Prevention

Youth Mental Health in Crisis

In October 2021, The American Academy of Pediatrics (AAP), the American Academy of Child and Adolescent Psychiatry (AACAP), and the Children's Hospital Association (CHA) declared a national emergency on children's mental health, citing the serious impact of the COVID-19 pandemic, in addition to the existing challenges. They urged policymakers to take swift action to address this current crisis. Lee Savio Beers, the President of AAP, noted, "Today's declaration is an urgent call to policymakers at all levels of government—we must treat this mental health crisis like the emergency it is" (AAP, 2021, p.1). Furthermore, in the same year, the AACAP President, Gabrielle Carlson, stated: "We are caring for young people with soaring rates of depression, anxiety, trauma, loneliness, and suicidality that will have lasting impacts on them, their families, their communities, and all of our futures" (AAP, 2021, p. 2).

DOI: 10.4324/9780429261527-10

The authors of the joint declaration agreed that the pandemic engendered physical isolation, fear, grief, and ongoing uncertainty (AAP, 2021). It was the tipping point for many already at-risk and overwhelmed youth. Collectively, these professional leaders reported that between March and October 2021, the emergency department visits for mental health emergencies rose by 24% for children ages 5–11 and 31% for youth ages 12–17. Moreover, emergency department visits for suspected suicide attempts increased by nearly 51% among girls ages 12–17 years compared to the same time period just in 2019 (Radhakrishnan, 2022).

Existing disparities in mental health emergencies were magnified by the pandemic for youth with disabilities, those from minoritized populations, and those from communities of poverty. One particularly striking example of this crisis is the spike in suicidality among Black teenagers (Davis et al., 2022). Similarly concerning, recent national surveys have shown that one in three high school students—and half of all female students—report persistent feelings of hopelessness or sadness, an overall increase of 40% from 2009 to 2019 (U.S. Surgeon General, 2021). This is a mental health emergency, and educational leaders must be part of the solution to bring it to an end.

Recent findings from the Institute of Education Sciences (IES) *2022 School Pulse Panel* indicate that not only are K–12 schools struggling with greater educator and chronic student absenteeism but also more than eight in 10 public schools have reported seeing delays in student behavioral and socioemotional development due to the COVID-19 pandemic.

Schools also report significant increases in student and staff need for mental health services. More specifically, 70% of schools reported seeing increases in students seeking such services, and approximately 29% reported increases in staff seeking mental health services. Clearly, as educators, we are all in it together. Because of this, we need to work together to address critically important but woefully unmet mental health needs in school communities.

Broad statistics can prove a point, but they can seem impersonal and miss the true human impacts of COVID-19 and its related sequelae. In a highly viewed CBS *60 Minutes* video (September 4, 2022), one 13-year-old student hospitalized for depression was asked what she lost most in the pandemic. She replied, "myself." In a nationwide study surveying school counselors, 94% of survey participants reported that students showed more signs of anxiety and depression than before the pandemic (Cain Miller & Pallaro, 2022). Approximately 88% of school counselors said their students had more trouble regulating their emotions, and nearly 75% said they observed students having more difficulty solving conflicts with friends. Counselors also noted increased difficulty focusing on classwork, breaking classroom rules, having trouble with time management, chronic absenteeism, and difficulties with social skills.

Sadly, the mental health crisis plaguing students existed long before the COVID-19 pandemic worsened things. Many researchers have suggested various reasons for this ranging from broad economic downturns that result in family stress to the breakdown in trust in institutions, to political factionalism and declines in civility, to the opioid endemic, to the increased use of social media among youth. You might be wondering: "Social media use?" However, in a compelling study, Jean Twenge (2020) controlled many of the former variables and found that adolescent depression rose in synch when social media use became ubiquitous and a dominant form of communication among school-aged youth. More specifically, Twenge found that rates of depression doubled between 2011 and 2019—a timeframe that parallels the unprecedented use of social media.

Whatever drives the mental health crisis among school-aged youth, one thing is clear: when the physical health risks associated with the COVID-19 pandemic abate, the mental health effects will not—and neither will the mental health risks that existed before the pandemic. Simply stated, opportunities were missed to support the mental health needs of a generation of students. Important mental health promotion and prevention practices were not neatly integrated into school culture, policy, and practice. However, this does not mean that school mental health cannot be centered as a primary responsibility of educational leaders. Anyone reading this book who has either personally experienced clinically significant depression or anxiety (or knows someone who has) will know how hard it is to learn and thrive in work and life while battling these demons. Educational leaders, the time is now for mental health promotion and preventive practice.

Promotion and Prevention to Deal with Big Problems

The timeless phrase that "an ounce of prevention is worth a pound of cure" was coined by Benjamin Franklin in 1736 to remind citizens to be vigilant about fire prevention. Still relevant today, this adage has been applied broadly to encompass countless other public safety and health initiatives. As the most recent massive public health initiative, the COVID-19 pandemic has underscored the importance of effective public health promotion and prevention—in this case, the promotion of accurate and actionable information and the prevention of a deadly global pandemic. Unfortunately, however, as illustrated by the devastating losses associated with major conflagrations such as the Great Chicago Fire of 1871 and the countless deaths attributable to misinformation and poor prevention during the COVID-19 pandemic, room for improvement still exists for public health promotion and preventive efforts.

With that said, public health should not be criticized for imperfection because it has saved millions of lives across countless generations and reduced incalculable suffering. Within the last century, everything from car seatbelt campaigns, smoking awareness, taking the lead out of gas, and mental health awareness can be classified as public health. Given the circumstances, educational leaders are at the forefront of school mental health initiatives modeled on a promotion and prevention public health model.

The Public Health Model

The public health model to address disease, injury, suffering, and mortality on a grand scale is hierarchical. Because health and mental health problems are highly variable within populations where some people display minimal risk and others are extremely at-risk, not everyone has the same needs. Because of various protective factors—and often just good luck—some people are highly resilient to problems and might just need minimum support. Conversely, individuals with significant vulnerabilities and bad luck may need extensive support. Thus, the public health model for providing goods and services to a population was developed to triage resources to match the needs of various individuals or groups.

The public health model is primarily depicted as having three levels. The first or foundational level is described as *universal* in providing all people with a resource or support. This is also known as *primary* prevention. Therefore, universal public health extends to an entire population and is preventive. In the case of COVID-19, accurate information about the transmissibility of the virus and the efficacy of vaccines are examples of universal prevention. However, despite the availability of vaccines and the ever-increasing dissemination of quality information about the virus, millions still got sick and died (Koh et al., 2021). These people needed *selective* or *secondary* public health approaches to take care of their health risks and needs and protect the public from the greater transmission of the disease.

Selective public health approaches to addressing COVID-19 included social distancing and quarantining as soon as symptoms were present. Additionally, getting tested for COVID-19 is an example of a selective public health approach that eventually became almost universal in many countries where tests were readily available. Lastly, *indicated* or *tertiary* public health approaches for COVID-19 involved hospitalizations, and for some, this involved being placed on a ventilator or receiving more intensive medical care. Thus, depending on the level of severity of symptoms and underlying risks, resources were triaged accordingly.

Multi-tiered Mental Health

Multi-tiered mental health promotion and prevention models map onto the previously described public health model. In schools, promotion involves efforts to support the entire community through initiatives that aim to promote mental health, resilience, and well-being. Tier 1 involves the universal delivery of preventive resources to stave off the development of mental health problems. Simply stated, everyone can benefit from these efforts.

In contrast, Tier 2 aims to address the needs of individuals who did not respond effectively to universal promotion and prevention efforts and need more support. In school settings, Tier 2 of multi-tiered mental health would involve selective efforts to address the problems afflicting certain individuals or groups in the school community. Individuals in Tier 2 need more than the general population. Lastly, Tier 3 involves triaging resources and supports for individuals who are most at-risk in the population or already display significant problems that clearly indicate that they need intensive resources and support. The multi-tiered approach to school mental health collectively provides everyone with something but channels the greatest resources to those who need them the most.

Figure 1.2 (see Chapter 1) shows a contemporary way mental health services are delivered in forward-thinking school districts using a promotion-focused multi-tiered support system. The National Association of School Psychologists first developed this model (without explicitly focusing on promotion). However, this text expands upon this model to focus more intently on school-based promotion. In addition, it dilates on how health services should be provided based on our current understanding of broad, pervasive, and cross-cutting issues impacting mental health and well-being in school populations. Essentially, the proposed model promotes school mental health by providing a solid foundation, a foundation that grounds multi-tiered school-based mental health in core belief systems (e.g., culturally responsible practices, support for every child). Everybody knows a structure is only as strong as its foundation.

Leaders and Mental Health Promotion

Promotion is about making good things happen, whereas prevention is forestalling bad things from happening. When leaders focus on fostering student mental health, it is important to consider promotion first—even though both proactive and reactive approaches are necessary. Mental health promotion can be seen as any activity that fosters an individual's or institution's emotional well-being. Though the distinction between promotion practices and primary prevention may seem semantic or permeable, as both involve all the students in the school, a focus on promotion can change the conversation and mindset of leaders. Promotion may encompass positive psychology practices, fostering healthy living (e.g., adequate sleep, exercise, nutrition), changing the environment to make it more conducive to children's learning and emotional well-being, and establishing a positive school culture and climate of care. As illustrated in previous chapters, these approaches to promoting mental health overlap with efforts to foster safe and supportive schools. For example, creating a positive school culture and climate (see Chapter 5) may be school leaders' most important promotion task. Harvey Mackay once opined, "If you have integrity, nothing else matters. If you don't have integrity, nothing else matters." The same could be said about school culture and climate. This is not a coincidence because positive school environments promote mental health and being mentally healthy makes it more likely for someone to flourish in life.

Practical Promotion Strategies

Many practical mental health promotion strategies exist that do not require extensive effort and can make a big difference. To kickstart mental health promotion, school leaders should meet with their faculty and discuss proactive strategies that promote positive mental health. A number of these approaches focus on using elements of positive psychology such as meditation, yoga, gratitude exercises, catching students doing good deeds, celebrating diversity, teaching calming techniques, practicing coping strategies, creating friendship circles, focusing on hope and optimism, promoting positive self-talk, working on problem-solving skills, and facilitating agency. Practices that focus on teaching students about emotional self-regulation have been particularly promising. As noted by Lazarus and Costa (2021), when students know how to control their emotions, rather than have their emotions control them, they experience a greater sense of personal agency. Like learning multiplication or how to read, learning how to control one's emotions opens unforeseen opportunities for students. Moreover, as just one example, the benefits of learning self-regulation make learning everything easier, including all the stuff that life will inevitably bring that is not taught in a traditional school curriculum. Have you ever had a class that taught you how to manage conflict effectively with a coworker, work well on a team, or overcome a tragedy?

As discussed in Chapter 6 on social connection and support, just about any activity that promotes a sense of belonging and connection can promote children's mental health. What needs to be emphasized is that promotion does not require school mental health professionals. All members of the school community can become involved. Following the pandemic, where students have been isolated from each other, this is more important than ever, and school leaders can work with their entire staff to develop creative approaches to facilitate social connection. One example is that many schools have developed a policy in which no one eats alone. Engaging in competitive team sports or student clubs has been shown to promote a sense of camaraderie and shared purpose among participants. Another simple, cost-free, and practical approach to mental health promotion is to have students interview each other as if they were reporters to learn about each other's backgrounds and experiences and find out where they have commonalities.

One free program leaders can encourage their entire staff to take is Youth Mental Health First Aid (National Council for Mental Wellbeing, n. d.). This is an evidence-based program endorsed by SAMHSA and it can be taken in three different ways: in person, where learners receive their training during a 6.5-hour instructor-led, in-person class; in a blended format with a 2-hour self-paced online course; and a 4.5 or 5.5 instructor-led training, either through an in-person class or a video conference.

In this class, participants learn (a) common signs and symptoms of mental health challenges in youth, including anxiety, depression, eating disorders, and attention deficit disorders (b) common signs and symptoms of substance use challenges, (c) how to interact with a child or adolescent in crisis, (d) how to connect the youth with help, and (e) expanded content related to trauma, substance use, self-care, and the impact of social media and bullying. In this class, all personnel who work with youth learn how to respond to the mental health first aid action plan (ALGEE). Assess for risk of suicide or harm, Listen nonjudgmentally, Give reassurance and information, Encourage appropriate professional help, and Encourage self-help and other support strategies. This course is not about diagnosing youth or treating mental health concerns. Instead, it focuses on intervening at the moment, listening with empathy, seeking relevant information, and getting the youth the help they need.

Promotion and Tier 1 Frameworks

In addition to practical preventive practices that school leaders can embrace and deploy, more cohesive frameworks exist that can provide a universal mental health foundation for school communities. Two in particular—positive psychology and social-emotional learning (SEL)—display considerable promise. Over the past 20 to 30 years, considerable research has accumulated to support these frameworks and their foundational application in school communities. These are discussed in detail below.

Positive Psychology

Positive psychology is both a theoretical and applied psychological movement that strives to help people function and excel at optimal levels—it aims at understanding the human aspects of happiness, fulfillment, and flourishing (Linley et al., 2006). It is a subset of mental health promotion with universal appeal and application. Positive psychology focuses on helping individuals lead more enriched lives, whereas clinical psychology focuses on ameliorating mental distress. Therefore, consistent with Tier 1 delivery, positive psychology focuses on promotion and universal prevention services, whereas clinical psychology focuses on behavioral and emotional Tier 2 and Tier 3 interventions. Consequently, both approaches complement each other, and each has applicability in the schools.

Foundational elements. Suldo (2013) notes that there are three foundational elements in positive psychology: 1) *positive* *subjective experiences,* 2) *positive character,* and 3) *positive institutions.* The first element, *positive subjective experiences* are composed of well-being, contentment, and satisfaction (in the past), happiness and flow (in the present), and hope and optimism (for the future).

The second element *positive character* relates to positive traits that an individual can develop. Researchers investigated the works of ancient spiritual leaders, moral philosophers, and educators to help identify universal virtues that existed across cultures and time periods (Peterson & Seligman, 2004). They determined that six core values constitute the broadest virtues and called them character strengths (Sulkowski & Lazarus, 2017, p. 173):

1) *wisdom and knowledge,* including creativity, curiosity, open-mindedness, love of learning, and perspective
2) *courage,* including authenticity, bravery, perseverance, and zest
3) *humanity,* including kindness, love, and social intelligence
4) *justice,* including fairness, leadership, and teamwork
5) *temperance,* including forgiveness, modesty, prudence, and self-regulation
6) *transcendence,* including appreciation of beauty and excellence, gratitude, hope, humor, and religiosity.

Individuals interested in determining their character strengths may take the VIA Inventory of Strengths at http://viacharacter.org/www/The-Survey.

Finally, the third component of positive psychology is called *positive institutions.* This component describes the concept of optimal living experiences at the *universal* level. It brings together the first two components and incorporates them into the larger context of life as well as the overall community in which individuals live. These communal institutions exist within families, places of work, society, culture, and especially within schools. To properly fit within the framework of positive psychology, positive institutions such as schools must nurture and support the individuals they serve. Further, they must help foster healthy living, harmony, and sustainability (Linley et al., 2006). Ultimately, positive institutions emphasize that well-being and quality of life can be enhanced at the systems level to benefit those who are part of the system. Thus, each of the three components of positive psychology—positive emotions, positive character, and positive institutions—all function independently yet in unison to contribute to the well-being of individuals (Sulkowski & Lazarus, 2017, p. 174).

Benefits of positive psychology. In application, positive psychology aims to help students by building competencies rather than correcting flaws or weaknesses (Seligman, 2002). Positive psychology can increase students' hopes about the future, levels of optimism, ability to live mindfully, experience gratitude and forgiveness, and engage in meaningful activities (Miller et al., 2014). Meta-analyses of positive psychology interventions have linked this concept to increased subjective and psychological well-being as well as decreased symptoms of depression (e.g., Boiler et al., 2013).[1] In turn, increasing well-being in children can lead to increased learning, academic motivation and self-efficacy, life satisfaction, and a decreased risk for depression (Seligman et al., 2009).

Positive psychology's focus on fostering strengths and adaptive abilities has been linked with healthy self-esteem, vitality, positive affect, and lower perceived stress (Wood et al., 2011). Moreover, fostering such strengths can lead to fulfillment, academic achievement, and decreased psychopathology in youth (Park & Peterson, 2008). Likewise, learning optimism has been shown to prevent anxiety and depression in children and adults, and positive affect can lead to increased attention, creative thinking, and critical thinking in children (Seligman et al., 2009). As such, positive psychology, its various components (e.g., flow, gratitude, mindfulness, optimism), and its focus on strengths and virtues can benefit students' overall well-being, mental health, learning, and functioning in and beyond the classroom. In other words, applying positive psychology to support healthy academic and psychosocial development confers many advantages with no established problems.

Programs and practices. Recently Suldo et al. (2021) described programs and practices that schools could engage in that promote students' positive emotions, character, and purpose. Current methods that help generate positive emotions in schools with evidence-based results include programs and practices designed to cultivate mindfulness, kindness, gratitude, and character strengths. Some examples are discussed below: Shankland and Rosset (2017) describe *mindfulness* activities as well-suited to classrooms. These include the mindful bell, brief body scan, mindful breathing, and caring mindfulness. Lyubomirsky et al. (2005) encourages students to select one day of the week when they perform five acts of *kindness*. They emphasize that the students should engage in behaviors to make others happy; these acts can be small to large. Students are provided a log where they plan their activity and record each act of kindness. The act of helping others, helps oneself in turn.

The *gratitude letter* is an activity in which students write a letter to a person to properly thank them for being helpful or kind (Froh et al., 2009). In their letter, students can explain how the person has helped them in the past, served as a role model, or otherwise had been there for them. Students are then encouraged to deliver the letter in person to the recipient and read it out loud with expression.

Another approach to engendering gratitude was discussed by Molony et al. (2014). Students were given Post-it Notes in a variety of colors, shapes, and sizes, to give to others to surprise the recipients with notes of appreciation. They noted that students who received notes experienced positive feelings. As a result, they then left positive notes to others—thus resulting in passing it forward. Engaging in these activities can change a school's climate and engender a culture of caring. Moreover, school personnel can implement a school-wide intervention where students are instructed to list five things they are grateful for before they leave school. Or teachers can encourage students to keep a journal to notice and appreciate feelings of gratitude daily and they can share in class (in small groups) or as a whole class. Additionally, as demonstrated in a study by Froh et al. (2009), gratitude practice among children has a significant relationship with increasing life satisfaction, positive affect, prosocial behavior, social support, and optimism.

Researchers (e.g., Seligman et al., 2009) believe that students can get more satisfaction out of life if they learn to identify which of the character strengths they possess in abundance. Then, they use these strengths as much as possible with friends, and family, during hobbies, and in school. This activity is called Using Signature Strengths in a New Way and is based on each student's assessment of their signature strengths. Moreover, the website authentichappiness.com includes several lessons in the curriculum that focus on helping youth identify character strengths in themselves and others, as well as using the identified strengths in new ways and/or applying them to overcome personal challenges.

It is impossible to do justice to the wealth of information on positive psychology. However, interested leaders may wish to read *Promoting Student Happiness: Positive Psychology Interventions in Schools* by Suldo (2016) or her aforementioned chapter (Suldo et al., 2021) where the author discusses and describes positive psychological activities and interventions including those that promote hope, optimism, flow, savoring, and a sense of purpose. The *Journal of Positive Psychology* also provides studies on positive psychology interventions, and the recently edited *Handbook of Positive Psychology in Schools: Supporting Process and Practice* by Allen et al. (2022), which focuses on integrating positive psychology into educational environments through the voices of leading experts.

Leadership in action. Leaders can ensure that teachers have the requisite training, support, consultation, materials, and resources to implement positive psychology into the daily curriculum. Leaders can put together a team to promote the delivery of positive psychology in their schools and foster positive psychology clubs. Regarding character strengths, they can provide ways for students to highlight their strengths, develop a sense of school community, and facilitate conjoint parent meetings to display how schools highlight student strengths. Moreover, leaders can provide continuing education opportunities and time for staff to use positive psychology to help change the culture and climate of the school for the better. As previously discussed, having a healthy school climate and culture is integral for students to feel emotionally supported. Further, leaders should always remember to use positive psychology with all teachers and staff; through recognition and delivering kind words, pats on the back, genuine compliments, displays of respect and acknowledgment, and "thank-yous" for tasks well-done. By doing so, school leaders can have a transformative effect. Positive psychology, through its optimistic focus on human thriving, has immense potential to engender mental health across entire school communities.

Social Emotional Learning

In 1994, the term "social-emotional learning" was coined by members of the Fetzer Institute, an organization that focuses on facilitating positive relationships among people because of a desire to increase health promotion and problem prevention efforts in schools (Macklem, 2014). In the following years, others developed what SEL entailed, involved, and influenced in school settings. In 1997, Elias described SEL as a process of recognizing and managing emotions, establishing and maintaining positive interpersonal relationships, identifying and appreciating multiple perspectives, setting and pursuing positive goals, making responsible decisions, and effectively managing interpersonal conflicts. Essentially, SEL is a framework to learn prosocial skills to succeed in relationships and life that traditionally are not explicitly taught in schools. SEL is considered one of the most well-researched and supported Tier 1 approaches (Elias et al., 2021).

Foundational elements. The Collaborative for Academic, Social, and Emotional Learning (CASEL.org), an organization that aims to advance the development of academic, social, and emotional competence for all students, redefined the goal of SEL as fostering the development of five key skills. These are *self-awareness* (knowing one's strengths and limitations), *self-management* (remaining in control of one's emotions while facing challenges), *social awareness* (understanding the emotional states of others and empathizing with them), *relationship skills* (being able to work with others and manage interpersonal conflicts), and *responsible decision-making* (making choices that ensure safety and ethical behavior. Thus, simply stated, SEL is an umbrella term that applies to preventive efforts associated with enhancing students' learning and reducing emotional and behavioral problems (CASEL.org). In no way does it proselytize or indoctrinate students. In fact, SEL does just the opposite—it teaches students skills that make them more autonomous and interpersonally effective on their own terms by better controlling their thoughts, feelings, and behaviors.

Benefits of SEL. Overall, the implementation of SEL has been associated with positive student outcomes and has no drawbacks. It is associated with improvements in students' emotional well-being and school performance. In contrast, a failure to achieve competence in SEL's key domains is associated with impairment in academic, social, and family functioning (Greenberg et al., 2003). To date, the best summary of research on SEL is a meta-analysis by Durlak et al. (2011). In this study, the researchers investigated 213 school-based SEL programs that included 270,034 K–12 students. Study results indicated that SEL programs were effective at all educational levels assessed (e.g., elementary, middle, high school) and across the different types of communities in which they were implemented (e.g., urban, suburban, rural). Moreover, as a testament to the important link between the development of social-emotional competence and academic achievement, students participating in SEL programs displayed an 11-percentile-point gain in academic achievement as well as improvements in social-emotional skills, attitudes about school, and school behavior compared to students in control schools that did not have SEL in place. This truly is a remarkable finding. Even interventions that directly try to increase academic achievement by this magnitude often fail. A student with the skills they need to maintain their mental health is a student who is primed and ready to learn.

Programs and practices. Well-designed SEL programs are grounded in solid theory, have empirical support, and involve developmentally appropriate directions and instructional techniques. Essentially, these programs encourage students to learn, apply, and generalize the skills they acquire across multiple settings (CASEL.org). Furthermore, Macklem (2014) writes that the acronym "SAFE" can be used to inform educators about what makes for an effective and empirically supported SEL program: S = sequenced set of activities, A = active listening, F = focus on developing personal and social skills, and E = explicit targeting of skills.

Researchers have conducted empirical studies to evaluate the effectiveness of specific SEL programs. These include the Caring School Community Program (Battistich et al., 2004), the I Can Problem Solve Program (Boyle & Hassett-Walker, 2008), the Promoting Alternative Thinking Strategies Program (Bierman et al., 2010), and the Social Decision-Making and Problem-Solving Program (Elias, 1991). Currently, there is an increasing emphasis on ensuring that SEL is more culturally responsive. This is well-intentioned and needed. Perhaps McCallops et al. (2019) opened this door most fully with their review of research. To date, according to their review, SEL literature does not incorporate

TABLE 7.1 Selected Social-Emotional Learning Programs that Have Empirical Support

Program	Grade Level	Brief Description	Developers
Caring School Community	Elementary Middle	A program that builds classroom and school-wide communities while developing students' social and emotional skills and competencies.	Developmental Studies Center (DSC)
I Can Problem Solve	Preschool Elementary Middle	A universal school-based program designed to enhance interpersonal cognitive processes and problem-solving skills.	Shure 2001
Promoting Alternative Thinking Strategies	Preschool Elementary Middle	A program that helps students resolve conflicts, peacefully handle emotions, positively empathize, and make responsible decisions.	Channing Bete Company
Second Step	Preschool Elementary Middle	A program that helps reduce school violence and improve social-emotional skills in students.	Committee for Children
Incredible Years	Elementary Middle	A developmentally based risk factor reduction program that targets parents, teachers, and children.	Incredible Years, Inc.
Al's Pals/The Wingspan Approach	Preschool Elementary	A program that aims to develop children's social-emotional skills, problem-solving abilities, and healthy decision-making.	Wingspan, LLC.
Interpersonal Cognitive Problem Solving	Elementary	A curriculum that focuses on effective social skill development.	Shure, 2001
Responsive Classroom	Elementary	A program that aims to facilitate the development of social, emotional, and academic skills.	Northeast Foundation for Children
Steps to Respect	Elementary Middle	A program that teaches children how to make friends; recognize feelings; recognize, refuse, and report bullying.	Committee for Children
Lions Quest	Elementary Middle High	A program that promotes SEL, character education, bullying prevention, drug awareness, and service-learning.	Lions Clubs International Foundation

Adapted from Sulkowski and Lazarus (2017).

the effects of discrimination on socio-emotional development or functioning. Thus, further work is needed to address this omission. Table 7.1 provides more information on SEL programs.

Leadership in action. To get started, leaders can visit CASEL. org. This website has information on selecting a program most suitable to a specific school or district and implementing high-quality programs. It also has a program guide, videos, lesson plans, and other materials to help guide leaders throughout the selection and implementation process.

Currently, the program guide lists 86 programs that apply to schools. To be considered for inclusion in the guide, programs must be universal, that is, for all enrolled students, delivered during the regular school day, and designed for Pre-K–12th grade students. Programs must also have written documentation that provides evidence that their approach promotes students' social and emotional development. Moreover, the program must provide guidance and detail to ensure consistency and quality for implementation. Lastly, the program must be developmentally appropriate and provide rigorous documentation regarding its effectiveness, which must include one high-quality evaluation with a comparison group.

The guide continues to be updated, and in 2020, new features were added. These are: 1) inclusion of strategies that directly support educational equity, 2) a greater emphasis on student voice, 3) a strategic focus on the importance of promoting and assessing students' connection to school (e.g., engagement, belonging, climate), and 4) inclusion of strategies offered by each program at the classroom, school, family, and community levels. These new features are totally consistent with the approach espoused in this book. Due to the new focus on equity and student voice in SEL programs, these features may prove promising in addressing issues related to discrimination's impact against marginalized and minoritized groups.

School leaders, after consulting with the SEL guide and after selecting an approach or a program, can also capitalize on the benefits of SEL by doing the following: 1) infusing SEL in teaching practices; 2) infusing SEL into the academic curriculum; 3) creating organizational structures and policies that support students' social and emotional development; and 4) directly teaching SEL in free-standing lessons while ensuring that the SEL approach (or program) fits the culture of the student population (CASEL.org; Sulkowski & Lazarus, 2017). For example, adopting an approach for a community with a large southeast Asian community would be different from one selected for a majority rural Midwest community. Moreover, a combination of these approaches can be applied. At the middle- or high-school level, SEL can be implemented as has been discussed. However, it can also take place through character education, health promotion classes, or through targeted approaches that focus on violence prevention, substance use, dropout prevention, or anger management.

Research also indicates that SEL yields the best outcomes when the skills are embedded into the day-to-day curriculum and relate to other school activities (Greenberg et al., 2003). In this regard, studies have also found that high-quality SEL implementation is necessary for ensuring successful outcomes—just adopting a program does not guarantee positive student outcomes. Thus, program implementation is an area where leaders can really shine. They can be involved in SEL training as well as ongoing support through coaching, consulting, and following up with stakeholders (CASEL.org). Additionally, school leaders can help ensure effective program implementation by setting high standards and allocating the necessary resources to program development, execution, and maintenance.

Tier 2

Tier 2 initiatives are scaffolded above a school mental health foundation and Tier 1 universal promotion and preventive efforts.

Although a comprehensive discussion of Tier 2 mental health initiatives is beyond the scope of this chapter, a few promising ones that are easy to implement in schools are included. These include small group interventions and mental health check-in/check-out (MH-CICO). However, prior to implementing Tier 2 mental health strategies, it is important to identify students who need and could benefit from them.

Consistent with the promotion-focused multi-tiered school mental health model introduced in Chapter 1, optimal candidates for Tier 2 support include students who have not responded adequately to universal or Tier 1 efforts, yet do not display critical concerns that warrant more intensive attention. Essentially, these at-risk students show signs of mental health problems, but these problems are not clinically significant. Typical estimates suggest this could be about 15% of the total student population. Common problems they may be experiencing include bereavement, social skills deficits, peer relational conflicts, and mood and anxiety concerns. Of course, depending on the composition of a school population, many other problems can be addressed through Tier 2 support. It is up to educational leaders (such as school counselors and psychologists) to decide who should be included.

Small group interventions. School-based small group interventions usually 1) include a handful (e.g., 3–6) of individuals experiencing similar problems or going through similar experiences; 2) have a trained group leader, coordinator, or counselor; 3) encourage participation and collaboration from all members; 4) have predetermined ground rules for participation (e.g., only one person speaks at a time); 5) never force members to share information they are uncomfortable discussing or not yet ready to disclose; and 6) require confidentiality of all group members (i.e., "what is shared with the group, stays with the group").

It is hard to determine how and why mental health-related small-group interventions work because of the heterogeneity of the problems students face and the diversity of characteristics shared among members. To complicate matters further, it typically is unclear what results in positive mental health outcomes associated with group participation. Is it the therapeutic approach (e.g., cognitive-behavioral therapy, solution-focused therapy, multicultural counseling)? Is it from feeling less alone by meeting and identifying with other individuals with similar issues? Is it from receiving social connection and support? Is it from learning coping skills and strategies? Is it from a combination of the former and other reasons? Despite ambiguity around the therapeutic mechanisms of small group interventions, they have become the mainstay of school counseling, and this underscores their utility as a Tier 2 mental health intervention. For more information on small group interventions, Keperling et al. (2017) provide a helpful guide entitled *Group Interventions in Schools: A Guide for Practitioners.*

Mental health check-in/check-out. The Individuals with Disabilities Educational Improvement Act (IDEIA, 2004) requires educational practices that are promotional, preventive, and positive. Additionally, it encourages multi-tiered systems of support consistent with the promotion-focused multi-tiered school mental health model. From this legislation came a push to identify Tier 2 interventions for students who do not respond to Tier 1 efforts, especially related to their behavior. Check-in/check-out (CICO) then gained popularity for addressing student behavior because of its relative ease of use and effectiveness (Filter et al., 2007). However, this Tier 2 intervention has recently been applied to support mental health in at-risk students (Sulkowski & Lazarus, 2017).

Mental health check-in/check-out (MH-CICO) builds on the typical CICO steps that have the student: 1) check in with a favored adult and pick up a daily behavior card; 2) ask a teacher for feedback on his or her behavior at the end of each class/block; 3) check out at the end of the day and receive a pre-determined reward if a daily goal is met; 4) take the behavior report card home to get parent/caregiver feedback and get the card signed;

and 5) return the signed card the next day while signing in. Thus, MH-CICO holds students accountable, but perhaps more importantly, it provides them with additional contact, support, and feedback from caring adults.

To address mental health concerns, MH-CICO can be tailored to focus more on students' social and emotional functioning and less on their behavior across the day. Thus, with this goal in mind, checking in can be an opportunity to make sure that the student's basic needs are met (e.g., did they have breakfast, sleep well enough, have hygienic supplies), as well as their physical safety and emotional needs (e.g., are they feeling depressed or suicidal? Do they feel safe at home? Do they need to see a counselor or therapist? Do they need to see the nurse for medication?). Thus, an ethic of care undergirds MH-CICO. This Tier 2 intervention allows at-risk students to receive more immediate and regular support to ensure that their mental health needs are being attended to and addressed. Some days MH-CICO may be a minimal "hello" and "goodbye" between a student and a trusted individual at school. However, on other days, MH-CICO can route students to needed support and resources such as counseling and crisis intervention to protect their mental health (Sulkowski & Michael, 2014). With that said, in contrast to traditional CICO, it is critically important for a crisis plan to accompany the intervention in case a student is suicidal or at risk for serious harm. Text Box 7.1 includes additional considerations for MH-CICO.

Text Box 7.1: Additional Considerations for Mental Health Check-in/Check-out (MH-CICO)

- ◆ Develop a safety or crisis plan that can easily and effectively be activated.
- ◆ Make sure that parents/caregivers are aware of the intervention and have contingencies at home if the student is in crisis.

206 ◆ The Mental Health Pillar

- Confirm that the MH-CICO adult at school is trusted and liked by the student.
- Establish that the MH-CICO adult at school is available every day and during the most important times of the day (typically before and after school) to meet with the student.
- Arrange for all needed resources to be available for students experiencing hardships like a crisis at home, residential instability, or homelessness, which may require such items as food, clothing, hygienic supplies, and bus passes.
- Communicate the plan to all key stakeholders (e.g., teachers, counselors, school psychologists, administrators, caregivers) are aware of the plan.
- Designate an alternate in case the MH-CICO adult is not available for whatever reason.
- Make extra time available for the student if they need to meet with a counselor or process something impacting their well-being.
- Use secondary reinforcers (e.g., snacks, toys, games) for good compliance with the plan.
- Keep a social worker or truancy officer on speed dial in case a student does not check in for several consecutive days.

Tier 3

The following chapter focuses on providing and delivering school-based mental health services in the form of crisis prevention and management and trauma-informed care. Therefore, it covers providing resources for individuals who need intensive resources and support—and they need this immediately. Therefore, they should not be thought of as students who did not respond to Tier 2 services and then need Tier 3 intervention. Instead, their needs should be addressed outside the promotion-focused multi-tiered school mental health model discussed in this chapter. However, this begs the question: "What should be done with students who need more than is available at Tier 2?"

Tier 3, or indicated interventions, typically are individually administered for the most at-risk students in a school population. These students usually comprise about 3–5% of the total school population, and they are vulnerable to experiencing long-term negative academic and life outcomes if their concerns are not addressed. However, as discussed at the beginning of the chapter, these percentages may be underestimated because of the mental health crisis that currently is afflicting school-aged populations due to the COVID-19 pandemic and other significant stressors.

Individualized Therapeutic Approaches

Individualized therapeutic approaches for addressing student mental health problems have been evolving to become increasingly evidence-based or grounded in research. Because they are time and resource-intensive and the students who receive these interventions display the most extensive risks and needs, they must be effective. To date, two therapeutic approaches that have overlapping components have received the most widespread application in school settings to help students with mental health problems at Tier 3. These include cognitive-behavioral therapy (CBT) and solution-focused therapy (SFT).

School-based CBT. The efficacy of CBT in treating a range of internalizing (e.g., depression, anxiety, social withdrawal) and externalizing (e.g., anger, impulsivity, aggression) mental health problems is widely established and uncontestable (for review see Kendall, 2011). However, its application in school settings has lagged far behind that in clinical settings, which is unfortunate because schools are where most youths receive mental health services (Sulkowski et al., 2011). Additionally, compared to clinical settings, delivering CBT at school provides some additional advantages such as improving access to children and families experiencing transportation and financial barriers, which includes millions.

TABLE 7.2 Core CBT Components, Specific Intervention Approaches, and Brief Intervention Description

Core CBT Components	Specific Intervention Approaches	Brief Intervention Descriptions
Emotional and physiological trigger reaction	Recognizing/understanding feelings and physiological triggers/precursors	Involves identifying feelings in oneself and others as well as physical triggers that influence negative moods
Relaxation training	Diaphragmatic breathing	Structured deep/belly breathing that helps produce a sense of calm
	Progressive muscle relaxation	Involves systematically tensing and releasing muscles to engender physiological release and feelings of relief
	Guided imagery	Involves imaging safe, enjoyable, or comfortable places to help calm distress in the moment
Mindfulness training	Cultivation practice	Involves finding gratitude, connection to others or a higher power, and seeing the "big picture"
	Acceptance	Accepting things that are unchangeable yet still cause frustration/distress as if they could be changed
Cognitive interventions	Thought records	Used to identify stimuli and situations that contribute to cognitive distortions as what happens after these thoughts
	Socratic questioning	In dialogue, a therapist challenges maladaptive thoughts and self-limiting beliefs
	Cognitive restructuring	Involves identifying and challenging cognitive distortions and maladaptive thoughts
Behavioral interventions	Exposure therapy	Involves being exposed to aversive, feared, or avoided stimuli and situations to habituate to the former through repetition
	Behavior modification	Principles include self-management, token economies, positive reinforcement, differential reinforcement, shaping, chaining, etc.

Adapted from Joyce-Beaulieu & Sulkowski (2020).

In a book entitled *Cognitive Behavioral Therapy in K–12 School Settings: A Practitioner's Workbook,* Joyce-Beaulieu and Sulkowski (2020) identify the following CBT components as being most applicable for school-based practice: 1) emotion and physiological trigger recognition; 2) emotion regulation and relaxation training; 3) mindfulness training; 4) cognitive interventions; and 5) behavioral interventions. Table 7.2 lists each core CBT component, specific intervention approaches, and brief intervention descriptions.

School-based SFT. A good body of research also supports the efficacy of SFT. This therapeutic approach is short-term, and goal focused. It incorporates positive psychology principles and practices and helps students make important changes to maladaptive behaviors or patterns by constructing solutions rather than focusing on problems. Essentially, SFT is a hope-driven, positive emotion eliciting, and future-oriented therapeutic approach that involves formulating, encouraging, motivating, achieving, and then sustaining desired behavioral change through identifying and achieving measurable goals. See *Solution-focused Counseling in Schools* by Murphy (2015) for more information on school-based SFT.

Delivering CBT and SFT requires training in mental health service delivery, which limits the ability of all educational leaders to deliver these services directly; however, they should know the people in their building or district with such training. This requires educational leaders to keep up-to-date referral lists and sources to expeditiously connect at-risk students with mental health professionals. Moreover, consistent with the promotion and prevention theme of the chapter, it is important for leaders to collaborate with their mental health colleagues—not just to coordinate Tier 3 services—with all universal and selected support and service initiatives. Moreover, for particularly serious or dangerous situations, such as when students are suicidal or threatening the school community, educational leaders must rely on experienced mental health professionals and SRO's or other police officers to protect student safety and coordinate out-of-school services such as emergency hospitalizations. School leaders must establish these relationships well before the occurrence of a mental health crisis. Yet again, the sage words of Benjamin Franklin are apropos.

Conclusion

School-aged students are currently suffering from an unprecedented mental health crisis (AAP, 2021). Millions of students are experiencing overwhelming feelings of depression, anxiety, and other mental health problems, which have only been exacerbated by the COVID-19 pandemic (St. George & Strauss, 2022). Essentially, this crisis is a public health disaster requiring a public health approach to supporting students. In this vein and following a promotional and preventive school-based multi-tiered framework, this chapter discusses practical promotional strategies and a preventive mental health model. At the promotional level and at Tier 1, this model includes positive psychology and SEL. At Tier 2, small group interventions and MH-CICO are discussed; and lastly, CBT and SFT are presented as Tier 3 mental health interventions. Despite the staggering challenges contemporary school-aged youth face, school leaders have a dynamic array of promising options to support students' mental health.

Note

1 A meta-analysis is a type of statistical analysis that aims to compare and contrast results from different studies to identify patterns among study results. Through using this approach, sources of disagreement among results can be understood and contextualized. In addition, use of meta-analytic techniques can elucidate other interesting relationships or patterns that can be established within the context of multiple studies.

References

Allen, K. A., Furlong, M. J., Vella- Broderick, D., & Suldo, S. M. (2022). *Handbook of positive psychology in schools: Supporting process and practice* (3rd ed.), Routledge.

American Academy of Pediatrics (2021). *AAP, AACAP, CHA declare national emergency in children's mental health.* Author. https://publications.aap.org/aapnews/news/17718

Battistich, V., Schaps, E., & Wilson, N. (2004). Effects of an elementary school intervention on students' "connectedness" to school and social adjustment during middle school. *Journal of Primary Prevention, 24,* 243–262.

Bierman, K. L., Coie, J. D., Dodge, K. A., Greenberg, M. T., Lochman, J. E., McMahon, R. J., & Pinderhughes, E. (2010). The effects of a multiyear universal social–emotional learning program: The role of student and school characteristics. *Journal of Consulting and Clinical Psychology, 78*(2), 156–168. https://doi.org/10.1037/a0018607

Bolier, L., Haverman, M., Westerhof, G. J., Riper, H., Smit, F., & Bohlmeijer, E. (2013). Positive psychology interventions: A meta-analysis of randomized controlled studies. *BMC Public Health, 13,* 119–139. doi:10.1186/1471-2458-13-119

Boyle, D., & Hassett-Walker, C. (2008). Reducing overt and relational aggression among young children: The results from a two-year outcome evaluation. *Journal of School Violence, 7,* 27–42.

Cain Miller, C., & Pallaro, B. (2022, May 29). 362 school counselors on the pandemic's effect on children: 'Anxiety is filling our kids'. *New York Times.* https://www.nytimes.com/interactive/2022/05/29/upshot/pandemic-school-counselors.html

CBS news 60 minutes (2022, September 4). American kids in a mental health crisis. https://www.cbsnews.com/video/american-kids-in-a-mental-health-crisis-sunday-on-60-minutes/

Davis, A., Bastien, R., & Lazarus, P. J. (2022, February). *Suicide among Black girls: Addressing the growing mental health crisis.* A poster presented at the annual convention of the National Association of School Psychologists. Boston, MA.

Durlak, J. A., Weissberg, R. P., Dymnicki, A. B., Taylor, R. D., & Schellinger, K. B. (2011). The impact of enhancing students' social and emotional learning: A meta-analysis of school-based universal interventions. *Child Development, 82*, 405–432. doi: 10.1111/j.1467-8624.2010.01564.x

Elias, M. J. (1991). An action research approach to evaluating the impact of a social decision-making and problem-solving curriculum for preventing behavior and academic dysfunction in children. *Evaluation and Program Planning, 14*, 397–401.

Elias, M. J., Powlo, E. R., Lorenzo, A., & Eichert, B. (2021). Adopting a trauma-informed approach to Social-Emotional Learning. In P. J. Lazarus, S. Suldo, & B. Doll (Eds.), *Fostering the emotional well-being of our youth: A school-based approach* (pp. 96–116). Oxford University Press. doi: 10.1093/med-psych/9780190918873.003.006

Elias, M. J., Zins, J. E., Weissberg, R. P., Frey, K. S., Greenberg, M. T., Haynes, N. M . . . Shriver, T. P. (1997). *Promoting social and emotional learning: Guidelines for educators.* Danvers, MA: ASCD.

Filter, K. J., McKenna, M. K., Benedict, E. A., Horner, R. H., Todd, A., & Watson, J. (2007). Check in/check out: A post-hoc evaluation of an efficient, secondary-level targeted intervention for reducing problem behaviors in schools. *Education and Treatment of Children, 30*(1), 69–84.

Froh, J., Yurkewicz, C., & Kashdan, T. (2009). Gratitude and subjective well-being in early adolescence: Examining mechanisms and gender differences. *Journal of Adolescence, 32*, 633–650.

Greenberg, M. T., Weissberg, R. P., O'Brien, M. U., Zins, J. E., Fredericks, L., Resnik, H., & Elias, M. J. (2003). Enhancing school-based prevention and youth development through coordinated social, emotional, and academic learning. *American Psychologist, 58*, 466–474. doi: 10.1037/0003-066X.58.6-7.466

Individuals With Disabilities Education Improvement Act of 2004, Pub. L. No. 108–446.

Institute for Education Sciences (IES) School Pulse Panel (2022). Mental health and well-being of students and staff during the pandemic. https://ies.ed.gov/schoolsurvey/spp/SPP_April_Infographic_Mental_Health_and_Well_Being.pdf

Joyce-Beaulieu, D., & Sulkowski, M. L. (2020). *Cognitive behavioral therapy in K–12 school settings: A practitioner's workbook.* Springer Publishing Company.

Kendall, P. C. (2011). *Child and adolescent therapy: Cognitive-behavioral procedures,* (4th ed.). Guilford Publications.

Keperling, J. P., Reinke, W. M., Marchese, D., & Ialongo, N. (2017). *Group interventions in schools: A guide for practitioners.* Guilford Publications.

Koh, H. K., Geller, A. C., & VanderWeele, T. J. (2021). Deaths from COVID-19. *JAMA, 325*(2), 133–134.

Lazarus, P. J., & Costa (2021). Teaching emotional self-regulation to children and adolescents. In P. J. Lazarus, S. Suldo, & B. Doll (Eds.), *Fostering the emotional well-being of our youth: A school-based approach* (pp. 264–337). Oxford University Press. doi: 10.1093/med-psych/9780190918873.003.0014

Linley, P. A., Joseph, S., Harrington, S., & Wood, A. M. (2006). Positive psychology: Past, present, and (possible) future. *The Journal of Positive Psychology, 1,* 3–16. doi: http://dx.doi.org.ezproxy.fiu.edu/10.1080/17439760500372796

Lyubomirsky S., & Sheldon, K. M., & Schkade, D. (2005). Pursuing happiness: The architecture of sustainable change. *Review of General Psychology, 9,* 111–131. doi:10.1037/1089-2680.9.2111

Macklem, G. L. (2014). *Preventive mental health at school.* Springer.

McCallops, K., Barnes, T. N., Berte, I., Fenniman, J., Jones, I., Navon, R., & Nelson, M. (2019). Incorporating culturally responsive pedagogy within social-emotional learning interventions in urban schools: An international systematic review. *International Journal of Educational Research, 94,* 11–28. https://doi.org/10.1016/j.ijer.2019.02.007

Miller, D. N., Nickerson, A. B., & Jimerson, S. R. (2014). Positive psychological interventions in U.S. schools: A public health approach to internalizing and externalizing problems. In M. J. Furlong, R. Gilman, & E. S. Huebner (Eds.), *Handbook of positive psychology in schools* (2nd ed.) (pp. 478–494). Routledge.

Molony, T. M., Hilbold, M., & Smith, N. D. (2014). Best practices in applying positive psychology in schools. In P. L. Harrison, & A. Thomas (Eds.), *Best practices in school psychology: Student-level services* (pp. 199–212). NASP.

Murphy, J. J. (2015). *Solution-focused counseling in schools* (3rd ed.). American Counseling Association.

National Council for Mental Well Being (n.d.) *Youth mental health first aid.* https://www.mentalhealthfirstaid.org/wp-content/uploads/2022/07/22.06.17_Youth-MHFA-Flier.pdf

Park, N., & Peterson, C. (2009). Strengths of character in schools. In R. Gilman, E. S. Huebner, & M. J. Furlong (Eds.), *Handbook of positive psychology in schools.* (pp. 65–76). Routledge.

Peterson, C., & Seligman. M. E. P. (2004). *Character strengths and virtues: A handbook and classification.* Oxford University Press.

Radhakrishnan, L. (2022). Pediatric emergency department visits associated with mental health conditions before and during the COVID-19 Pandemic—United States, January 2019–January 2022. *MMWR. Morbidity and Mortality Weekly Report, 71.*

Seligman, M. E. P. (2002). Positive psychology, positive prevention, and positive therapy. In C. R. Snyder, & S. J. Lopez (Eds.), *Handbook of positive psychology*, (pp. 3–9). Oxford University Press.

Seligman, M. E., Ernst, R. M., Gillham, J., Reivich, K., & Linkins, M. (2009). Positive education: Positive psychology and classroom interventions. *Oxford Review of Education, 35,* 293–311.

Shankland R., & Rosset, E. (2017). Review of brief school-based psychological interventions: A taster for teachers and educators. *Educational Psychology Review, 29*(2), 363–392.

Shure, M. B. (2001). I can problem solve (ICPS): An interpersonal cognitive problem-solving program for children. *Residential Treatment for Children & Youth, 18*(3), 3–14.

St. George, D., & Strauss, V. (2022, December 5). The crisis of student mental health is much vaster than we realize. *Washington Post.* https://www.washingtonpost.com/education/2022/12/05/crisis-student-mental-health-is-much-vaster-than-we-realize/

Suldo, S. M. (2013, October 30). *Positive people & positive practices: Insights from the field of positive psychology.* Presentation at the FASP Annual Conference, Omni Resort, Orlando, FL. PowerPoint presentation flash-drive obtained at FASP Conference.

Suldo, S. M. (2016). *Promoting student happiness: Positive psychology interventions in schools.* Guilford Press.

Suldo, S. M., Mariano, J. M., & Gilfix, H. (2021). Promoting students' positive emotions, character, and purpose. In P. J. Lazarus,

S. Suldo, & B. Doll (Eds.), *Fostering the emotional well-being of our youth: A school- based approach* (pp. 282–312). Oxford University Press. doi: 10.1093/med-psych/9780190918873.003.0015

Sulkowski, M. L., & Lazarus, P. J. (2017). *Creating safe and supportive schools and fostering students' mental health*. Routledge.

Sulkowski, M. L., & Michael, K. (2014). Meeting the mental health needs of homeless students in schools: A multi-tiered system of support framework. *Children and Youth Services Review, 44,* 145–151. https://doi.org/10.1016/j.childyouth.2014.06.014

Sulkowski, M. L., Wingfield, R. J., Jones, D., & Coulter, W. A. (2011). Response to intervention and interdisciplinary collaboration: Joining hands to support children's healthy development. *Journal of Applied School Psychology, 27*(2), 118–133. https://doi.org/10.1080/15377903.2011.565264

Twenge, J. M. (2020). Why increases in adolescent depression may be linked to the technological environment. *Current Opinion in Psychology, 32,* 89–94.

U.S. Department of Health and Human Services (2021). *Protecting youth mental health: The U. S. Surgeon General's Advisory.* Author. https://www.hhs.gov/sites/default/files/surgeon-general-youth-mental-health-advisory.pdf

Wood, A. M., Linley, P. A., Maltby, J., Kashdan, T. B., & Hurling, R. (2011). Using personal and psychological strengths leads to increases in well-being over time: A longitudinal study and the development of the strengths use questionnaire. *Personality and Individual Differences, 50,* 15–19.

8

Crisis Recovery and Advocacy

Strong leadership is often most apparent during a crisis or following a disaster. Often, before a crisis, leadership potential is latent or maybe even unknown. Thus, in the same way, that adversity tests people's mettle, crisis events test the resilience of educational leaders and school systems. Ironically, despite the unanticipated distress, pain, and devastation, a crisis can also be an opportunity for educational leaders to help their school communities recover and advocate for positive change and better policies and practices to protect students and foster their mental health.

This chapter completes the book by weaving together overlapping yet distinct topics about school crisis response, trauma-informed care, and advocacy. These topics encourage educational leaders to dig down and be their best selves during difficult times when others are overwhelmed, decompensating, or traumatized. Even though this is not easy work, crisis response and disaster recovery can be immeasurably rewarding and the apogee of effective leadership. This work also aligns with the Three Pillar Model for creating safe and supportive schools

DOI: 10.4324/9780429261527-11

and fostering students' mental health. Thus, crisis response and disaster recovery are not separate from ensuring safe, supportive, and emotionally healthy schools—it is an extension of this aim for educational communities afflicted by adversity.

Large-Scale Disaster Response

This section discusses three major types of large-scale disasters or crises—school shootings, natural disasters, and the COVID-19 pandemic—with implications for necessary action to be taken by school leaders.

Impacts of Crises

All crises have unique characteristics and affect individuals in different ways. Some individuals will struggle to cope in the aftermath of a crisis, while others will be relatively unaffected. Rates of post-traumatic stress disorder (PTSD) following crisis events are highly variable. According to a meta-analysis that examined 72 peer-reviewed studies, 16% of crisis victims developed PTSD (Alisic et al., 2014).

The variability in developing PTSD following trauma is due to the myriad of contextual factors. Some include physical and emotional proximity to the event, trauma history, types of loss experienced, the extensiveness of the injuries sustained, and the actual experience of significant injury or death of friends or loved ones (Sulkowski & Lazarus, 2017). Trauma or PTSD risk is also modulated by feelings of helplessness and the fear of death or dying during the crisis. Moreover, disrupted family functioning, separation from parents after the event, and ongoing family impairment associated with the crisis increase trauma risk. Considering these and numerous other contextual factors, a rule of thumb for educational leaders to follow in the aftermath of a crisis is the 20/60/20 heuristic. This heuristic suggests that 20% of individuals will be seriously affected in a large-scale crisis,

60% will be moderately affected, and 20% will be relatively unaffected (Lazarus et al., 2005).

Crisis Response

All schools must prepare for crisis events. Brock (2013) argues that "it is not a matter of if, but rather when a school will be required to respond to a crisis" (p. 19). Although this task may seem daunting, school leaders can develop plans and policies that reduce the devastation associated with crises and disasters and foster healthy post-crisis recovery (Lazarus & Sulkowski, 2010; Sulkowski & Lazarus, 2013). Thus, school crisis prevention and response should be central to every school leader's plan for creating safe schools and fostering students' mental health.

Preparing for a crisis. Current approaches to school crisis response have been shaped by both successful and unsuccessful crisis response efforts. Thus, school crisis prevention strategies have been mainly influenced by what has been learned from large-scale crisis response and management efforts. From this bank of knowledge, the U.S. Department of Homeland Security's Incident Command System (ICS) has structured crisis response and management around the different roles of various school leaders. These individuals include command members (i.e., trained senior leaders), thinkers (i.e., planners), doers (i.e., operators), getters (i.e., logistics managers), payers (i.e., financers), and general staff such as medical support personnel (e.g., nurses), school-based mental health professionals (e.g., school psychologists, counselors, social workers), security personnel (e.g., school resource officers, school security officers), and school service/maintenance staff (e.g., food service staff, janitorial staff). Figure 8.1 presents the U.S. Department of Homeland Security's ICS.

Crisis response teams. Obtaining administrative support is vital for establishing crisis response teams; these individuals should be primary team leaders. However, they also must empower other educational leaders involved with crisis response. Crisis response teams should generally include individuals who

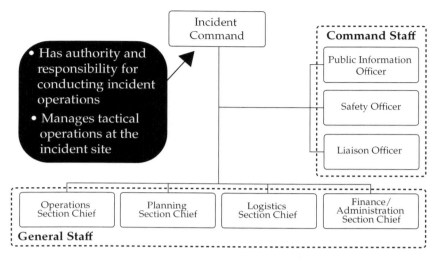

FIGURE 8.1 The U.S. Department of Homeland Security's Incident Command System

know the school culture and climate well and have connections to the district administration and community partners such as emergency first responders. This is especially true for responding to large-scale disasters and crisis events.

For large-scale events such as school shootings and significant natural disasters, crisis response teams should designate school leaders in roles following the U.S. Department of Homeland Security's ICS. Therefore, at a minimum, teams need an incident commander, an operations section chief, a planning section chief, a logistics section chief, and a finance/administration section chief (Reeves et al., 2012). The incident commander is the person who is ultimately in charge and is most directly responsible for crisis response efforts. This individual must have leadership skills and manage people effectively in stressful settings. Command staff members take orders from the incident commander under the ICS model but also function autonomously in their respective roles. For example, a school administrator might serve as the incident commander and lead the rest of the team, whereas a school psychologist works individually with crisis victims. Their roles are complementary yet distinct.

Crisis response plans. Crisis response plans and initiatives must be developed for a range of crises that vary in scope, magnitude, and duration. Following recommendations by Brock et al. (2009), leaders must determine who should be involved in crisis response at different hierarchical levels, including at the school building, district, and regional levels. This ultimately involves having crisis plans before an event that delineates who is involved and what roles they will fulfill. Furthermore, these plans should designate alternative leaders who can execute the plan in case a key team member is unavailable or compromised by the disaster.

Crisis management plans must include forward-thinking preparedness protocols. These include visitor sign-in, crisis exercises/drills, student evacuation and assembly, student accounting and caregiver reunification, communications, and media relations (Sulkowski & Lazarus, 2017). Text Box 8.1 lists key considerations for each element above as part of a crisis management plan that is especially relevant to school shootings. Because each crisis presents unique challenges, school leaders must be regularly educated and trained to handle the circumstances influencing the crisis, its fallout, and the recovery process. The specifics of each crisis will require decisions regarding the nature and scope of the response.

Text Box 8.1: Key Considerations for Crisis Response Plans

Visitor Sign-in

- Make sure that members of school communities are quickly and easily identified.
- Create badges for school visitors.
- Scan driver's licenses and other official IDs.
- Take photos of new school visitors and store pictures safely.
- Collect signatures from students and caregivers when students sign out early.

222 ◆ The Mental Health Pillar

- ◆ Have sign-in only occur at one location at the school.
- ◆ Set up notification systems or alerts in case an unknown, hostile, or threatening individual enters the school.
- ◆ Minimize contact points to ensure school safety and reduce the spread of diseases.

Crisis Exercises and Drills

- ◆ Provide a detailed orientation for all involved team members.
- ◆ Train regularly to improve the knowledge and efficiency of all crisis team members.
- ◆ Include tabletop exercises and discussion-based exercises.
- ◆ Run exercises with alternative team members and educators involved.
- ◆ Do not implement any practices that may trigger trauma reactions in students or staff. Ensure everyone knows *ahead of time* that this is a practice and *not* a real event—Announce "THIS IS A DRILL!"
- ◆ Exercises and drills should never be mistaken for a real event.
- ◆ Exercises and drills should be part of a broader long-term school safety and security plan.
- ◆ Exercises and drills should follow protocols from the National Incident Management System's Incident Command System and activate an Emergency Operations Center.
- ◆ Include a debriefing after the exercises and drills are conducted.

Student Evacuation and Assembly

- ◆ Multiple plans should be devised for different-sized crisis events.
- ◆ Evacuation locations (e.g., different schools, libraries, fire stations, and churches) must be thoroughly briefed and prepared.
- ◆ Plans should be regularly reviewed, practiced, and revised.
- ◆ Students with disabilities must be considered in plans.
- ◆ Essential resources (e.g., food, water, appropriate clothing) must be available.

The assembly location must be safe, secure, organized, and accessible by relevant parties.

Key community partners (e.g., first responders) must be aware of all evacuation and assembly procedures.

Students, educators, and school staff should be protected from potentially harmful outside influences during evacuations and assemblies.

Student Accounting and Caregiver Reunification

Attendance records must be always accessible.

Attendance information should be accessible in multiple formats (e.g., electronically, written down on physical logs).

Clear communication is needed about any missing or harmed students or staff.

Social media should only be used to provide concrete and factual information to prevent the spread of rumors, falsehoods, and misinformation.

Students and staff should be discouraged from the excessive use of their cell phones and social media so they can appropriately follow accounting and reunification procedures.

Reunification must follow an orderly plan that ensures that all students and staff are accounted for and documented.

School leaders and emergency responders should make sure that reunification occurs systematically, and that the area does not become clogged with traffic and concerned individuals who could hobble the accounting and reunification process.

Caregivers should be provided with regular updates on the accounting and reunification process as it evolves.

Communication

A single voice or platform should coordinate public communication to reduce the spread of rumors or misinformation.

Multiple modes and channels of communication (e.g., emergency warning systems, text messaging, tweets, email, landlines, walkie-talkies, K–12 Alerts, reverse 9–1-1 calling systems) must be built into crisis plans as one or two could be compromised during a crisis.

♦ Aside from quick safety check-ins, social media posts and digital message use should be discouraged.

♦ Credible school leaders should be the "face" of public statements as the crisis response evolves.

♦ Misinformation, rumors, or falsehoods must be quickly and efficiently addressed by a credible source to prevent panic or other problems.

♦ Toxic rumors and conspiracy theories should be promptly dismissed with factual information and not overly indulged.

♦ Crisis-related communication templates should be developed in advance so they can quickly be modified and employed during a crisis.

Media

♦ Only leaders trained in media relations should address media for statements and interviews.

♦ Students and staff should be protected from giving statements and interviews during a crisis.

♦ Media should have a staging area where they do not interfere with the crisis response process.

♦ Members of school communities should be prepared for media requests after an acute crisis ends through interview requests, emails, or digital messages on social media.

♦ School leaders should develop templates for replying to media requests that can speak for most of the school community.

Crisis Response Procedures

Consistent with the goal of crisis prevention, school leaders must also develop crisis response procedures and preparedness plans.

This often involves planning to (a) assess crises, (b) identify and assist crisis victims, (c) implement crisis intervention services, (d) triage these services, (e) refer to outside agencies and providers as needed, and (f) debrief and evaluate the crisis response (Brock, 2013).

Assessing crises. The first step in assessing a crisis is determining who is immediately at risk, how pervasive it is, and how it will impact the school community. The incident commander or the crisis team's primary leader must make these determinations and then communicate the expected impact to other crisis response team members and district personnel. Similarly, the incident commander must also determine the level of response that likely will be needed to address a crisis. Some crises can be managed effectively at the building level by utilizing members of the crisis response teams. In contrast, other crises require response services from outside agencies, school districts, or community personnel. Lastly, widespread crises that impact a community or region will require response services from external agencies (or even state and federal organizations) such as the American Red Cross or the Federal Emergency Management Agency (FEMA).

Identifying victims. In the aftermath of a crisis or disaster, it is relatively easy to identify students who sustained physical injuries. Yet, identifying students who have been psychologically injured is often challenging. According to Brock (2013), the most critical factor determining the degree of psychological distress or trauma a student will experience during a crisis is their immediate proximity to the crisis event. Proximity might involve being personally close to the crisis and seeing victims or fearing for security. However, it also might include having close relationships with others impacted or threatened. To ensure that crisis victims are accurately identified, school crisis team leaders should educate all members of school communities on the signs that a student may be experiencing post-crisis distress. Text Box 8.2 lists factors that place students at risk of having an adverse outcome associated with crisis exposure.

Text Box 8.2: Factors that Place Students at High Risk

Individual Crisis Experience Factors During the Event

Close to the crisis event
Long exposure to the crisis event
Close relationship with victim(s)
Individual was injured during the crisis
High perceived threat. That is, the individual thought he or she might die or be seriously injured during the crisis.
Initial response was severe (e.g., panic, shock, disassociation)
Suffers significant losses

Individual Crisis Responses After the Event

Over time the individual does not emotionally self-regulate their feelings or thoughts
Has suicidal thoughts or engages in suicidal or self-destructive behaviors
Attempts self-medication (e.g., alcohol, drugs, or prescription medication)
Experiences symptoms related to depression, anxiety, PTSD
Significant negative changes in behavior
Withdrawal from social interaction

Vulnerability Factors within the Family

Parental incarceration
Family dysfunction
Ineffective or uncaring parenting
Not living with nuclear family
Parental mental illness
Child abuse or maltreatment
Lack of financial resources
Lack of social support or social resources
Family displacement following crisis
Family suffers significant losses

Vulnerability Factors within the Individual

External locus of control
Preexisting mental illness
Low developmental level
Ineffective or avoidant coping skills
Poor emotional self-regulation
Low self-esteem
History of prior traumatization
Previously suffered recent or multiple losses

Adapted from Brock (2002).

Crisis intervention services. Critical decisions must be made about what services will be delivered to identified crisis victims. If there are many victims, services must be triaged to students with the most significant needs (Sulkowski & Lazarus, 2013). This may include students in shock, displaying signs of acute psychiatric symptoms, or feeling overwhelmed by severe anxiety and distress. After this, students experiencing more general and less severe adjustment problems in the aftermath of the crisis should be assisted. Further, students who display more severe issues than many school-based mental health professionals are accustomed to handling need to be referred to community-based specialists.

Evaluate and debrief. Despite being harmful and disruptive, crises also provide opportunities for learning and growth. Considering this, leaders of crisis response teams should review crisis management plans and procedures following a crisis to determine areas for further refinement and improvement. A debriefing should occur daily during an ongoing crisis to ensure everyone is on the same page. As part of this process, team members can discuss (a) what went well and what did not, (b) plans for the following day, (c) who is at high risk and needs to be seen or referred (which may also include faculty and staff), and (d) the emotional reactions of team members (Sulkowski & Lazarus, 2017). A crucial yet often overlooked aspect of crisis response involves ensuring that crisis response team members feel supported throughout the response and afterward. This is especially important during crises of long duration because the ongoing stress of dealing with the emotional pain of victims can cause feelings of burnout among crisis responders and team leaders. A balanced approach to crisis recovery—for all affected members—is key to reestablishing a sense of normality at school, healing, and future growth as the effects of the crisis abate in acute intensity.

Instilling and inspiring hope. In 2007, an international and interdisciplinary panel of experts was convened to find a consensus on effective intervention principles for individuals impacted by a crisis (see Hobfoll et al., 2007). This group identified five principles that had empirical support for influencing individual outcomes after a crisis or disaster: 1) promoting a sense of safety; 2) promoting calming; 3) promoting a sense of self and collective efficacy; 4) promoting connectedness; and 5) promoting hope. Text Box 8.3 lists a few selected intervention strategies that leaders can use for each of the five principles related to crisis response. Some of these have been discussed in more depth in previous chapters; however, what warrants further discussion is promoting hope.

Text Box 8.3: Interventions Based on the Five Essential Elements of Crisis Response

Element	Suggestions for Interventions
Promoting a sense of safety	◆ Ensure and reassure students of their safety ◆ Share accurate, up-to-date information with students regarding the crisis ◆ Help students re-establish familiar routines ◆ Find balance between academic demands and social-emotional needs
Calming and supporting fearful individuals	◆ Identify trusted adults that students can seek for support when they are ready to talk about their experiences and emotions ◆ Teach positive coping actions (e.g., deep breathing, journaling, positive self-talk) ◆ Refer highly-impacted students to community agencies and mental health providers ◆ Reassure students that reactions to a crisis can be different for each person ◆ Normalize faculty and student reactions so that individuals do not feel like they are "going crazy"

Engendering a sense of self and collective efficacy	♦ Engage students in post-disaster, clean-up efforts when appropriate, if impacted by a natural disaster
	♦ Encourage volunteer opportunities with local community agencies
	♦ Involve students in collaborative group projects that help the community and each other
Increasing feelings of connectedness with others	♦ Build caring relationships with students and families
	♦ Use social media and related platforms to maintain ongoing connections with students and families
	♦ Provide highly impacted students the opportunity to check in regularly with a trusted adult or school mental health professional
	♦ Have students engage in helping their peers, as one of the best ways to help oneself is by helping others
Instilling and inspiring hope in victims	♦ Promote an optimistic outlook
	♦ Help students create attainable goals and discuss ways they can overcome challenges to achieve their goals
	♦ Engage students, if appropriate, in creating positive messages to share with family, friends, school staff, or other community members
	♦ Share stories of others who have successfully overcome similar challenges

Based on suggestions from Brymer et al., 2012; Lazarus & Costa, in press; Sulkowski & Lazarus, 2017; Zakrzewski, 2012.

When affected individuals heal in the aftermath of a crisis, they may find meaning and a purpose from the traumatic event. This is called post-traumatic growth. Individuals with favorable outcomes after experiencing a crisis tend to be optimistic, expect a positive future, and feel they have the skills to cope with the crisis (Brymer et al., 2012). In other words, they are hopeful about the future and their ability to handle adversity.

While trying to instill hope in crisis victims, school leaders must strike a delicate balance between validating crisis-related suffering and highlighting potential opportunities for personal, social, and emotional growth that can be derived post-crisis (Sulkowski & Lazarus, 2013). On the one hand, prematurely highlighting "silver linings" may be insensitive and invalidating to victims and may minimize the distress they are experiencing. On the other, sharing legitimate hope about the future is crucial to post-crisis recovery and adjustment (King & Miner, 2000). Thus, even if students are not ready to feel hopeful about the future, educational leaders can project an optimistic and grounded view of crisis recovery.

Helping Victims of Natural Disasters

In 2021, the Emergency Event Database (EM-DAT) recorded 432 natural disasters (2021_EMDAT_report.pdf). The year 2021 was marked by an increase in the number of disasters and economic losses from previous years. Five of the top ten economically costly disasters occurred in the U.S., resulting in a total economic cost of $112.5 billion. According to CoreLogic, a company that analyzes financial and property data, natural disasters impacted one in ten homes in the U.S. In 2017, in the United States alone, 1,762,103 people were affected by natural disasters (Centre for Research on the Epidemiology of Disasters [CRED], 2017). As a result, communities often experienced physical and emotional losses, displacement from everyday life, and relocation to shelters or relatives' homes (Felix et al., 2020; Lazarus & Costa, in press).

The associated outcomes that individuals and communities experience will also be impacted by the specific type and scope of the natural disaster (e.g., flood, fire, earthquake, tornado, hurricane, etc.). For example, the magnitude of a response will depend on the number of schools involved, such as one school impacted by a tornado in Kissimmee, FL, in contrast with an entire school district impacted by multiple losses of school buildings, as with Hurricane Katrina in New Orleans, LA.

Consequently, school leaders must ensure that their district has active crisis intervention plans to help students and families prepare for natural disasters and respond in the aftermath (Lazarus & Costa, in press). This is especially important as natural disasters have historically been associated with psychological sequelae and a decline in the mental health of those impacted (Jimerson et al., 2012). Children and youth may experience mood changes, heightened arousal, sleep disturbances, lack of concentration, and impaired social and academic functioning (Tang et al., 2018). Not only is development impacted, but children and youth's social-emotional health and the availability of social supports may also be negatively affected in the short and long term (Felix et al., 2020).

Following large-scale disasters, leaders, especially principals, can become emotionally and physically exhausted by the number of new tasks and responsibilities they must add to their daily calendar. They often take on the role of a social worker, psychologist, homeless liaison, shelter coordinator, pastor, and property clean-up specialist to coordinate the repair of their building if damaged. While leaders support their entire school community, they often need to support themselves. Thus, the district administrator should bring in extra principals or assistant principals to help manage the school's day-to-day functioning while dealing with the disaster's repercussions. Retired administrators who know the system are especially recommended for this role.

In the aftermath of a disaster, leaders must support their faculty, other school personnel, and students. Following a natural disaster, usual behavioral expectations and school rules can become compromised as schools reestablish new norms, and members of the school communities adjust. As such, school leaders must be flexible and realistic and make the necessary adjustments to campus and classroom operational protocol. For example, in August 2004, Hurricane Charlie, a category 4 hurricane, severely impacted a vast swath of land in Southwest Florida, including many schools in Hardee County School District in Wauchula, Florida. As a result, the school system was shut down for weeks. Several days before reopening, Dennis Jones, the District Superintendent, addressed his entire instructional staff of nearly 800 individuals. Excerpts of his heartfelt message follow:

> Until further notice, I am instituting the following measures. No homework will be given, for many of our students have no home in which to complete it. Attendance will be taken, but all absences and late arrivals will be excused. Cafeteria lunches will be free of charge for students and employees. There will be no fundraising activities since our community has been financially depleted. Lastly, I want each of you to focus on the social and emotional healing of our students at this critical time, not on preparing for high-stakes testing. (Zenere, 2005)

Moreover, the dress code was relaxed for both students and faculty because many individuals had lost all their clothing in the wake of the hurricane. Also, the schools became centers for increased community activities, as many other support sources were destroyed and had yet to be rebuilt. Text Box 8.4 lists various crisis interventions to support students, staff, and families following a natural disaster.

Text Box 8.4: Crisis Interventions Following a Natural Disaster to Support Students, Faculty, and Families

Actions to take prior to opening schools

- Establish effective means of communication as communication may be compromised.
- Immediately contact all members of the crisis response team so they can coordinate with school administrators to determine the level of response needed.
- Assess the damage from the natural disaster and make appropriate accommodations.
- Assess and address the survival and emotional needs of faculty and staff.
- Designate a spokesperson to provide information to the media.
- Identify staff needs and provide assistance (e.g., food, shelter, clothing, water, laundry, babysitting, transportation, pet sitting, legal advice, Employee Assistance Programs, etc.).
- Contact all families needing help (same as above).
- Coordinate with the homeless liaison.
- Provide critical information to families.
- Conduct staff trainings on such topics as (a) what has happened in the community, (b) common reactions of children, adolescents, and families, (c) how to identify students who may be at high risk, (d) how to proceed when school opens, (e) where and how students, families, and faculty can get help, (f) what to expect in the coming weeks and months, and (g) how to promote recovery.

Actions to take on the first day of school and beyond

- Do not expect to do school right away.
- Adjust academic demands.

234 ◆ The Mental Health Pillar

- ◆ Reach out to every student in the building.
- ◆ Conduct a group crisis intervention in each class.
- ◆ Engage in post-disaster activities that promote healing.
- ◆ Encourage creative instructional methods using lessons learned following the disaster.
- ◆ Secure all types of personnel and support as necessary (e.g., a second principal, substitute teachers, maintenance staff).
- ◆ Ensure adequate mental health support.
- ◆ Identify students who are at high risk and plan interventions.
- ◆ Debrief all members of the crisis response team.
- ◆ Practice self-care.

Source: Jimerson et al. (2012); Lazarus & Costa (in press); Lazarus et al. (2002).

Crisis Response and COVID-19

On March 11, 2020, the COVID-19 pandemic was declared a public health emergency (CDC COVID-19 Response Team, 2020). Shortly thereafter, school closures followed. During the 2019–20 school year, closures impacted at least 55.1 million students in 124,000 public and private schools across the United States (Wang et al., 2020). As a result of the pandemic, uncertainty abounded. Not only did students have to cope with remote learning, but they also had to deal with the fear that they or their family members would get ill or die. According to the CDC COVID Data Tracker, more than one million people have died from the virus in the U.S. alone, and more than 98 million have been infected (https://covid.cdc.gov/covid-data-tracker/?CDC_#datatracker-home). This was and continues to be the most prominent educational crisis that has impacted our nation.

Major crisis events, such as the COVID-19 pandemic, engender widespread anxiety, pain, and helplessness. At the outset, nobody knew how harmful the virus would be. Unfortunately, millions died worldwide, misinformation proliferated, and countless people became cynical about social institutions that struggled to adjust to the unknown. This chaos led to the distrust of well-respected institutions such as schools, hospitals, and the medical science establishment. This erosion in trust also created novel challenges for educational leaders, especially when conspiracy theories and quack cures—rather than science-based practice—entered the discourse and were amplified by bad actors. Decisions regarding opening schools, vaccines, and wearing masks became controversial and often made school board meetings highly contentious. This conflict created challenges for school leaders because a segment of the population did not support educational decisions and devalued the expertise of medical leaders.

The COVID-19 pandemic is similar to a natural disaster because it has caused continuing social disruption, financial insecurity, family challenges, and community disruption (Nickerson & Sulkowski, 2021). At-risk and vulnerable students are at the greatest risk for adverse outcomes associated with the pandemic (Condon et al., 2020; Meckler, 2022; Prime et al., 2020). However, the COVID-19 pandemic also differs from other crises because there is no recovery endpoint. Moreover, long COVID presents a unique challenge, and suffering and death will continue to happen worldwide.

Further, according to a study of 1,000 teachers and 957 principals in K–12 public schools in late April and early May of 2020, multiple factors limited the transition to distance learning, with the most common being students' lack of access to the internet and concerns about equity (Hamilton et al., 2020). Moreover, only 12% of teachers reported covering "all" or "nearly all" of the curriculum they would have had schools remained open.

In the same study, only 59% of teachers and 77% of principals reported being able to contact "all" or "nearly all" of their students and families. For various reasons, a sizable segment of the school-age population (often from low-income and minority backgrounds) was not in contact with their school. These findings highlight marked disparities in service access and delivery. These are structural problems—structural problems related to inequity that encourage educators to stand up and lead.

The psychosocial and mental health effects of the pandemic cannot be understated. These include stress, anxiety, fear, depressive symptoms, and profound grief for those who have lost loved ones. In 2020, about 40% of surveyed youth reported experiencing psychological problems; 32%, 31%, and 34% of adolescents reported clinically significant symptoms of depression, anxiety, and PTSD, respectively (Murata et al., 2021).

Further, in addition to immediate risks associated with COVID-19, related concerns should be monitored, given that the pandemic resulted in reduced social and school connectedness. Brief longitudinal studies assessing changes from pre-lockdown to during and after a lockdown have found decreases in children's emotional and behavioral functioning and increased depression and anxiety (Magson et al., 2021). Research shows an association between loneliness and mental health problems (Loades et al., 2020), and loneliness predicts depression, anxiety, PTSD, and suicidal ideation among youth (Murata et al., 2021). Collectively, pandemic-related difficulties with learning online and increased parent-adolescent conflict exacerbated mental health problems, whereas adherence to stay-at-home orders and feelings of social connectedness protected adolescents from depression and anxiety (Magson et al., 2021).

Overall, the COVID-19 pandemic became an abrupt and chronic stressor that caused a toxic stress response among many. This shocked the educational system and other institutions (Condon et al., 2020). Families from marginalized, minoritized, and disadvantaged communities were especially hurt (Condon et al., 2020; Prime et al., 2020). It has been estimated that more than 230,000 students are grieving the loss of a loved one, and the deaths from COVID-19 for Black and Hispanic families were near twice the rate of those from White families (St George & Strauss (2022). Moreover, academic achievement in math and reading for these more vulnerable populations suffered the most (National Center for Education Statistics, 2022).

The COVID-19 pandemic spotlights inequity in K–12 schools and communities. So, what can leaders do? Leaders can (a) be transparent in their communication, (b) ensure that students and families know that they are being heard and respected, (c) communicate as frequently as possible, (d) do their best to support children's learning and appreciate the sacrifices made by faculty, (e) reach out to the community to get resources for those students needing additional help, (f) if necessary, try to serve as a mediator among segments of the population that have different views, and (g) ensure counseling and tutoring services are available to help the most impacted students. With current crisis response knowledge, educational leaders can help address problems associated with the pandemic. Text Box 8.5 highlights what has been learned from responding to COVID-19's impact on the educational system thus far. With optimism, this information may help with responding to future large-scale public health crises.

Text Box 8.5: What we have learned about the COVID-19 pandemic

Pandemic points related to schooling.

1. All children were impacted emotionally, socially, and academically by the pandemic.
2. Students from low-income communities, those with handicapping conditions, and those from marginalized populations will have more academic challenges than other youth. They will suffer the most.

238 ◆ The Mental Health Pillar

3. If schools are closed, students will have less opportunity for socialization and their social skills will be negatively affected. Also, more behavioral challenges will become apparent in the classroom when the children return.
4. The stress on teachers and school leaders will increase, often dramatically. They will be working longer hours, and more teachers will consider leaving the profession.
5. Accommodations will need to be made so that all students have take-home laptop computers.
6. State and federal governments need to invest in broadband access so that all students can access the internet if schools get closed.

Pandemic points related to medical-decision making.

7. Decisions are complex and multi-layered and often depend on a tradeoff between students' health, economics, and political considerations.
8. Science is a process. Findings are published at a point in time. Health decisions should change as science changes. We need to follow the trajectory of science in order to make the best medical decisions.
9. Some epidemiologists and medical leaders will get criticized by some segments of the public, no matter what they recommend. Often, the most extreme voices become the loudest.
10. Individuals should consult with family physicians and follow procedures the CDC recommends.
11. Decisions regarding closing schools are made at a point in time and depend on the spread of the pathogen, the availability of a vaccine, the number of cases in a specific regional population, the current science, and national, state, and regional politics.

Pandemic points related to interventions.

12. Vaccines have proven to be a miracle in the past and have effectively eliminated smallpox and rinderpest, and significantly reduced polio, tuberculous, cholera, and measles.
13. The use of vaccines in reducing the severity of disease and deaths from COVID-19 has been substantiated in the medical literature.
14. Masks and social distancing have proven effective in decreasing infections.
15. Indoor air quality filtration is beneficial in reducing transmission.

Pandemic points related to interventions are based on research conducted by Abaluck et al. (2022); Huang & Kuan (2022); Nazarenko (2020).

Recovery

Trauma-Informed Care

Childhood trauma is one of the most significant causes of mental health problems afflicting youth (Blodgett, 2012; Rossen & Cowan, 2013). Childhood trauma has been defined by SAMHSA "as an event, a series of events or a set of circumstances that is experienced by an individual as physically or emotionally harmful or life-threatening that has lasting adverse effects on the individual's functioning and mental, physical, emotional, or spiritual well-being" (2014, p. 7). Much of the research on this topic came from the original Adverse Childhood Experiences (ACE) Study conducted by Felitti et al. (1998). These researchers focused on the following seven ACEs categories: emotional abuse, physical abuse, sexual abuse, mother treated violently, substance abuse in the household, mental illness in the home, and incarcerated household members. Current ACE studies include three other categories: parental separation or divorce, emotional neglect, and physical neglect.

Since the seminal Feletti et al. (1998) study, other types of potentially traumatic experiences that students may experience have been recognized (Lazarus et al., 2021a). These include the death of a family member (especially due to violence); becoming homeless; going into foster care; being impacted by community and school violence (e.g., witnessing drive-by shootings, being mugged, seeing friends and neighbors being shot, being raped, experiencing a school shooting); enduring hurricanes, fires, earthquakes, tornadoes, and other natural disasters; and surviving vehicular and other accidents. Moreover, chronic or repetitive stress and adversity such as ongoing sexual abuse or neglect are likely to have a variety of symptoms and be experienced differently and often more severely by an individual than going through a single potentially traumatic incident (e.g., a school shooting, a bus accident, or a hurricane). Each person's trauma response depends on their coping skills and resources and the context and circumstances in which the stressful event(s) occur.

Based on a systematic review of existing research (Perfect et al., 2016) on the 10 ACEs, approximately two out of every three school-age children are likely to have at least one potentially traumatic experience by age 17. Similarly, a national study concluded that about 34 million children in the United States had experienced at least one potentially traumatic event in their lifetime (Bethell et al., 2017). Exposure to adverse and traumatic events in childhood has significant negative implications for youths' consequent development and social-emotional well-being (Diamanduros et al., 2018). It has been associated with lower cognitive abilities, higher rates of special education placement, poorer academic functioning, and increased risk for mental health and behavioral problems (Perfect et al., 2016; Porche et al., 2016). For example, based on the original Feletti data, about 2% of individuals with zero ACEs will attempt suicide, whereas 18% of individuals with four or more ACEs will attempt suicide. This is a 900% increase between the two groups.

Based on this research, many schools have adopted a trauma-informed approach that focuses on building a school culture and learning environment that is sensitive to the needs of youth who have been traumatized. This approach also has the added benefit of supporting all students (Chafouleas et al., 2016). Moreover, though this is a relatively new movement, research results supporting its effectiveness have been promising but not conclusive. For example, Dorado and colleagues (2016) analyzed the effect of a trauma-informed intervention program that included a professional development component. The researchers found that the program increased the staff's understanding and use of trauma-informed practices. This, in turn, led to significant drops in students' trauma-related symptoms, disciplinary office referrals, incidents involving physical aggression, and out-of-school suspensions.

What can leaders do? Leaders must understand that a trauma-informed school approach provides a framework for interventions, effective practices, and system reform (Lazarus et al., 2021b). It aligns well with the PF-MTSS framework as it "provides effective practices to all students and intensive supports to those who need it" (Phifer & Hull, 2016, p. 202).

Leaders can implement policies, strategies, and interventions based on the eight common elements of trauma-informed practices (Lazarus et al., 2021b): 1) whole-school safety planning, 2) whole-school prevention planning, 3) whole-school trauma planning, 4) classroom strategies, 5) early intervention trauma planning, 6) targeted trauma programming, 7) staff self-care, and 8) community involvement. Many trauma-informed policies, training examples, and practices recommended in the research literature have already been addressed in this text (e.g., assessment of campus physical safety, bullying prevention strategies, clearly defined processes for students to report concerns about peers). However, several recommendations focus directly on trauma, such as 1) All school staff are educated on the prevalence and impact of trauma, 2) Student support teams utilize an approach to examine trauma as it relates to student performance, 3) School- and evidence-based treatments are available for students exposed to trauma, 4) Discipline policies are sensitive to students exposed to trauma.

Trauma-informed care implies that instead of using punitive measures such as embarrassing or shaming students and over-relying on suspensions and expulsions, educators instead set up support teams to investigate the cause of a student's behavioral issues and offer valuable links to mental health professionals and use behavioral supports and therapeutic interventions. Nonetheless, leaders still need to follow district discipline codes unless otherwise modified. To reiterate the point made at the book's outset, trauma-informed schools focus on "what happened in the life of a child" rather than "what is wrong with the child." The emphasis is on how educational leaders and the whole school community can help.

Ultimately, healing and recovery through school-based, trauma-informed care involve strong leadership and policies. In a review of two decades of research, Thomas et al. (2019) call for the greater application of trauma-informed practices in schools by educational leaders in collaboration with related professionals (e.g., mental health professionals, community agencies). Regarding trauma-informed care and consistent with the Three Pillar Model espoused in this book, they conclude: "Because school-based practitioners confront the impacts of trauma in the lives of students on a daily basis, we urge that this work moves forward expediently with prevention and recovery at every level of the system in mind" (p. 448). The onus is for educational leaders to advocate for practices that foster students' safety, security, and mental health.

Advocacy

So how well-educated, powerful, socially connected, rich, or old does one need to be to become an advocate and leader? Perhaps retelling the story of Caitlyne Gonzalez can answer this question. In an exclusive 20-page profile by John Woodrow Cox (2022) in the *Washington Post*, Cox tells the story of Caitlyne Gonzalez, a 10-year-old child who survived the Uvalde school shooting and became an advocate and a voice for her slaughtered friends. Caitlyne was a 4th grader when she lost her best friend, Jackie, in the shooting at Robb Elementary School where the perpetrator killed 19 students and two teachers on May 24, 2022. As Cox (2022) notes, Caitlyne was a uniquely American amalgam, a child who had not yet learned to ride a bike without training wheels but knew about bulletproof backpacks and bulletproof windows, and how to argue about banning assault weapons.

Caitlyne, a four-foot-eight-inch, 75-pound young girl, thought of herself as one who helps others and aspired to become a teacher when she got older. Yet, despite the horror she experienced, she became Uvalde's most public survivor. In the months following this tragedy, she gave speeches at rallies in Uvalde and Austin; she later traveled to Washington, D.C., to speak with Senators and Congress members about the need to make schools safer for all children. Caitlyne wrote her speeches in neat block letters and at rallies, often stood alone on tippy toes before a microphone. Caitlyne said, "A school is a place where a teacher and a child should feel safe. I should feel safe. My friends should feel safe. But we don't. . . . I can't imagine the pain my friends and teacher felt in their last moments. Jackie and the rest of the classmates and teachers died because law enforcement did not protect us like they should have. I am so mad. So many lives could have been saved. I'm here to be their voice since we can no longer hear their voice." Will you stand up with Caitlyne? As an advocate and leader, will you help elevate her voice?

Advocating for Mental Health Services

School mental health services are a necessity, not a luxury. However, there are not—and perhaps will never be—enough school-based mental health professionals to meet the needs of today's youth. Each profession (e.g., school psychologists, school counselors, school social workers, school nurses) has training and ethical standards, roles, and skill sets. When these professionals are appropriately integrated into the schools, they complement each other and can offer more comprehensive and integrated services. Yet, to do so, they must have a manageable caseload. The National Association of School Psychologists (2021) recommends a ratio of 1 professional for every 500 children. However, the current ratio is well beyond that, and the national average is 1 school psychologist to 1,162 students, and it is not unusual for there to be a ratio of 1 school psychologist to 2,000 students, and in some districts, 1 to 5,000 (Eklund et al., 2020). Only 8% of districts nationwide meet the recommended ratio. The American School Counselor Association (2021) recommends 1 school counselor to 250 students, yet the national average ratio for 2020–21 was 1 to 415.

As noted by Cowen et al. (2013), high ratios of school-based mental health professionals to students restrict the ability of these professionals to provide comprehensive, integrative, and preventive mental health services. These include important initiatives such as social-emotional learning, dropout prevention, school-wide positive behavioral supports, violence prevention, safety promotion, threat assessment, suicide prevention, and intervention. As a result of inadequate ratios, many districts may not include prevention and early intervention services that link mental health, school safety, and school climate (Sulkowski & Lazarus, 2017). Is it no wonder we have a student mental health

Crisis Recovery and Advocacy ◆ 245

problem in the U.S.? In Text Box 8.6 are listed comprehensive services that can be provided by school-based mental health professionals when the district meets the recommended ratios.

> ### Text Box 8.6: Comprehensive Services Provided by School-Based Mental Health Professionals
>
> ◆ Collecting, analyzing, and interpreting data to improve the availability and effectiveness of mental health services.
> ◆ Evaluating students for disability determination.
> ◆ Designing and implementing interventions to meet the behavioral and mental health needs of students.
> ◆ Promoting early intervention services.
> ◆ Providing individual and group counseling.
> ◆ Providing staff development related to positive discipline, behavior, and mental health (including mental health first aid).
> ◆ Providing risk and threat assessments.
> ◆ Supporting teachers through consultation and collaboration.
> ◆ Coordinating with community service providers and integrating intensive interventions into the schooling process.
>
> Cowen et al. (2013).

To reduce ratios based on the concerns addressed in this text, mental health programs and supports in schools will now begin to receive significantly more funding. This is primarily due to strong advocacy by concerned citizens and President Biden's commitment to mental health. On June 25, 2022, President Biden signed the Bipartisan Safer Communities Act (BSCA) into law. According to the Office of Elementary and Secondary Education (2022) (https://oese.ed.gov/bipartisan-safer-communities-act/), "this legislation expands vital mental health services and provides additional support for States and districts to design and enhance initiatives that will promote safe, more inclusive, and positive school environments for all students, educators, and school staff." There are basically two major grant programs funded under this Act with a combined total of $1 billion. The first is the BSCA, the Stronger Connections Grant Program. This includes monies for state educational agencies to competitively fund subgrants to high-need local educational agencies to establish safer and healthier learning environments and to prevent and respond to acts of bullying, violence, and hate that impact our school communities at the individual and systemic level. The second is the BSCA School-Based Mental Health Services (SBMG) grant program. The purpose of this grant is to increase the number of credentialed mental health services professionals to provide services to local educational agencies or districts with demonstrated need, increase the number of service providers from diverse backgrounds or from the communities they serve, and ensure that all service providers are trained in inclusive practices, including providing access to services for children and youth who are English learners.

These federally supported training grants can make a strong impact in increasing the number of mental health professionals to support children and youth, and school leadership teams should strongly consider applying for new grants when they become available. As one example, over the past five years, the School Psychology Program at Florida International University (FIU), where the first author (PJL) has served for more than four decades as the Program Director, has received $8 million in funding in training grants to support graduate student education in the mental health field. The first Project SPECIAL ($1 million over five years) funded two cohorts of school psychology students and special education students to complete their graduate programs and take selected courses together to increase collaboration and the ranks of both professions. The second Project CRYSTAL ($1 million over five years) funded two cohorts of school psychology graduate students to meet the needs of bilingual PK to 12th grade students. And the third, recently funded by the aforementioned Bipartisan Safer Communities Act called Project DIG ($6 million over five years), will enable five cohorts of school psychology and school social work students to receive tuition reimbursement and financial stipends to complete their degrees. They will then be able to provide services to meet the needs of underserved, low income, and minority PK to 12th grade students in Miami-Dade County Public Schools (M-DCPS). In addition, M-DCPS where FIU is located recently received $15 million over five years under the BSCA School-Based Mental Health Services (SBMG) grant program. Yet, even with these federal grants, the mental health needs among the district's children and youth will still require significantly more resources. Consequently, leaders should support the continued infusion of state and federal dollars into mental health training and services to support the well-being of our next generation.

It is not uncommon for School Psychology Program Directors to receive emails and calls every week requesting our graduates to come work in their local school districts. Unfortunately, there is a national shortage of mental health service providers, especially those from minority backgrounds. Why is that? There are multiple reasons, and the National Association of School Psychologists (NASP) has developed research summaries (NASP, 2021) and a Task Force to help mitigate this problem. First, all programs require at least three years of graduate study, including a full school-year internship. However, after completing a degree, graduates in many districts will often earn only $5,000 to $8,000 more in salary than a teacher with a bachelor's degree and can be saddled with large student loans. A law school graduate who attends a program for the same number of years can earn vastly more.

Second, not all required internships are paid positions (or are paid at a rate considerably lower than a teacher's salary). Therefore, the graduate student must work for a full academic year for a small stipend or no salary. Third, there is a shortage of graduate programs in school psychology. Some states have no programs, and others may have only one. These graduate programs are expensive to administer; therefore, universities find few incentives to expand the number of programs. Also, the clinical skills required to enter the profession are challenging to deliver remotely or online. Therefore, an individual who wishes to enter the profession may find the nearest program hundreds of miles away, which would be a significant barrier to someone who is place-bound. Fourth, the profession often recruits from the ranks of current teachers, and now fewer recent college graduates are entering the teaching profession.

So, what are some potential remedies? One can see that both the problems and solutions are connected to funding and resources. Lazarus et al. (2021a) provide some solutions that the profession can only solve. However, there is much that other leaders can do. First, lobby school districts to offer or expand well-paying school psychology internships and pay small stipends to school district supervisors of interns. Second, advocate for free tuition for state university internship credits for school-based mental health providers. Florida does provide free tuition waivers for internship credit for school psychology students. Third, have local school districts financially support their current teachers or other school personnel in becoming school-based mental health providers; and fourth, urge Congress to continue to finance the Bipartisan Safer Communities Act to help expand and fund school mental health services.

Educational Leaders and Advocacy

At this point, you might wonder: "What can I do about structural problems like a shortage of trained mental health professionals?" Although invoking structural change is beyond the influence of any single individual, each individual can inspire change in their realm of influence, which is true for educational leaders. Whether a superintendent or a proactive teacher, each educational leader makes a difference and is needed. Collectively, and in collaboration with mental health professionals, educational leaders are among the most crucial allies in efforts to make schools safer, more supportive, and conducive to fostering student mental health. So how can educational leaders do this through advocacy?

Educators are most often the first professionals to come into contact with students who need mental health supports. First, educational leaders must advocate for themselves and their profession and ensure that they have highly qualified and credentialed teachers in the classroom and the appropriate supports and resources to do their job. They can advocate for higher salaries and better working conditions in collaboration with concerned stakeholders. These incentives will enable more young people to enter the profession and for current educators to remain in schools. The American Teacher Act was recently introduced by Representative Frederica Wilson, a Democrat from Florida, on December 14, 2022. Wilson noted that the proposed act would set a salary floor of $60,000 to help recruit qualified teachers and support a national campaign to renew awareness of teaching as an essential and economically viable profession. According to the Economic Policy Institute, teachers currently work under a "pay penalty." This economic concept means educators earn lower weekly wages and overall compensation for their work compared to other college-educated graduates. They now earn 76.5 cents on the dollar compared to their peers (Stanford, 2022).

Second, educational leaders can advocate at the individual or school level to improve services to today's youth. Educational leaders can go to bat for necessary services for children with disabilities, reach out to homeless and foster children, and have conversations with students about treating others, especially those different from themselves, with dignity and respect. Educational leaders can serve on a school committee that focuses on improving the school culture and climate. Proactive educators can incorporate activities and practices associated with positive psychology into their classrooms. They can listen and respond empathetically to students' concerns. They can reach out to a young person who shows signs of mental distress and potentially refer the student to a school-based mental health provider. Educational leaders can become aware of the signs of suicide risk and help ensure that the affected student gets the necessary help. They can confront racism, bigotry, and anti-Semitism when it lifts its ugly head. Educational leaders can work to ensure that their office or their classroom is a safe place for LGBTQ+ students. Teachers can incorporate social-emotional learning into their classrooms. They can study how adverse childhood experiences impact their students' daily lives and functioning. They can forge stronger connections with families and community supports. All educational leaders can make it a priority to learn about different cultures and communities.

Although strong advocacy is needed to respond to crises and disasters, you might have noticed that advocacy is key to success for all initiatives and topics covered in this book. Thus, advocacy is key to ensuring that all components of the Three Pillar Model come to fruition. It is the cement that holds the pillars in place and together.

Consequently, educational leaders need to advocate for

- ♦ school safety practices that facilitate healthy learning environments and not draconian institutional settings that send the message that school is not safe
- ♦ evidence-based bullying prevention and intervention practices that are proactive and pertain to physical and cyber settings
- ♦ policies that ensure all threats of violence and suicide are taken seriously and that all students are safe and protected from violence
- ♦ policies and practices that result in a healthy school climate and support a school culture that is welcoming to all students

- practices that facilitate social connectedness among students and ensure that all students feel socially supported
- mental health practices that are culturally responsive, promotive, preventive, and accessible to all students
- effective crisis prevention and intervention teams, policies, and practices.

Concluding Comment

Three sturdy pillars are needed to stabilize students and schools that were on shaky ground before the COVID-19 pandemic, and after the recent spate of school shootings in the U.S., students need to feel safe (Section 1—The Safety Pillar). They need to know that educational leaders are engaged in initiatives to prevent and respond to school violence. However, this is not enough to stabilize students or schools. They must also be in supportive environments (Section 2—The Supportive Pillar). With this in mind, educational leaders must create positive and healthy school climates and cultures that are inclusive of all students. However, this too is not enough to put students on a solid footing. Lastly, students need strong and sturdy mental health supports (Section 3—The Mental Health Pillar) to foster their mental health and emotional well-being.

Perhaps daunting but ultimately beneficial and rewarding, educational leaders are uniquely positioned to stabilize students and schools. They can begin to make the Three Pillar Model a reality. As Marian Wright Edelman, the Children's Defense Fund founder noted, "The greatest threat to America's national security comes from no enemy without but from our failure to protect, invest in, and educate all our children who make up all our futures." Though posterity will be the ultimate beneficiary of these efforts, leadership begins with us today. We have work to do—we must support all the Caitlyne Gonzalezes. As the Spanish cellist, Pablo Casals, once wrote, "You must work—we must all work—to make the world worthy of its children." It's now time to get to work.

References

Abaluck, J., Kwong, K. H., Styczynski, A., Haque, A., Mobarak, A.M. + 17 authors (2022, December 2). Impact of community masking on COVID-19. A cluster randomized trial in Bangladesh. *Science, 375*(6577). doi:101126/science.abi9069

Alisic, E., Zalta, A. K., van Wesel, F., Larsen, S. E. Hafstad, G. S., Hassanpour, K., & Smid, G. E. (2014). Rates of post-traumatic stress disorder in trauma-exposed children and adolescents: Meta-analysis. *British Journal of Psychiatry, 204,* 335–340.

American School Counselor Association (2021). Roles and ratios. https://www.schoolcounselor.org/About-School-Counseling/School-Counselor-Roles-Ratios

Bethell, C. D., Davis, M. B., Gombojav, N., Stumbo, S., & Powers, K. (2017). *Issue brief: A national and across state profile on adverse childhood experiences among children and possibilities to heal and thrive.* Johns Hopkins Bloomberg School of Public Health. http://www.cahmi.org/wp-content/uploads/2017/10/aces_brief_final.pdf

Blodgett, C. (2012). *Adopting ACEs screening and assessment in child serving systems.* Working Paper. WSU Area Health Education Center. http://extension.wsu.edu/ahec/trauma/Documents/ACE%20Screening%20and%20Assessment%20in%20Child%20Serving%20Systems%207-12%20final.pdf

Brock, S. E. (2013). Preparing for the school crisis response. In J. Sandoval (Ed.), *Crisis counseling, intervention, and prevention in the schools* (3rd ed.) (pp. 19–30). Routledge.

Brock, S. E., Nickerson, A. B., Reeves, M. A., Jimerson, S. R., Feinberg, T., & Lieberman, R. (2009). *School crisis prevention and intervention: The PREPaRE model.* National Association of School Psychologists.

Brymer, M. J., Pynoos, R. S., Vivrette, R. S., & Taylor, M. A. (2012). Providing school crisis interventions. In S. E. Brock, & S. R. Jimerson (Eds.), *Best practices in school crisis prevention and intervention* (2nd ed., pp. 317–336). National Association of School Psychologists.

CDC COVID-19 Response Team (2020). Preliminary estimates of the prevalence of selected underlying health conditions among patients with coronavirus disease 2019—United States, February 12–March 28, 2020. *Morbidity and Mortality Weekly Report, 69,* 382–386. https://stacks.cdc.gov/view/cdc/87230.

Centre for Research on the Epidemiology of Disasters (CRED). (2017). Economic losses, poverty and disasters 1998–2017. https://www.cred.be/sites/default/files/CRED_Economic_Losses_10oct.pdf

Chafouleas, S. M., Johnson, A. H., Overstreet, S., & Santos, N. M. (2016). Toward a blueprint for trauma-informed service delivery in schools. *School Mental Health, 8*, 144–162.

Condon, E. M., Dettmer, A. M., Gee, D. G., Hagan, C., Lee, K. S., Mayes, L. C., . . ., & Tseng, W. L. (2020). Commentary: COVID-19 and mental health equity in the United States. *Frontiers in Sociology.* 5:584390. https://doi.org/10.3389/fsoc.2020.584390

Cowen, K. C., Vaillancourt, K., Rossen, E., & Pollitt, K. (2013). *A framework for safe and successful schools* [Brief]. National Association of School Psychologists.

Cox, J. W. (2022, October 24). *An American girl. At 10, Caitlyne Gonzalez survived Uvalde's school shooting. Then she became a voice for her slain friends.* Washington Post. https://www.washingtonpost.com/dc-md-va/2022/10/24/uvalde-survivor-caitlyne-gonzales-victims/

Diamanduros, T. D., Tysinger, J., & Tysinger, P. D. (2018). Trauma and its impact on children. *Communiqué, 46*(6), 1, 24–25.

Dorado, J., Martinez, S., McArthur, M., & Leibovitz, L. (2016). Healthy Environments and Response to Trauma in Schools (HEARTS): A whole-school, multi-level, prevention and intervention program for creating trauma-informed, safe and supportive schools. *School Mental Health, 8*, 163–176.

Eklund, K., DeMarchena, S. L., Rossen, E., Izumi, J. T., Vaillancourt, K., & Rader Kelly, S. (2020). Examining the role of school psychologists as providers of mental and behavioral health services. *Psychology in the Schools, 57*, 489–501. https://doi.org/10.1002/pits.22323

Felitti, V. J., Anda, R. F., Nordenberg, D., Williamson, D. F., Spitz, A. M., Edwards, V., . . . & Marks, J. S. (1998). The relationship of childhood abuse and household dysfunction to many of the leading causes of death in adults: The adverse childhood experiences (ACE) study. *American Journal of Preventive Medicine, 14*, 245–258.

Felix, E. D., Nylund-Gibson, K., Kia-Keating, M., Liu, S. R., Binmoeller, C., & Terzieva, A. (2020). The influence of flood exposure and subsequent stressors on youth social-emotional health. *American Journal of Orthopsychiatry, 90*(2), 161–170. http://dx.doi.10.1037/ort0000418

Hamilton, L. S., Kaufman, J. H., & Diliberti, M. (2020). *Teaching and leading through a pandemic: Key findings from the American Educator Panels Spring 2020 COVID-19 Surveys.* RAND Corporation.

Hobfoll, S. E., Watson, P., Bell, C. C., Bryant, R. A., Brymer, M. J., Friedman, M. J., . . . & Ursano, R. J. (2007). Five essential elements of immediate and mid–term mass trauma intervention: Empirical evidence. *Psychiatry, 70*(4), 283–315.

Huang, Y. Z., Kuan, C. C. (2022, March). Vaccination to reduce severe COVID-19 and mortality in COVID-19 patients: a systematic review and meta-analysis. *Eur Rev Med Pharmacol Sci, 5,* 1770–1776. doi: 10.26355/eurrev_202203_28248. PMID: 35302230.

Jimerson, S. R., Brown, J. A., Sacki, E., Watanabi, Y., Kobayashi, T., & Hatzichristou, C. (2012). Natural disasters. In S. E. Brock, & S. R. Jimerson (Eds.), *Best practices in school crisis prevention and intervention* (2nd ed.) (pp. 573–595). National Association of School Psychologists.

King, L. A., & Miner, K. N. (2000). Writing about the perceived benefits of traumatic events: Implications for physical health. *Personality and Social Psychology Bulletin, 26,* 220–230.

Lazarus, P. J. & Costa, A. (in press). Supporting students and schools in the aftermath of natural disasters. In L. A Theodore, M. A. Bray, M. A., & B. A. Bracken (Eds.), *Desk Reference for School Psychologists.* Oxford University Press.

Lazarus, P. J., Doll, B., Song, S. Y., & Radliff, K. (2021a). Transforming school mental health services based on a culturally responsible dual-factor model. *School Psychology Review.* https://doi.org/10.1080/2372966X.2021.1968282

Lazarus, P. J., & Jimerson, S. R., & Brock, S. E. (2002). Natural disasters. In S. E. Brock, P. J. Lazarus, & S. R. Jimerson (Eds.), *Best practices in school crisis prevention and intervention* (pp. 435–450). National Association of School Psychologists.

Lazarus, P. J., Overstreet, S., & Rossen, E. (2021b). Building a foundation for trauma-informed schools. In P. J. Lazarus, S. Suldo, & B. Doll (ds.), *Fostering the emotional well-being of our youth: A school-based approach* (pp. 313–337). Oxford University Press. doi: 10.1093/med-psych/9780190918873.003.0016

Lazarus, P. J., & Sulkowski, M. L. (2010). Oil in the water, fire in the sky: Responding to technological/environmental disasters. *Communiqué, 39*(7), 16–17.

Lazarus, P. J., Zenere, F., & Feinberg, T. (2005, November). *Helping students and faculty cope in the aftermath of Hurricane Katrina.* Presentation to Plaquemines Parish Schools, New Orleans, LA.

Loades, M. E., Chatburn, E., Higson-Sweeney, N., Reynolds, S., Shafran, R., Brigden, A., . . . & Crawley, E. (2020). Rapid systematic review: the impact of social isolation and loneliness on the mental health of children and adolescents in the context of COVID-19. *Journal of the American Academy of Child & Adolescent Psychiatry, 59*(11), 1218–1239.

Magson, N. R., Freeman, J. Y. A., Rapee, R. M., Richardson, C. E., Oar, E. L., & Fardouly, J. (2021). Risk and protective factors for prospective changes in adolescent mental health during the COVID-19 pandemic. *Journal of Youth and Adolescence, 50*, 44–57. https://doi.org/10.1007/s10964-020-01332-9

Meckler, L. (2022, November 23). The science on remote schooling is now clear. Here's who it hurt the most. *The Washington Post.* https://www.washingtonpost.com/education/2022/11/23/covid-research-remote-school-poverty/

Murata, S., Rezeppa, T., Thoma, B., Marengo, L., Krancevich, K., Chiyka, E., . . . & Melhem, N. M. (2021). The psychiatric sequelae of the COVID-19 pandemic in adolescents, adults, and health care workers. *Depression and Anxiety, 38*(2), 233–246. https://doi.org/10.1002/da.23120

National Association of School Psychologists. (2021). *Shortages in school psychology: Challenges to meeting the growing needs of U.S. students and schools* [Research summary].

National Center for Education Statistics (2022). The nation's report card. NAEP long term trend assessment results: Reading and mathematics. https://www.nationsreportcard.gov/highlights/ltt/2022/

Nazarenko, Y. (2020). Air filtration and SARS-CoV-2. *Epidemiol Health.* 42:e2020049. doi:10.4178/epih.e2020049. Epub 2020 Jul 4. PMID: 32660218; PMCID: PMC7644931.

Nickerson, A. B., & Sulkowski, M. L. (2021). The COVID-19 pandemic as a long-term school crisis: Impact, risk, resilience, and crisis management. *School Psychology, 36*(5), 271–276. https://doi.org/10.1037/spq0000470

Perfect, M. M., Turley, M. R., Carlson, J. S., Yohannan, J., & Saint Gilles. M. P. (2016). School-related outcomes of traumatic event exposure and traumatic stress symptoms in students: A systematic review of research from 1990 to 2015. *School Mental Health, 8,* 7–43.

Phifer, L. W., & Hull, R. (2016). Helping students heal: Observations of trauma- informed practices in the schools. *School Mental Health, 8*(1), 201–205. https://doi.org/10.1007/s12310-016-9183-2

Prime, H., Wade, M., & Browne, D. T. (2020). Risk and resilience in family well-being during the COVID-19 pandemic. *American Psychologist, 75,* 631–643. doi: 10.1037/amp0000660

Porche, M. V., Costello, D. M., & Rosen-Reynoso, M. (2016). Adverse family experiences, child mental health, and educational outcomes for a national sample of students. *School Mental Health, 8,* 44–60.

Reeves, M. A., Conolly-Wilson, C. N., Pesce, R. C., Lazzaro, B. R., & Brock, S. E. (2012). Preparing for comprehensive school crisis response. In S. E. Brock, & S. R. Jimerson (Eds.), *Best practices in school crisis prevention and intervention, second edition* (pp. 245–283). National Association of School Psychologists.

Rossen, E. & Cowan, K. (2013). The role of schools in supporting traumatized students. *Principal's Research Review, 8*(6), 1–8.

Stanford, L. (2022, December 15). Teachers would make at least $60K under new federal bill. *Edweek.* https://www.edweek.org/policy-politics/teachers-would-make-at-least-60k-under-new-federal-bill/2022/12

St. George, D., & Strauss, V. (2022, December 5). The crisis of student mental health is much vaster than we realize. *The Washington Post.* https://www.washingtonpost.com/education/2022/12/05/crisis-student-mental-health-is-much-vaster-than-we-realize/

Sulkowski, M. L., & Lazarus, P. J. (2013). Five essential elements of crisis intervention to respond to technological/ecological disasters. *International Journal of School and Educational Psychology, 1,* 3–12. doi: 10.1080/21683603.2013.780192

Sulkowski, M. L., & Lazarus, P. J. (2017). *Creating safe and supportive schools and fostering students' mental health.* Routledge.

Tang, W., Lu, Y., & Xu, J. (2018). Post-traumatic stress disorder, anxiety, and depression symptoms among adolescent earthquake victims: Comorbidity and associated sleep-disturbing factors. *Social Psychiatry and Psychiatric Epidemiology: The International Journal for Research in Social and Genetic Epidemiology and Mental Health Services, 53*(11), 1241–1251.

Thomas, M. S., Crosby, S., & Vanderhaar, J. (2019). Trauma-informed practices in schools across two decades: An interdisciplinary review of research. *Review of Research in Education, 43*(1), 422–452. https://doi.org/10.3102/0091732X18821123

Wang, G., Zhang, Y., Zhao, J., Zhang, J., & Jiang, F. (2020). Mitigate the effects of home confinement on children during the COVID-19 outbreak. *Lancet, 395,* 945–947. doi: 10.1016/S0140-6736(20) 30547-X

Zakrzewski, V. (2012). How to help students develop hope. https://greatergood.berkeley.edu/article/item/how_to_help_students_develop_hope

Zenere, F. (2005). Hurricane experiences provide lessons for the future. *Communiqué, 33*(5).

Index

Page numbers in **bold** denote tables, those in *italics* denote figures.

AACAP *see* American Academy of Child and Adolescent Psychiatry
AAP *see* American Academy of Pediatrics
AAS see American Association of Suicidology (AAS)
AASA see American Association of School Administrators
Abaluck, J. 239
abuse, emotional/physical/sexual 239, 240
academic achievement: and COVID-19 pandemic 7, 237; expectations 136; and mental health 95, 194; and school climate and culture 131–132; and social connection and support 161; and social-emotional competence 199
access: internet 7, 235, 238; to health care 6; to mental health services 22; to school campus, control of 39, 42, **43**
action planning 142
active shooter drills 12, 44, 47–51, 55; best practices **50**
Adams, John 9

Addington, L. A. 39
adverse childhood experiences (ACEs) 146, 239–241, 250
advocacy 217, 243–251; educational leaders and 248–251; mental health services 244–248
AERA *see* American Educational Research Association
AFSP *see* American Foundation for Suicide Prevention
After a Suicide: Toolkit for Schools (AFSP/SPRC) 97
agency collaboration 44, 47, 55
aggression 83, 130, 136, 144; microaggressions 128; physical 62, 75, 76; relational 62, 75, 76; sexual 62, 75, 76; verbal 62; *see also* abuse; bullying; school violence
Ahram, R. 168
Alessandrini, K. A. 93
Alisic, E. 218
all children approach 19–20
Allen, K. A. 196
Al's Pals/The Wingspan Approach **200**
Alter, P. 138

American Academy of Child
  and Adolescent Psychiatry
  (AACAP) 183
American Academy of Pediatrics
  (AAP) 183, 184, 210
American Association of School
  Administrators (AASA) 139
American Association of
  Suicidology (AAS) 93, 95
American Educational Research
  Association (AERA) 66
American Foundation for Suicide
  Prevention (AFSP) 92, 96, 97
American Psychological
  Association (APA) 67
American Red Cross 225
American School Counselor
  Association (ASCA) 96, 244
American Teacher Act (2022)
  249
Americans with Disabilities Act
  (1990) 65
Anderman, L. H. 162
Anderson, C. 167
anxiety 4, 77, 160, 162, 164, 183,
  185, 191, 194, 210
APA *see* American Psychological
  Association
Arizona School Facilities Board
  42
armed assailant/intruder drills
  47–48, **50;** *see also* active
  shooter drills
Aronowitz, N. W. 49
ASCA *see* American School
  Counselor Association
Asher, S. R. 157, 163, 164

Association for Supervision and
  Curriculum Development
  (ASCD) 19
attendance records 223
authentichappiness.com 196
authoritarian school climate 124,
  125, **133**
authoritative school climate 124,
  125, **133**
Authoritative School Climate
  Survey **140**
autonomy 3, 9, 124

Banerjee, D. 166
Barnard, C. 126
Barrett, P. 37
Battistich, V. 199
Baumeister, R. F. 156
Baumrind, D. 123–124
Beers, Lee Savio 183
behavioral interventions **208,**
  209
behaviors: expected 132, **133,**
  137–139, 144, 146, 148;
  prosocial 68–69, 81, 136, 196
beliefs 132, **133,** 134, 148
belongingness 156, 162, 167, 191
Benbenishty, R. 130
Benson, P. L. 5
Berger, A. 126
Berguno, G. 163
Berkowitz, R. 131
Berman, A. L. 92, 93
Bethell, C. D. 26, 240
biases 134
Biden, Joe 245
Bierman, K. L. 199

Bipartisan Safer Communities Act (BSCA) (2022) 245–246, 247
Black families, and COVID-19 6, 236–237
Black, Indigenous, and People of Color (BIPOC) *see* Black families; Black students; Hispanic students/families; Latino students; minoritized groups
Black Lives Matter 5
Black students 6, 25, 131; exclusionary discipline 20–21; suicidality among 184
Blodgett, C. 239
Blueprints for Healthy Youth Development 67
Blum, R. W. 94
Bokhorst, C. L. 160
Bolier, L. 194
Borum, R. 53
Bosworth, K. 42, 64
Boucher, M. 169
Boyle, D. 199
Brackett, Marc 3
Bradshaw, C. P. 43–44
Brock, S. E. 39, 47, 93, 219, 221, 225, 226
broken windows/doors **41**, 44
Bronfenbrenner, U. 7
Brown, E. C. 67
Brymer, M. J. 229, 230
Buck, S. 53
Bully Busters 71
Bully Proofing Your School 71
bullying 61–74, 75, 83–84, 105, 120, 136, 144, 191;

bystander interventions ("upstanders") 67–68, 71; definition of 61–62; forms of 62; legal considerations and student rights 65–66; myths and facts about children who bully 72–73; nature of 62–63; and power 61–62, 65, 71; prevalence of 62–63; prevention and intervention 12, 17–18, 64, 65–71, 73–74, 78, 94, 145, 242, 250; reporting **41**, 70; and school leadership 64–74; students vulnerable to 64–65; *see also* cyberbullying
burnout, educators 9

Cacioppo, J. T. 154, 164
California School Climate Survey **140**
campus access, controlling 39, 42
caregivers *see* parents/caregivers
caring communities, schools as 26, **171–2**, 174, 189, 196
Caring School Community Program 199, **200**
Carlson, Gabrielle 183
Carrington, S. 127
Casals, Pablo 251
CASEL *see* Collaborative for Academic, Social, and Emotional Learning (CASEL. org)
Catalano, R. F. 163
Centers for Disease Control and Prevention (CDC) 5, 6, 18–19, 91, 92, 93, 94, 95, 97, 102–103

262 ◆ Index

Centers for Disease Control and Prevention (CDC) COVID Data Tracker 234
Centers for Disease Control and Prevention (CDC) COVID-19 Response Team 165, 234
Centre for Research on the Epidemiology of Disasters (CRED) 230
Chafouleas, S. M. 26, 241
Channing Bete Company **200**
character strengths 193, 195, 196, 197
check-in/check-out (CICO) *see* mental health promotion and prevention, check-in/check-out
Children's Hospital Association (CHA) 183
Children's Hospital of Philadelphia (CHOP), Center for Violence Prevention 76
Cholera, R. 6
chronosystem 7–8
civic education 122, 130
Civil Rights Act (1964) 65
classroom rules or expectations 137–138; and student buy-in and collaboration 138
classroom–based strategies for improving school climate and culture 143–144
Clauss-Ehlers, C. S. 22
cleanliness 44
clinical psychology 192
Cognitive Behavioral Therapy in K–12 Settings (Joyce-Beaulieu and Sulkowski) 209

cognitive interventions **208**, 209
cognitive restructuring **208**
cognitive-behavioral therapy (CBT) 207–209, **208**, 210
Cohen, J. 120
Cokley, K. 21
Cole, S. F. 25
collaboration, and devising of classroom rules 138
Collaborative for Academic, Social, and Emotional Learning (CASEL.org) 198, 201, 202
collective efficacy 229
collectivist cultures 167
Collins, T. A. 69
Combes, B. 127
comfort 39, 44, 55
Committee for Children **200**
communications **40**, **41**; crisis–related 221, 223–224
community partnerships 13, 26–27, 146
Condon, E. M. 235, 236
conflict resolution 71, 80, **100**
connectedness, increasing feelings of after crisis 229; *see also* interconnectedness; school connectedness; social connectedness
contagion effect, suicide 95
control 124, *125*
Cook-Harvey, C. M. 140–142
CorLogic 230
Cornell, D. G. 46, 54, 63–64, 103, 104, 105, 107–108, 109, 111, 112n, 124, **140**

Costa, A. 190, 229, 230, 231
courage 193
Couture, M. C. 76
COVID-19 pandemic 3, 5, 6–7, 9, 21, 183–186; and academic achievement 7, 237; crisis response 218,220, 234–239; interventions 187–188, 239; learning from 237–239; and marginalized/minoritized groups 6, 165, 236–237; and medical decision-making 238; and mental health 4, 21, 207, 210, 236; and online learning 6–165, 235, 236; and social connectedness 165–166, 174, 236
Cowan, K. 26, 239
Cowen, K. C. 244, 245
Cowie, H. 68
Cox, J. W. 48, 55, 243
Creating Safe and Supportive Schools and Fostering Students' Mental Health 10
CRED *see* Center for Research on the Epidemiology of Disasters
Crenshaw, K. 128
crime prevention through environmental design (CPTED) 12, 42–44, 55
crime reporting **40**
criminal justice practices 81–82, **83**
crises: 20/60/20 heuristic 218–219; assessing 225; factors that place students at high risk during/after 226; impacts of 218–219

crisis exercises and drills 22; *see also* active shooter drills
crisis plans 44, 47, 55, 205, 221–224; caregiver reunification 221, 223; communications 221, 223–224; crisis exercises and drills 221, 222; media relations 221, 224; student accounting 221, 223; student evacuation and assembly 221, 222–223; visitor–sign in 221–222
crisis recovery *see* trauma-informed care
crisis response 217, 218–239; calming and supporting fearful individuals 228; connectedness, increasing feelings of 229; and COVID-19 pandemic 218, 234–239; hope, instilling and inspiring 228, 229, 230; intervention strategies 228–229, 233–234; natural disasters 218, 220, 230–234; preparing for a crisis 219; school shootings 218, 220; sense of safety, promoting 228; sense of self and collective efficacy, engendering 229; teams 219–220, 227
crisis response procedures 224–230; assessing crises 225; evaluation and debriefing 227; intervention services 227; victim identification and assistance 225
Critical Race Theory (CRT) 128–130

264 ◆ Index

Crowley, B. 54, 104, 107, 108, 111
cultural differences, respecting and celebrating 13
cultural responsiveness 21–22, 126–130, 251; social-emotional learning (SEL) 199, 201
culture, and social connection and support 167–168, 174
Cummings, J. R. 22
curricula, representative and multicultural 146–147
cyber safety 8
cyber-system 8
cyberbullying 8, **41**, 62, 63–64, 70; disinhibition effect 63–64, 73; strategies to prevent being victimized by 73–74

Dads on Duty program 169
Danelski, D. 130
Darling-Hammond, L. 140–141
Darling-Hammond, S. 83
Davis, A. 184
Davis v. Monroe County Board of Education (1999) 65
DeAngelis, Frank 54
debriefing, crisis 227
decision-making: responsible 198; shared 139, **173**
deficit approach 20
Degol, J. L. 130, 139
del Mar Sánchez-Fuentes, M. 135
Delaware School Climate Survey **140**
delinquency 42, 75, 130, 163
Demaray, M. K. 160
DeMary, J. L. 46

democracy 128, 129
Dempsey, A. G. 62
depression 4, 77, 93, 95, 160, 162, 164, 183, 185, 191, 194, 210, 236
Developmental Studies Center (DSC) **200**
Devlin, D. N. 52
Diamanduros, T. D. 240
DiAngelo, R. 167
Diliberti, M. K. 9
disability approach 20
disabled students 7, 64, 127, 184, 249; *see also* Individuals with Disabilities Education Improvement Act (IDEIA) (2004)
disaster response *see* crisis response
discrimination 128, 131, 165; and social-emotional development 201
distance learning *see* online (distance) learning
diversity 20–22, 130; respect for 122, *123*
Doll, B. 17, 23
Dorado, J. 241
Dornbusch, S. M. 163
Doumas, D. M. 68
dress code 39, **40**, 232
drills, crisis *see* crisis exercises and drills
drug use *see* substance use
dual-factor model of mental health 23–24
Dunbar, R. 155, 158

Duong, M. T. 8
Durlak, J. A. 17, 23, 198–199

Eccles, J. S. 159, 160, 161
Eckert, T. 93
Economic Policy Institute 249
ED School Climate Surveys **140**
Edelman, Marian Wright 251
Edsall, T. 10
educators *see* teachers/educators
efficacy: collective 229; self-efficacy **100**, 167, 194
Eisenberger, N. I. 157
Eklund, K. 51, 244
Elhai, J. D. 62
Elias, M. J. 24, 197, 198, 199
Emergency Event Database (EM–DAT) 230
Emergency Operations Center **40**, 222
emergency responders 47, 103
emotional abuse 239
emotional behavior disorder (EBD) 23
emotional and physiological trigger reaction **208**, 209
emotional regulation 24, 25, 185, 190
emotional well-being 3, 4, 5, 15, 19, 23, 24, 28, 156, 159, 164, 189, 251
emotions, positive 194, 195
engagement, student 13, 122, 131, 143–144, 159
entry points 39, 42
environmental design 37–44
Epstein, J. A. 94, 97

equity 20–22, 130, 201, 235; *see also* inequity
Erbacher, T. A. 48, 49
Erikson, E. 3
evacuation plans 222–223
evidence-based interventions (EBIs) 22–23
exclusionary discipline 20–21
exosystem 7
expected behaviors 132, **133**, 137–139, 144, 146, 148
exposure therapy **208**
expulsions 21
extra-curricular activities 147
extroverts 154

Facebook 74
families 26, **173**, 174; and crisis events 218; minoritized, and COVID-19 236–237; school-family partnerships 13, 26–27; *see also* parents/caregivers
Farmer, E. M. Z. 8
Federal Emergency Management Agency (FEMA) 225
Fein, R. 109
Felitti, V. J. 239–240
Felix, E. D. 230, 231
Fetzer Institute 197
Filter, K. J. 204
Finn, P. 51
firearms: possession policies **40**; providing teachers with 53–55, 103; *see also* gun violence; school shootings
First Star Academy, University of California, LA 169–170

Index

Fisher, B. W. 20, 52, 55
Flannery, D. J. 67
Flemming, E. G. 154
Florida International University (FIU), School Psychology Program 246–247
Florida School Toolkit for K–12 Educators to Prevent Suicide 97
flow 193, 194
foster children 93, 127, 169–170, 240, 249
Franke, T. M. 127, 132
Franklin, Benjamin 186
free and appropriate education (FAPE) 127, 134–135
Froh, J. 195, 196
Fronius, T. 82
Furrer, C. 160

Gallou, L. 167
Garcia-Reid, P. 159
Garrity, C. 73
gender identity 21, 127, 146, 167
Georgia School Climate Survey **140**
Girouard, C. 52
Gonder, P. O. 139
Gönültaş, S. 65
Gonzalez, Caitlyne 243–244
Gore, F. 5
Gottfredson, D. C. 52
graffiti **41**, 44
gratitude 190, 193, 194, 195–196
Greenberg, M. T. 198, 202
Greenberg, S. F. 103
Greenwald, A. G. 134
Gregory, A. 46

Grewenig, E. 21
grief 6, 236
Group Interventions in Schools (Keperling et al.) 204
guided imagery **208**
gun violence 102–103; *see also* school shootings
Gun Violence Archives 102
Gun-Free School Zone Act (1994) **40**
guns *see* firearms
Guterres, Antonio 3

Hagborg, W. J. 161
Hamilton, L. S. 235
Handbook of Positive Psychology in Schools (Allen et al.) 196
Harnsich, T. L. 103
Harris, B. 22
Harris, R. 127
Hart, S. 95
Hartman, S. 169
Hassett-Walker, C. 199
Hatzenbuehler, M. L. 130
Hawkley, L. C. 164
Haydon, T. 138
health *see* mental health; physical health
health care 141; access to 6; discrimination in 165
healthy lifestyle instruction 13, 189
Helmes, E. 167
helplessness 93, **99**, 218, 234
Hinduja, S. 63
Hispanic students/families 6, 236–237

history 129, 130
Hobfoll, S. E. 228
Hoffman, J. 104
homeless students 20, 93, 127, 132, 206, 240, 249
Homer, E. M. 20, 52
hope 190, 193, 196, 209; instilling and inspiring, after crises 228, 229, 230
hopelessness 5, 93, 95, **99**, 110, 184
Hopkins, M. 6
Hoy, W. K. 126
Huang, F. L. 63–64, 124
Huang, Y. Z. 239
Hull, R. 241
humanity 193
Hurricane Charlie, Southwest Florida 232
Hurwitz, J. 131
Hymes, D. 139

I Can Problem Solve Program 199, **200**
IDEIA *see* Individuals with Disabilities Education Improvement Act
identity checks 39, **41**, 42
IES *see* Institute of Education Sciences
Imagine Charter School 2
immigrant students 64, 127
Implicit Association Test (IAT) 134
inclusion 20–22, 127–128
inclusive language 146
Incredible Years Program **200**

individualistic cultures 167
individualized therapeutic approaches 14, 207–210
Individuals with Disabilities Education Improvement Act (IDEIA) (2004) 19, 65, 204
inequity 20–21, 28, 165
influence, systems of 7–8
Instagram 74
Institute of Education Sciences (IES) 2022 *School Pulse Panel* 184
interconnectedness 8
internet 8, 22; access to 7, 235, 238
introverts 154
intruder assessment 46
isolation *see* social isolation
Ivey, C. 92, 96, 97

Ji, Y. 165
Jimerson, S. R. 76, 77, 231
job losses 6
Johnson, S. 43
Jones, Dennis 232
Jones, J. 18, 19
Journal of Positive Psychology 196
Joyce-Beaulieu, D. 209
Juhnke, G. A. 95
justice 193; restorative *see* restorative justice

Kalafat, J. 97
Kann, L. 76
Kataoka, S. H. 5
Katic, B. 79, 82
Kendall, P. C. 207
Kendi, I. X. 128

Kennedy, B. R. 131
Keperling, J. P. 204
Khalifa, M. A. 128
Khubchandani, J. 93
kindness 193, 195
King, L. A. 230
KiVa 67, 145
Klein, J. 130
knowledge 193
Koh, H. K. 187
Kohli, R. 135
Konold, T. 131
Koope, C. Everett 4
Kowalski, R. M. 62
Kratochwill, T. R. 125, 126
Kuan, C. C. 239

Lamoreaux, D. 39
Langman, P. F. 24, 164
language, respectful, inclusive and accurate 146
Latino students 21, 25, 131
law enforcement officers 103; as threat assessment team members 106, 107, 108–109; *see also* police; School Resource Officers (SROs)
Lazarus, Jane 111
Lazarus, P. J. 2, 3, 4, 5, 16, 20, 24, 53, 54, 62, 71, 73, 74, 91, 93, 97, 102, 104, 105, 111, 190, 193, 194, 202, 204, 218, 219, 221, 227, 229, 230, 231, 240, 241, 244, 248
Leach, J. B. 155
learning 122, 194, 195; online (distance) 6–7, 165, 170, 235,

236; service 122; *see also* social-emotional learning (SEL)
Learning Policy Institute 140
Leary, M. R. 156
Lee, Harper 129
Lee, R. M. 156, 158
legislation: to combat bullying 65–66; *see also individual pieces of legislation*
Lenzi, M. 76
LGBTQ+ students 64, 65, 66, 67, 93, 94, 120, 127, 129, 145, 250
Lieberman, R. A. 92, 96, 97
life satisfaction 194, 196
Limber, S. P. 62, 67
Lindsey, M. A. 92
Linley, P. A. 192, 194
Lions Clubs International Foundation **200**
Lions Quest Program **200**
litigation, and suicide risk 95–96
Loades, M. E. 236
lockdowns 44, 47–48, 55; best practices **50**
locker room policies 39, **40**, **41**
loneliness 157, 163–164, 165, 183, 236
Louvar Reeves, M. A. 106, 107
low-income communities 7, 25, 235, 237
Lowenhaupt, R. 6
Luo, Y. 164
Lyubomirsky, S. 195

Mackay, Harvey 190
Macklem, G. L. 197, 199
MacNeil, A. J. 132

macrosystem 7

Magson, N. R. 236

Malamut, S. T. 64

Malecki, C. K. 160

marginalized groups 5, 9, 28, 147, 167, 201; and COVID-19 pandemic 165, 236–237; and curricula 147; health care access 6; and school culture 126, 127, 130

Margolius, M. 6

Marjory Stoneman Douglas High School (MSD) shooting (2018) 1–2, 27, 103

Marks, H. M. 160

Maryland Safe and Supportive Schools Climate Survey **140**

Maslow, A. 3–4, 156

Masten, A. S. 24

math skills 7, 237

Maxwell, T. W. 132

Mayer, M. J. 76, 77

McCallops, K. 199

McDevitt, J. 51

McLesky, J. 131–132

Meckler, L. 235

media relations 221, 224

Meloy, J. R. 104

mental health 2, 3, 249; and academic achievement 95, 194; and adverse childhood experiences (ACEs) 241; and COVID-19 pandemic 4, 21, 207, 210, 236; crisis among youth 4–5, 183–186, 207, 210; dual-factor model of 23–24; and natural disasters 231;

school shooters 94, 104; and school violence 77; and social connection and support 156, 159–160, 161–162, 191; and suicide 93–94, 95

Mental Health Pillar 10, 13–14, 251

mental health professionals 209, 242, 244–245, 246–248, 249; as threat assessment team members 106–107, 108, 109; *see also* school counselors; school psychologists

mental health promotion and prevention 251; check-in/ check-out (MH-CICO) 204–206, 210; cognitive-behavioral therapy (CBT) 207–209, **208**, 210; culturally responsive 251; individualized therapeutic approaches 14, 207–210; multi-tiered system of support 16, *17*, 188–189, 192–210 (Tier 1 *17*, 188, 192–202, 210; Tier 2 *17*, 188, 202–206, 210; Tier 3 *17*, 188, 206–210); positive psychology 13, 24, 189, 192–197, 209, 210, 249; practical promotion strategies 190–192; school leaders and 189–192; small group interventions 14, 203–204, 210; social-emotional learning (SEL) 13, 23, 24, 78, 82, 144, 192, 197–202, **200**, 210; solution–focused therapy (SFT) 207, 209–210 mental health services 8, 13, 21–22, 141, 147, 184; advocating for 244–248; continuum of *17*; inclusive 147

Merikangas, K. R. 5

mesosystem 7

meta-analysis 23, 210n

metal detectors 38, 39

Miami-Dade County Public Schools (M-DCPS) 247

Michael, K. 205

microaggressions 128

microsystem 7

Midgett, A. 68

Miller, D. 92, 93

Miller, D. N. 93, 194

mindfulness 194, 195, **208**, 209

Miner, K. N. 230

minoritized groups 5, 7, 20–22, 120, 201; and bullying 64–65, 120; and COVID-19 pandemic 165, 236–237; and curricula 147; and mental health 184; and school culture and climate 127, 130, 131; and social connection and support 167–168; and special education 21, 168

Miranda, A. H. 18, 19

Mitchell, R. M. 131

Model Programs Guide 67

Molony, T. M. 195

Montag, C. 63

Monteiro, D. L. M. 62

Moore, G. F. 120

Moyano, N. 135

multi-tiered system of support (MTSS) 10, 141, 144; *see also* promotion-focused multi-tiered system of support (PF-MTSS)

multicultural curricula 146–147

Mulvey, K. L. 65

Murata, S. 236

Murphy, J. J. 209

Murthy, V. 6, 157

Musu-Gillette, L. 38, 48

Myers, C. A. 68

Nagle, R. J. 160

Nansel, T. R. 62

NASP President's Call to Action to Prevent Suicide 102

National Academies of Sciences, Engineering, and Medicine 5, 6, 20

National Association of School Psychologists (NASP) 21, 27, 44, 48–49, 50, 67, 96, 102, 139, 168, 189, 244, 247

National Association of School Resource Officers (NASRO) 44, 48, 50

National Center for Education Statistics 7, 21, 48

National Center for Safe Supportive Learning Environments 143

National Council for Mental Wellbeing 191

National Foster Youth Institute 169

National Incident Management System, Incident Command System 222

National Registry of Evidence-Based Programs and Practices 67
National School Climate Center 122, 143
National School Climate Council (NSCC) 121, 141–142
National Survey of Child Health 25
National Threat Assessment Center 49
natural disasters 218, 220, 230–234, 240
natural surveillance 42, **43**
Nazarenko, Y. 239
needs: hierarchy of 156; primary/basic 3–4, 156
negligent school climate 124, *125*, **133**
Nekvasil, E. 102, 109
Nelson, H. J. 65
Nickerson, A. B. 7, 8, 160, 235
Niehaus, K. 161
Nieuwenhuys, A. 53
norms 121, 122, 126, 132, **133**, 135–137, 144, 146, 148
Northeast Foundation for Children **200**
NSCC *see* National School Climate Council

Obeng, C. 53
Office of Elementary and Secondary Education 245–246
Olweus Bullying Prevention Program 67, 71, 145
Olweus, D. 61, 67

online disinhibition effect 63–64, 73
online (distance) learning 6–7, 165, 170, 235, 236
optimism 193, 194, 196
Orme, J. G. 52
Osterman, K. F. 161
Ostrov, J. M. 62
Oudejans, R. R. 53

Paquette, J. A. 157, 163, 164
parents/caregivers 3–4; job losses 6; loss of 6; reunification with, after crisis 223; social support 155, 156, 159, 160–161; *see also* families
Park, N. 194
parking policies 39
Patchin, J. W. 63
PATHS (Providing Alternative THinking Strategies) 71
Patrick, H. 160
Patrick, W. 154
Pazey, B. 127
PeaceBuilders 67
Pearman, F. A. 20
peer aggression *see* school violence
peer mediation 80, 81
peer reporting, positive 68–69
peer social support 155, 156, 159, 160–161
peer-reviewed research 22–23
Peffley, M. 131
Perfect, M. M. 26, 240, 241
Perkins, Adrian 169
permissive school climate 124, *125*, **133**

272 ◆ Index

personality, and social networks 154
Perumean-Chaney, S. E. 39
Peterson, C. 193, 194
Pfohl, W. 71
Phifer, L. W. 241
physical abuse 239
physical aggression 62, 75, 76
physical environment 37–44, 55, 122, *123*
physical health 3, 156; and social disconnectedness 164
physical safety 37–60, 68, 121, 122, *123*, 242; strategies to increase **40–41**
physiological needs 4
Plucker, J. 22
Poland, S. 48, 49, 93, 96, 97
Polanin, J. R. 68, 75, 76–77
police 38, 47
Pollack, W. S. 103
Porche, M. V. 241
positive affect 194, 196
Positive Behavior Intervention Support (PBI) 144
positive character 193, 194
positive emotions 194, 195
positive institutions 193–194
positive peer reporting 68–69
positive psychology 13, 24, 189, 192–197, 209, 210, 249; benefits of 194–195; foundational elements 192–194; programs and practices 195–196; school leaders and 197
positive subjective experiences 192–193

post-traumatic growth 230
post-traumatic stress disorder (PTSD) 218, 236
Postman, Neal 10
power, and bullying 61–62, 65, 71
Preventing Suicide: A Toolkit for High Schools (SAMHSA) 94
prevention approaches 15–18
Price, J. H. 92
primary prevention 16, 18, 187, 189
Prime, H. 235, 236
proactive approaches 15–16, 189
Project DIG 247
Project SPECIAL 246
Promoting Alternative Thinking Strategies Program 199, **200**
Promoting Student Happiness (Suldo) 196
promotion-focused multi-tiered system of support (PF-MTSS) 15–18, 188–189, 241; and mental health 16, *17*, 188–189, 192–210
prosocial behaviors 68–69, 81, 136, 196
psychological distress 24
psychopathology 23, 24
public health promotion and prevention model 186–188; indicated or tertiary approaches 188; selective or secondary approaches 187–188; universal level (primary prevention) 187

race and racism 5, 20–22, 131, 167, 250; Critical Race Theory (CRT) 128–130; structural racism 165; systemic racism 21

racial and ethnic minorities 5, 20–22, 131, 167–168; and COVID-19 pandemic 165, 236–237; mental health 184; *see also* Black families; Black students; Hispanic students/families; Latino students

Radhakrishnan, L. 184

Rai, M. 166

reactive approaches 15–16, 189

reading skills 7, 237

Reeves, M. A. 44, 47, 220

referral sources 14

Rehabilitation Act, Section 504 (1973) 65

relational aggression/violence 62, 75, 76

relationship skills 198

relationships 122, *123*; *see also* social connectedness; social support

relaxation training **208**, 209

research-supported interventions 22–23

Resnick, H. S. 161

responsible decision-making 198

Responsive Classroom Program **200**

responsiveness 124, *125*; *see also* cultural responsiveness

restorative circles 80, 81

restorative conferences 80, 81

restorative conversations 79–80

restorative justice 78, 79–83, 84, 141, 145; and criminal justice practices compared 81–82, **83**

Rich, S. 48, 55

right-wing politics 128, 129

Roach, A. T. 125, 126

Roach, K. 82

Robb Elementary School shooting 27, 103, 243–244

Robbins, S. B. 158

Roberts, S. 39, 62

Rogers, J. 129–130

Rosenfeld, L. B. 159

Ross, D. M. 62

Rossen, E. 26, 239

Rosset, E. 195

Rubin, J. 130

Rueger, S. 160

Ryan, A. M. 160

sadness 5, 93, 95, 184

Safe Pillar 10, 12, 251; *see also* bullying; physical safety; suicide/suicidality; school violence; threat assessment

safety audits 12, 44, 45–47, 55

safety drills 38; *see also* active shooter drills; armed assailant drills

safety policies and approaches 44–51, 55, 250

safety teams 44–45, 46, 55

safety-related needs 4

Salmivalli, C. 67

SAMHSA *see* Substance Abuse and Mental Health Services Administration

Sandy Hook Elementary School shooting 52, 103
Saylor, C. F. 155
Schmidt, E. M. 18
Schneider, T. 43
school climate 12, 44, 46, 64, 69, 82, 94, 119–125, 196, 197, 244, 249; and academic achievement 131–132; components 122; data 139–142; definition of 119–120, 120–123, 148; improving 139–147; inclusive 127–128; influence of 130–132; measures 139–140, **140**; positive/healthy 64, 78, 119, 121, 127, 129, 130–131, 134, 137, 139, 143, 148, 190, 197, 250, 251; and school leadership 132, 134–139; types of 123–124, *125*; and aspects of school culture **133**
School Climate Measure **140**
school connectedness 122, 158, 159, 163, 170, 236
school counselors 13, 106, 185, 203, 244; *see also* American School Counselor Association
school culture 12, 119, 120, 197, 249, 250; and academic achievement 131–132; culturally responsive 126–130; definition of 125–126, 148; improving 139–147; inclusive 127–128; influence of 130–132; positive/healthy 128, 130, 132, 137, 139, 143, 148, 189, 190, 197, 251; school climate styles

and aspects of **133**; and school leadership 132, 134–139
school handbooks **40**
school improvement 122
school leaders, role of 9–10
school psychologists 203, 220, 244; graduate programs 246–247, 248; internships 247, 248; *see also* National Association of School Psychologists (NASP)
School Resource Officers (SROs) 38, 51–52, 55, 103, 209; as threat assessment team members 107, 108–109
school security officers 51
school security personnel *see* School Resource Officers (SROs); school security officers
school shooters 23, 92; characteristics of 104; drills to protect students/staff from *see* active shooter drills; mental health issues 94, 104; social disconnectedness 164; suicidal ideation 94, 104, 112
school shootings 1–2, 4, 27, 52, 54, 102–104, 243–244, 251; crisis response 218, 220
school social workers 247
school violence 75–84, 169, 240, 250, 251; conceptualizing 75; and leadership 77–83; prevalence and impact 75–77; prevention and intervention 78–83, 94, 103–104, *see also* threat assessment;

restorative justice approach 78, 79–83, 84; student outcomes 76–77; transdisciplinary approach 77–78; *see also* bullying

School-Based Mental Health services (SBMG) grant program 246, 247

schools, role of 7–8

Second Step Program **200**

secondary prevention 16, 18, 187–188

security personnel see School Resource Officers (SROs); school security officers

security technologies 38–39, 103

selective public health 187–188

self-awareness 198

self-concept 159, 166

self-efficacy **100**, 167, 194

self-esteem 72, 77, **100**, 159, 161, 194, 226

self-management 198

Seligman, M. E. P. 193, 194, 196

sense of self 229

September 11 (2001) 27

service learning 122

Seth, A. 74

sexual abuse 239, 240

sexual aggression/violence 62, 75, 76

sexual orientation 21, 66, 92, 167; *see also* LGBTQ+ students

Shah, K. 6

Shankland, R. 195

Shelton, A. J. 42

Sheras, P. 107, 112n

Shochet, I. M. 162

Shure, M. B. **200**

60 Minutes (September 4, 2022) 185

Skinner, E. 160

Slopen, N. 25

small group interventions 14, 203–204, 210

Snapchat 74

social awareness 198

social competence 159

social connectedness 94, 122, 153–174, 251; and academic achievement 161; and COVID-19 pandemic 165–166, 174, 236; cultural considerations 167–168, 174; individual level fostering of 170–173; local, state, and national level fostering of 168–170; "meaningful" connections 155, 158; and mental health 161–162, 191; protective factors 162, 163; research 160–168; web 158–159, 174

Social connectedness–Support Matrix *156*, 156–157, 162

Social Decision-Making and Problem-Solving Program 199

social disconnectedness 157, 159, 163–164, 165–166, 174; signs of 166

social distancing 165–166, 187–188, 239

social isolation 6, 156, 157, 159, 163, 165, 184

social media 8, 22, 62, 74, 120, 156, 157, 185, 191; and crisis response 223, 224, 229

276 ◆ Index

social networks 154; factors influencing 154
social relationships *see* social connectedness; social support
social support 122, 153–174, 196; and academic achievement 161; balloons 159–160, 174; cultural considerations 167–168, 174; definition of 155; individual level fostering of 170–173; local, state, and national level fostering of 168–170; and mental health 156, 159–160, 161–162, 191; protective factors 162, 163; research 160–168
social-emotional learning (SEL) 13, 23, 24, 78, 82, 144, 192, 197–202, **200**, 250; benefits of 198–199; foundational elements 198; programs and practices 199–201, **200**; school leaders and 201–202
social-emotional safety 121, 122
social-emotional well-being 19, 240
socioeconomic background 131
Socratic questioning **208**
Solution-focused Counseling in Schools (Murphy) 209
solution-focused therapy (SFT) 207, 209–210
Southwood High School, Shreveport, LA 169
special education 19, 21, 168, 240

Spencer, M. B. 20
Spirito, A. 94, 97
SPRC *see* Suicide Prevention Resource Center
SROs *see* School Resource Officers
standards 132, **133**, 135–137, 148
Stanford, L. 249
Steps to Respect Program 67, 71, **200**
stereotype threats 128
Stern, M. 6
Stop Bullying Now 71
Strassman, M. 169
Strauss, V. 6, 210, 237
St. George, D. 6, 210, 237
stress 5, 6, 164, 194, 236
Stronger Connections Grant Program 246
structural racism 165
student accounting 223
student engagement 13, 122, 131, 143–144, 159
student evacuation and assembly 222–223
Substance Abuse and Mental Health Services Administration (SAMHSA) 94, 95, 97, 191, 239
substance use 94, 122, *123*, 130, 161, 163, 191
suicide/suicidality 4, 77, 91–102, 105, 112, 161, 183, 191, 236; attempts 92–93, 184; contagion effect 95; as global phenomenon 92; high-risk

groups 92, 94; hotline and crisis response system 97; legal responsibilities 95–96; and mental health 93–94, 95; plan for 92, 93; possible precipitants 97, **98**, 102; prevention and intervention 12, 94–97, **100**, 101–102, 250; protective factors 97, **100**; questions to ask a student with a suicide plan 101; rates 92; risk assessments 96, 97, 102; risk factors for 93–94, 97, **99**, 102; and school shooters 94, 104, 112; scope of the problem 92–94; and

social disconnectedness 164; warning signs 96, 97, **98**, 102, 250

Suicide Prevention Resource Center (SPRC) 96, 97

Suldo, S. M. 23, 192–193, 195, 196

Sulkowski, M. L. 4, 5, 8, 16, 39, 53, 54, 62, 74, 91, 93, 104, 105, 111, 193, 194, 202, 204, 205, 207, 209, 218, 219, 221, 227, 229, 230, 235, 244

Sumter, S. R. 160

supportive communities 26

Supportive Pillar 10, 12–13, 251; *see also* school climate; school culture; social connectedness; social support

surveillance, natural 42, **43**

Sutton, L. M. 39

Swearer, S. M. 62

systemic racism 21

Tang, W. 231

Tanner-Smith, E. E. 55

Taquette, S. R. 63

target hardening 39, 54, 55

teachers/educators: burnout 9; role of 9–10; social support 155, 159, 160, 161; as weapon-carrying personnel 53–55, 103

temperance 193

territoriality/maintenance 42–43

tertiary prevention 16, 18, 188

Thapa, A. 122, 130, 139

Theriot, M. T. 52

Thomas, A. R. 132

Thomas, H. J. 75

Thomas, M. S. 242

thought records **208**

threat assessment 91–92, 104–112; process 107–111; questions when conducting 109, 110; safety plan 110, 111; teams 106–107

threats: anticipating 44; reporting 12, **41**, 111–112; stereotype 128; substantive 108; transient 108

three pillars of safe, supportive and healthy schools 2, 3, 10–14, *11*, 28, 141, 217–218, 250, 251; foundational principles 14–27

To Kill a Mockingbird (Lee) 129
Tokunaga, R. S. 167
transcendence 193
trauma-informed care 24–26, 146, 206, 217, 239–243
Trevor Foundation 96
Trump, K. S. 39
trust 3, 8, 27, 121, 142, 185
Turanovic, J. J. 75, 76

U.S. Capitol, storming of 5, 27
U.S. Department of Education (U.S. DOE) 104, 121; Safe and Supportive Schools 122; school climate model 122, *123*, 127
U.S. Department of Health and Human Services 4, 71, 94
U.S. Department of Homeland Security Incident Command System (ICS) 219, *220*
U.S. Secret Service 104, 109, 111
U.S. Surgeon General 184
"upstanders" 68, 71
Using Signature Strengths in a New Way activity 196

Vagi, K. J. 44
values 121, 126, 132, **133**, 134–135, 144, 146, 148
Vella-Brodrick, D. A. 5
verbal aggression 62
VIA Inventory of Strengths 193
violence 161, 163; community 240; *see also* abuse; school violence

Virginia Student Threat Assessment Guidelines (VSTAG) 92, 107–108, 112n
visibility **41**, 42, **43**; *see also* natural surveillance
visitors: access 39, 42, **43**; identity checks 39, **41**, 42; sign-in 221–222
Völlink, T. 62
von Hirsch, A. 81
Vossekuil, B. 23, 94, 112, 164

Wagner, B. M. 92
Waldron, N. L. 131–132
Wang, G. 165, 234
Wang, K. 75
Wang, M. T. 130, 139, 159, 160, 161
weapons 76, 130; possession policies **40**; of war 103; *see also* firearms
welcoming environment 8, 39, **40**
well-being 7, 9, 10, 16, 21, 23, 194; emotional 3, 4, 5, 15, 19, 23, 24, 28, 156, 159, 164, 189, 251
wellness approach 20
Wenham, C. 165
whole-child approach 18–19
Williamson, E. 51
Wilson, Frederica 249
Wincentak, K. 76
Wingspan **200**
wisdom 193
Wit, D. J. D. 161
Wood, A. M. 194

Woodhouse, S. S. 164
World Health Organization
   (WHO) 5, 92
WSCC model 18, 19

Yoon, E. 156
Youth Mental Health First Aid
   191–192; action plan (ALGEE)
   191–192

Youth Risk Behavior Surveillance
   Survey 5, 92–93
Yule, K. 168

Zakrzewski, V. 229
Zenere, F. 102, 232
zero tolerance policies 20, 21, 66,
   145, 167–168
Zhang, A. 75